Gerrymandering the States

State legislatures are tasked with drawing state and federal districts and administering election law, among many other responsibilities. Yet state legislatures are themselves gerrymandered. This book examines how, why, and with what consequences, drawing on an original dataset of ninety-five state legislative maps from before and after 2011 redistricting. Identifying the institutional, political, and geographic determinants of gerrymandering, the authors find that Republican gerrymandering increased dramatically after the 2011 redistricting and bias was most extreme in states with racial segregation where Republicans drew the maps. This bias has had long-term consequences. For instance, states with the most extreme Republican gerrymandering were more likely to pass laws that restricted voting rights and undermined public health, and they were less likely to respond to COVID-19. The authors examine the implications for American democracy and for the balance of power between federal and state governments; they also offer empirically grounded recommendations for reform.

Alex Keena is Assistant Professor of Political Science at Virginia Commonwealth University.

Michael Latner is Professor of Political Science at Cal Poly San Luis Obispo, and Senior Fellow at the Union of Concerned Scientists' Center for Science and Democracy in Washington, DC.

Anthony J. McGann is Professor of Government and Public Policy at the University of Strathclyde, Glasgow.

Charles Anthony Smith is Professor in Political Science and Law at the University of California, Irvine.

D1570547

Gerrymandering the States

Partisanship, Race, and the Transformation of American Federalism

ALEX KEENA
Virginia Commonwealth University

MICHAEL LATNER
California Polytechnic State University

ANTHONY J. MCGANN
University of Strathclyde

CHARLES ANTHONY SMITH
University of California, Irvine

CAMBRIDGE
UNIVERSITY PRESS

CAMBRIDGE
UNIVERSITY PRESS

University Printing House, Cambridge CB2 8BS, United Kingdom

One Liberty Plaza, 20th Floor, New York, NY 10006, USA

477 Williamstown Road, Port Melbourne, VIC 3207, Australia

314–321, 3rd Floor, Plot 3, Splendor Forum, Jasola District Centre,
New Delhi – 110025, India

103 Penang Road, #05–06/07, Visioncrest Commercial, Singapore 238467

Cambridge University Press is part of the University of Cambridge.

It furthers the University's mission by disseminating knowledge in the pursuit of
education, learning, and research at the highest international levels of excellence.

www.cambridge.org
Information on this title: www.cambridge.org/9781316518120
DOI: 10.1017/9781108995849

© James Alexander Keena, Michael Steven Latner, Anthony J. McGann and
Charles Anthony Smith 2021

First published 2021

A catalogue record for this publication is available from the British Library.

ISBN 978-1-316-51812-0 Hardback
ISBN 978-1-108-99545-0 Paperback

Contents

Figures

Tables

Acknowledgments

The authors are grateful to many people and organizations for input and advice, not only for this project but also for our earlier book on gerrymandering. We all owe an enormous debt to Rein Taagepera for shaping how each of us thinks about politics. He has had a profound influence on each of us and we are grateful for the opportunity to have learned from him. We also are thankful to Bernie Grofman for his insight and guidance, on redistricting and many other topics and problems. We are fortunate to have had terrific discussants and co-panelists at many conferences, including the Midwest Political Science Association, American Political Science Association, and Southern Political Science Association, among others. We are grateful for the advice and support of Jack Santucci and for the data and research projects of Carl Klarner, Justin Levitt, Stephen Wolf, and others whose work we rely on.

The team at Cambridge University Press and the anonymous reviewers have improved the manuscript in both large and small ways. We concluded that the reviews were likely the most constructive any of us had ever seen, and we are very thankful for the careful, thoughtful, and thorough approach taken by the anonymous reviewers. We are also grateful to Common Cause for the input we received at their 2016 redistricting conference and to Emmett Bondurant, who shared terrific insights and fascinating war stories.

We also want to make individual acknowledgments to others who helped us.

Alex Keena: Thank you to my wife, Jessie, and daughters, Marlowe and Jolene, for their never-ending support and patience; my grandmother, Janet Keena; Brad, Heather, Larry, Shirley, and Renee (my parents);

Mike, Tony, and Tony; my research assistants, Taieba Kohistany, Capriana Phillips, and Adam Santiago. Special thanks are owed to Knight-Finley; Dierdre Condit, Judy Twigg, and Ravi Perry for helpful comments; to the discussants and co-panelists at SPSA 2019; to John Curiel and Tyler Steelman; to Elliot Fullmer, Hank Chambers, Nicholas Goedert, Rebecca Green, Michael D. Gilbert, Deborah Hellman, and A. E. Dick Howard; to Nakeina E. Douglas-Genn, and the Minority Political Leadership Institute at VCU; and to Brian Cannon.

Michael Latner: In addition to this amazing team, I wish to thank Frank, Shirley, and Brian, for early investment; Christina and my kids Violet and Chase, for all the love they bring; my best friend Sean Sanner, for saving my life; Russ Dalton and Pedro Hernandez for countless hours of advice and expertise; and the team at the Union of Concerned Scientists' Center for Science and Democracy, who supported this work through a Kendall Science Fellowship and many lasting friendships.

Anthony J. McGann: I would like to thank Jack Nagle and Rogers Smith for organizing a conference at University of Pennsylvania back in 2008 that turned out to be instrumental in getting this project going. I would like to thank so many people who have provided inspiration and support, including John Nagle, Keith Forsyth, Don Saari, and Bill Batchelder. And, in this uncertain hour, I would particularly like to thank the people who campaign for fair elections at Union of Concerned Scientists, Common Cause, and Fair Districts PA, and many other organizations.

Charles A. Smith: I am grateful to my husband, Julio Rodriguez. His insight, humor, and tenacity have made my life wonderful and have also made my work better. I'm also grateful for his tolerance of the very weird world of the academy! I also owe my coauthors on this and other projects an enormous debt. I am lucky to work with so many amazing scholars.

Redistricting Wars in the US States

On November 5, 2019, Democrats won control of Virginia state government for the first time in nearly 30 years. Although they had performed well during the preceding decade – they had won every statewide election held in Virginia after 2009 – the party's popularity statewide did not translate to a majority in the House of Delegates. Republicans managed to retain control of the House, even though Democrats won 10 percent more of the vote statewide in 2017. However, the party's fortunes changed when a federal court invalidated twelve of the house districts that were drawn by Republicans during the 2011 redistricting as illegally racially gerrymandered. The court implemented a remedial map for the 2019 elections that strengthened the voting rights of African Americans and, consequently, leveled the playing field for Democrats.

The story of Republicans' grip on power – and the Democrats' uphill battle to retake it – is not unusual. This happened in the 1993, 1995, and 1997 Virginia House of Delegates elections, when Democrats were able to keep their house majorities even though Republicans won more votes. And in the past decade, similar stories have played out in many other states: One party manages to win a majority of the seats in the legislature despite receiving a minority of the votes.

In Virginia, as in most other states, the balance of power in state government was not determined simply by the votes cast in biennial state legislative elections. Instead, the political balance of power was determined by *decennial* state legislative elections – those that decided who would control redistricting. In 1989, Democrats won control of Virginia's government, and they used this power in 1991 redistricting to deny seats to Republicans, who had been gaining popularity in the state.

But the Republicans eventually won. When it was their turn to redistrict in 2001, the Republicans rolled back the Democratic bias baked into the 1991-era maps. Republican victories in the 2009 elections won them control of the governorship and the House of Delegates, giving them a dominant position for 2011 redistricting, which they used to give themselves a partisan advantage in state house and congressional elections for years to come, as Democrats had done in 1991.

The federal courts eventually intervened to end the Republican gerrymander of the 2011 state house plan because the drafters had relied on an illegal tactic of racial vote dilution to achieve a partisan advantage. Anti-gerrymandering activists in Virginia succeeded in pressuring the legislature to advance unprecedented reforms, including a state constitutional amendment that transferred redistricting to a sixteen-member commission, staffed with four Republican legislators, four Democratic legislators, and eight citizens (selected by a panel of retired judges). However, achieving these reforms posed a formidable challenge.

Democratic legislators, who had overwhelmingly supported the reforms when they were in the minority, opposed them when their party won power. The legislature would advance the measure, but only nine Democratic delegates voted in favor of the reforms, sending them to voters in 2020 for final approval.

1.1 OPENING THE REDISTRICTING "BLACKBOX"

Although Virginia is one of many states to have debated changes to the redistricting process, surprisingly little in the scientific literature is known about the efficacy of such reforms. In the popular discourse, as well as in the scholarship, redistricting is treated something like a "black box." In political science, the research on redistricting has generally focused more on the outcomes of districting, and less on the determinants.

Scholarship since the 1970s has sought to answer questions about the effects of redistricting control, such as whether controlling parties gain a durable electoral advantage through redistricting, and whether gerrymandering undermines political competition or leads to legislative polarization (Abramowitz, Alexander, and Gunning 2006; Gelman and King 1994a). Case studies of redistricting in 1991 (when Democrats controlled most state legislatures) show that Democrats received surprisingly few electoral advantages from the maps they drew (e.g., Lyons and Galderisi 1995). After the 2001 redistricting cycle, similar investigations show that Republicans, who controlled redistricting in most states, drew only modest levels of bias into their maps. In many cases, the maps approved by Republicans did not prevent Democrats from eventually retaking power (Hood and McKee 2010, 2013).

In addition, the effects of redistricting on competition are estimated to be small (Masket, Winburn, and Wright 2012), although the magnitude of the effect depends on the institutional and political actors involved (Carson and Crespin 2004; Carson, Crespin, and Williamson 2014; Goedert 2017; Murphy and Yoshinaka 2009). And there is little evidence that redistricting bias has caused the long-term decline of electoral competition in congressional elections (Abramowitz, Alexander, and Gunning 2006).

Justice Sandra Day O'Connor asserted in her famous opinion in *Davis v. Bandemer* (1986) that partisan gerrymandering is "self-limiting" because the costs of drawing a partisan advantage across a large number of districts exposes the redistricting party to the potential for steep losses, a view advanced by Seabrook (2017). And the strategy of achieving a partisan advantage through the "cracking" and "packing" of the opposing party's voters means that the controlling party exposes itself to extraordinary risk if the electoral tides shift toward the opposition. Several storied examples of "dummymanders" demonstrate that political gerrymandering often backfires spectacularly on the ruling party in ways that the drafters fail to anticipate (Grofman and Brunell 2005).

Collectively, this literature suggests that the democratic harms of political districting are self-correcting and that partisan gerrymandering is not a particularly urgent problem. However, after the US House elections in 2012, perceptions about partisan gerrymandering changed. That year, Democratic candidates for the US House collectively received about one million more votes than Republican candidates, yet Republicans still managed to win a comfortable majority of seats. Since then, much of the redistricting literature has coalesced around the goal of challenging unlawful partisan gerrymandering in the federal courts.

1.2 THE "GREAT GERRYMANDER OF 2012"

The "Great Gerrymander of 2012," as Princeton professor Sam Wang put it, took many by surprise. The outcomes of 2011 redistricting were unique in terms of degree and scope of the partisan gerrymanders drawn, and it forced a revision of the commonly accepted ideas about partisan gerrymandering and its consequences.

Among the objectives of our 2016 volume, *Gerrymandering in America: The House of Representatives, the Supreme Court, and the Future of Popular Sovereignty*, was to update the scientific literature to reflect a new reality. Our analysis of partisan gerrymandering of US House districts showed that many states drew maps with extreme Republican bias. With the 2012 districts, Democratic candidates would need to win approximately 54 percent of the nationwide two-party vote to win control of the House.

After the book was published, the Democrats managed to retake the House in the 2018 midterm elections, with Democratic candidates receiving about 10 million more votes than Republicans (54 percent of the two-party vote). However, this lopsided margin of victory gave Democrats a majority of only thirty-six-seats. By contrast, only two years earlier, in 2016, the Republicans managed to win a forty-seven-seat majority with a two-party vote share advantage of less than 2 percent.

Despite large statewide vote swings in favor of the Democrats in 2018, not a single Republican US House incumbent lost a general election race in Ohio, Tennessee, Wisconsin, Missouri, or Indiana. In North Carolina, Republicans held onto nine of their ten seats and won back the tenth in a 2019 special election, after Representative Mark Harris' 2018 victory was invalidated by the courts for voter fraud.

Thus, the gerrymanders drawn in 2011 and 2012 were surprisingly durable. Despite the electoral advantage that Republicans were able to draw for their party, they still managed to draw plans that were unresponsive to swings in vote support for their opponents, thus undermining the myth that partisan gerrymanders are self-limiting. That the Democrats managed to retake the House in 2018, despite the widespread pro-Republican bias, was in large part due to successful legal challenges of gerrymandered congressional maps. In Virginia, after a federal court in 2016 invalidated the US House map as an unlawful racial gerrymander, Democratic challengers in 2018 managed to flip three seats previously held by Republican incumbents. Likewise, Democrats in Pennsylvania gained three additional seats after a state supreme court invalidated the congressional plan. In Florida, the congressional map was ruled an unconstitutional partisan gerrymander in state courts, after which Democrats gained one seat in 2016 and two more in 2018. These cases reveal the interconnectedness of racial gerrymandering and political gerrymandering, and they show that courts can have a significant impact on redistricting outcomes.

1.2.1 Answering Kennedy's Challenge in *Vieth*

As we argued in *Gerrymandering in America*, the roots of partisan gerrymandering in 2011 stem from a 2004 Supreme Court case, *Vieth* v. *Jubelirer*, which received relatively little attention from legal scholars at the time the decision was handed down by the Court.

The *Vieth* case was a partisan gerrymandering challenge by Democrats to the congressional map that was passed in Pennsylvania in 2001 with a Republican majority. In that ruling, the Supreme Court held that it was not capable of providing a legal remedy for citizens who claimed their constitutional rights were denied as a result of partisan gerrymandered districting maps, because no legal standard for adjudicating such claims currently existed.

This undermined previous Court decisions that found that political gerrymandering was unconstitutional, without strictly overturning them (there was no majority opinion in *Vieth* , except to affirm the lower court's judgment). In *Reynolds* v. *Sims* (1964, 563), the Court found that "weighting the votes of citizens differently, *by any method or means*, merely because of where they happen to reside, hardly seems justifiable" (italics ours). In *Bandemer* v. *Davis* (1986), the Court confirmed that this applied to political gerrymandering as well as malapportionment, while at the same time overturning a federal court decision to invalidate the 1981 Indiana districting plan.

While the *Vieth* decision did not overturn these decisions, it did make clear that the Supreme Court was unlikely to strike down districting plans for political gerrymandering and would likely overturn any federal court that attempted to do so. In a four-justice plurality decision, the late Justice Antonin Scalia asserted that the Court erred in *Bandemer* and that partisan gerrymandering represented a "political question" for which the Court could not provide relief. Scalia claimed that there existed no standard for partisan gerrymandering that is judicially "discernable and manageable." Because the Constitution does not explicitly prohibit partisan gerrymandering, such challenges should be left to the elected branches.

Justice Kennedy wrote a concurring opinion in which he agreed in part with Scalia that there currently existed no standard for detecting and adjudicating partisan gerrymandering. However, Kennedy disagreed that partisan gerrymandering is a "political question" beyond the purview of the judiciary. Instead, he suggested that one day a standard could be identified by social scientists and legal scholars.

We posited that the *Vieth* ruling marked a critical moment in redistricting, insofar as the Court signaled to state districting authorities that there would be no consequences for partisan gerrymandering. Before *Vieth*, lawmakers feared the possibility that a district plan could be overturned by the courts. After *Vieth*, lawmakers were free to gerrymander on a scale that they had previously not done. Because the Court held that there were no standards for adjudicating gerrymandering challenges, state governments had little reason to fear that the judiciary would strike down their maps as unlawful partisan gerrymanders. Indeed, from the perspective of partisan districting authorities, the threat of a successful partisan gerrymander challenge in federal courts was non-credible.

After the 2012 House elections, the unprecedented scale of partisan gerrymandering was revealed. Documentary evidence would show that the national Republican Party had coordinated efforts by Republican legislatures to approve dozens of aggressive gerrymanders across the country (Daley 2017). This prompted a renewed sense of urgency among scholars of redistricting about the problems posed by extreme partisan gerrymandering. After the 2012 House elections, redistricting scholars eagerly answered the challenge offered by Justice Kennedy in his concurring opinion in *Vieth*, which left open the possibility that a suitable standard for challenging partisan gerrymandering in the federal courts might one day be identified by social scientists and legal scholars.

Since then, the dominant focus of the redistricting scholarship has been to identify a "discernable and manageable" standard for partisan gerrymandering that Justice Kennedy would be willing to endorse. These collective efforts were joined by a diverse group of scholars from a range of disciplines, including political science, law, physics, economics, and mathematics (e.g., Arrington 2016; Best et al. 2018; Grofman 2018; Stephanopoulos and McGhee 2015, 2018; Warrington 2018, 2019).

However, these efforts were apparently in vain. Justice Kennedy abruptly retired after the 2017–18 term, and his replacement, Brett Kavanaugh, shifted the Court to the ideological right. The Court shifted even further to right after the death of Ruth Bader Ginsburg, who was replaced by Amy Coney Barrett just days before the 2020 Presidential Election. It is unlikely a majority on this Court would ever reconsider partisan gerrymandering.

1.2.2 Partisan Gerrymandering after *Rucho*

The Court closed the book on partisan gerrymandering standards when it ruled in *Rucho* v. *Common Clause* (2019) (a partisan gerrymandering challenge to the North Carolina congressional map) that partisan gerrymandering claims are beyond the purview of the federal courts.

Writing for the majority, Chief Justice Roberts echoed the logic of Justice Scalia's plurality decision in *Vieth* and claimed that, unlike the "one-person, one-vote" standard in reapportionment cases, a majority rule standard (a majority of persons must elect a majority of legislators) could not be derived from any "constitutionally discoverable" right, because majority rule claims pertain to groups, not persons. "Partisan gerrymandering claims," Roberts asserts, "rest on an instinct that groups with a certain level of political support should enjoy a commensurate level of political power and influence. ... But such a claim is based on a 'norm that does not exist' in our electoral system" which the Framers of the US Constitution "certainly did not think ... was required" (*Rucho* v. *Common Cause* 2019, 588 U. S. ____, at 16).

In her dissent, Justice Elena Kagan noted that "for the first time ever, this Court refuses to remedy a constitutional violation because it thinks the task beyond judicial capabilities."

For anti-gerrymandering advocates, the *Rucho* decision has prompted a refocusing of strategy. Rather than seeking a solution to partisan gerrymandering in the federal courts, the battle has shifted to the states, with some limited successes. Legal victories in Florida, Pennsylvania, and North Carolina show that the courts are willing to enforce state constitutional provisions that prohibit partisan gerrymandering (in Florida), and require "free and equal elections" in Pennsylvania (Grofman and Cervas 2018) and "free" elections in North Carolina.

In Colorado, Michigan, Missouri, Ohio, Utah, Virginia, and other states, reformers have won changes to redistricting processes. In Virginia, implementing redistricting reform was accomplished because reform groups, such as One Virginia 2021, Fair Maps VA, Common Cause, and the League of Women Voters, pushed back against politicians opposing reforms and battled misinformation.

A similar story played out in Missouri, where voters in 2018 approved the "Clean Missouri" redistricting reform package that would have delegated redistricting authority to an independent public demographer. However, Republican legislators opposed the reforms, and in 2020 promoted a constitutional amendment to voters that rolled back many of the changes.

1.3 A STUDY OF STATE LEGISLATIVE REDISTRICTING

These examples show that reforms are achievable when there is a groundswell of grassroots energy and public support, but the spread of misinformation can undermine their popularity. In this book, we hope to provide "best practices" in the design of redistricting institutions and processes, so that scholars, policymakers, and the public alike can have reliable and trustworthy data to weigh the pros and cons of reforms. We investigate the state legislative redistricting process that began in 2011 in order learn about how the design and architecture of redistricting institutions and processes affect redistricting outcomes.

The study of the state legislative redistricting presents enormous complexity, given the diversity and variation in the redistricting processes and institutions used by fifty state governments. In the fifty states, there are a total of ninety-nine state legislative assemblies, which collectively redistrict more than ninety state legislative maps, drawn by a variety of institutions, each of which is governed by distinct processes. The availability and accessibility of data on state legislative elections varies widely between states. What's more, compared to the congressional level, the scale of districting at the state level entails unique challenges. Whereas most congressional district maps include less than a dozen districts, many state legislative maps number in the hundreds.

However, the larger sample of districting outcomes gives us the means to assess the theoretical determinants of redistricting outcomes in a systematic way. A study of state-level redistricting provides important generalizable insights for those hoping to understand gerrymandering in other contexts, at the federal, state, and local levels, as well as in other legislatures that use single-member districts. This is simply not possible with a focus on the US House, for example, which has less variation and a relatively small sample of cases.

We hope our investigation of the institutions and practices of redistricting will inform the debate over redistricting reform that is unfolding in states across the country, such as those in Virginia and Missouri over 2020 redistricting reform ballot initiatives. Our findings suggest policy prescriptions for how redistricting systems can be altered to prevent partisan bias in elections so that policymakers can be more deliberate in their designing of institutions and processes.

We also believe that an important part of the story of redistricting in 2011 has thus far been overlooked. In *Alabama Legislative Black Caucus v. Alabama* (2015), the Supreme Court established legal standards for race and districting. Instead of drawing "majority-minority" districts that preserve mathematical majorities of voters from racial and ethnic minority communities, districting authorities should not dilute the value of a vote and must draw "minority influence" districts so that voters from minority communities can elect a representative of their choosing.

This decision was cited in subsequent racial gerrymandering challenges in North Carolina and Virginia, in which the courts installed remedial maps that eroded Republican bias.

In these states, gerrymanders were able to "waste" the votes of Democrats by diluting the votes of Black and Latinx citizens. These cases show how Republican lawmakers across the country were able to achieve a partisan advantage in districting by using race as a proxy for party, while claiming cynically to advance minority representation (see Waymer and Heath 2016). For the Republicans, it is easier to draw gerrymanders, because Democratic voters as well as Black and Latinx voters tend to live in cities (Chen and Cottrell 2016; Chen and Rodden 2013a; Goedert 2014; Rodden 2019).

1.4 OBJECTIVES OF THE BOOK

This book answers four basic questions about state legislative redistricting:

> First, what happened in 2011? Second, Why? Third, what are the consequences? And fourth, can gerrymandering be prevented?

1.4.1 What Happened after Redistricting?

First, we ask, what were the outcomes of 2011 state legislative redistricting? We know a great deal about how 2011 redistricting changed the congressional maps. Our own work (McGann et al. 2015, 2016) shows that, in many states, the maps were politically gerrymandered to give Republicans an edge in the US House. As well, several other studies have found similar results (Curiel and Steelman 2018; Engstrom 2020; Hood and McKee 2008; McKee, Teigen, and Turgeon 2006; Stephanopoulos and Warshaw 2020). However, to our knowledge, there does not exist a comprehensive, systematic analysis of the causes and effects of partisan gerrymandering of state legislatures. A number of case studies suggest that state legislatures drew their own maps with substantial partisan bias, and there is compelling anecdotal evidence to suggest this as well (Browning and King 1987; Burden and Snyder 2020; Makse 2012). Yet, thus far, no one has been able to produce a comprehensive, scientific assessment of the state legislative maps that were approved during 2011 redistricting.

1.4.2 Why Does Bias Occur?

Is it possible to predict redistricting outcomes? Evaluating the state legislative district maps that were redistricted in 2011 gives us unique insight into the causal determinants of partisan bias because the state legislatures provide a sample that is large enough to test hypotheses about the institutional and geographic determinants of redistricting outcomes.

In *Gerrymandering in America*, we posited that politics, in contrast to geography, was the most important variable in explaining whether and when we see bias. Our analysis then was limited to the thirty-eight maps drawn in states with more than two congressional districts. In this study, our sample size is much larger. With state legislative maps, we nearly triple our dataset, and we are able to use advanced statistical inference to disentangle the effects of political, institutional, and geographic variables. We particularly focus on the links between racial geography and political geography to understand tactics used by political parties to achieve partisan advantage.

1.4.3 What Are the Consequences of Bias?

What impact, if any, does the presence of partisan bias in state legislative district maps have on democracy in the United States? Because redistricting determines who gets into office, it has long-term ripple effects on the policies that are approved by state government. What sorts of policies do gerrymandered legislatures adopt? As well, bias in state-level redistricting impacts the balance of federalism in the United States. State legislatures regulate the administration of election laws in their states and can alter the costs of voting to affect voter participation in national elections. If the state-level architects of congressional gerrymanders are in fact gerrymandering themselves, this makes it possible for an entrenched minority party to hold power indefinitely through decennial redistricting and gives state-level actors an unprecedented reach into national affairs.

1.4.4 Do Reforms Work?

The fourth question we address in this volume is whether it is possible to reform redistricting institutions to achieve unbiased maps. Here, we draw upon our findings to evaluate which common reforms are more likely to succeed and which are less likely to succeed. In particular, we evaluate the effectiveness of two types of reform options: rules-based reforms, which impose additional restrictions or requirements on existing redistricting authorities, and procedural reforms that fundamentally change how and by whom redistricting is done. We also assess the effectiveness of the judiciary in dealing with districting bias and whether the courts are capable of stopping gerrymandering.

In our investigation of redistricting in 2011, we find that dozens of state legislative plans were drawn with extreme partisan bias. This bias gives Republican state legislative candidates about 9 percent more seats in the average state legislature than Democratic candidates for a similar share of the vote. This is comparable to the level of bias we observed in the gerrymandering of congressional maps (McGann et al. 2016). In nearly all cases, the most extreme bias occurred in states where Republicans controlled redistricting.

We also find that, while political control of redistricting is a powerful predictor of where bias is likely to occur, racial and political geography play a key role. In states with high levels of Black–white and Latinx–white segregation, Republicans are able to draw extreme levels of bias by diluting the voting power of racial minorities. However, we do not see this effect when Democrats, or bipartisan, or nonpartisan actors draw the maps.

We investigate the policy effects of partisan gerrymandering by looking at the legislators that were elected through biased maps and the laws they approved. The most gerrymandered legislatures were more likely to enact voting rights restrictions, pass restrictive abortion laws, and challenge the Affordable Care Act. Legislatures with extreme Republican gerrymanders also did less to respond to the COVID-19 pandemic or facilitate vote-by-mail for the 2020 elections.

However, we also find that, in spite of these costs, there are effective solutions to the problem of extreme bias. While the courts can provide a partial solution, particularly to the problem of racial gerrymandering, the most promising solutions are reforms that depoliticize redistricting. Reforms that prevent one party from monopolizing redistricting are likely to lead to less bias, and citizen redistricting commissions (those which bar politicians) in particular appear to hold promise as an effective reform option. Incorporating protections from the Voting Rights Act into multimember, proportional electoral districting can also depoliticize the redistricting process while ensuring fair representation.

1.6 THE PLAN OF THE BOOK

In Chapter 2, we consider the outcomes of the 2011 redistricting. We discuss our approach for measuring the extent of partisan gerrymandering in the ninety-five state legislative assemblies after the 2011 redistricting cycle and report the findings of this analysis. We compare the plans adopted after 2011 during the 2011–18 state legislative elections and compare the level of partisan symmetry and responsiveness with the plans that were enacted in the previous cycle, during the 2007–10 elections. Our results show that, like congressional maps, several state governments enacted plans that, with extreme bias, favor the Republican Party.

In Chapter 3, we investigate the effects of political redistricting on bias. We analyze the redistricting institutions in fifty states in order to understand whether politics can explain where we see bias. We find that, while the states use a great variety of methods and institutions for drawing the lines, including courts and independent commissions, most still delegate the task to politicians. We find higher levels of partisan bias associated with state legislative maps that were drawn by a single party in competitive states. Accordingly, predicting partisan gerrymandering is hardly rocket science; it occurs only when politicians, who stand to gain from biased maps, are in charge of the process and do not need bipartisan support to enact the district plan.

In Chapter 4, we illuminate the precise role of political geography on partisan bias. Whereas previous studies of geography and gerrymandering have dismissed gerrymandering as the "unintentional" consequence of demographic sorting (i.e., Democrats clustering in urban areas) rather than the deliberate decisions made by partisan mapmakers (e.g., Chen and Rodden 2013a), we show that politics play a fundamental role in districting outcomes. While it is true that geography can help or harm a political party in charge of redistricting, this does not make biased maps inevitable or natural. In short, geography is not destiny. Although geography constrains the options available, mapmakers choose the plans that best serve their interests.

In Chapter 5, we explore the effects of voting rights reforms, minority districting, and racial geography on bias. We find that achieving minority representation and unbiased districting are not mutually exclusive goals. Indeed, many of the states with the largest Black and Latinx populations managed to draw unbiased maps. Similarly, among the most racially segregated states, we do not observe a correlation between racial segregation and bias once we control for partisanship. Instead, we find that when Republicans control districting, they are often able to use racial segregation to gain a partisan advantage, through the drawing of majority-minority districts. However, when Republicans are not in control, we do not see a correlation between racial segregation and bias. Yet again, the key variable is politics.

In Chapter 6, we investigate the political and social consequences of political redistricting. We survey the policy outcomes that were adopted by the state legislatures after redistricting. We find that the legislatures with extreme Republican gerrymandering were more likely to pass laws that restrict voting rights, limit access to the polls, and erode public health and were less responsive during the COVID-19 outbreak. In Chapter 7, we discuss democratic harms of political redistricting and argue that gerrymandering of state legislatures undermines democracy and disrupts the balance of power between state and federal government in the United States.

In the last part of the book, we explore solutions to the problems of bias in districting. We assess the effect of the courts on redistricting outcomes in Chapter 8, and we evaluate common redistricting reforms adopted by the states in Chapter 9. In the conclusion, we argue that reforms are most effective at preventing gerrymandering when they prevent one party from controlling outcomes, such as independent redistricting. Accordingly, anti-gerrymandering reformers should pursue procedural reforms. By comparison, reforms that do not change who is in charge, but simply change the rules (e.g., criteria) have only limited success and are only as effective as the courts are willing to enforce them.

2

What Happened in 2011? The Other "Great Gerrymander"

On November 2, 2010, voters across the United States went to the polls to cast their votes in what may be the most consequential midterm election in recent memory, as many of the state-level races that were up for grabs determined who would control the decennial redistricting in 2011. Yet, for the millions who cast ballots in state-level races, redistricting was apparently not a relevant issue.

The focus of much of the country, instead, was on the congressional elections and national politics. A Gallup poll taken a week before Election Day suggests that the most important issues to voters were the economy and jobs, with large majorities also citing corruption in government, federal spending, healthcare, terrorism and immigration as "very important" issues (Jones 2010).

In the media, there was hardly any sustained focus on redistricting and little consideration of the broader, long-term implications of the state-level races and their critical importance. A Google search of "redistricting and the 2010 elections" with the search range set from January 1, 2010 to November 1, 2010 (the day before Election Day) shows that almost no news coverage was given to the issue in the months before the election, aside from a *Wall Street Journal* op-ed penned by Karl Rove in March of 2010, asserting the importance of 2010 elections for redistricting, as well as a few scholarly references to redistricting posted in obscure blogs.

In retrospect, the implications of the 2010 elections are difficult to overstate. The election came at a critical junction that occurs only once every 20 years, because it signified an "off-year" election, during which most state governments hold their legislative and gubernatorial elections, and it occurred during a census year, which marks the beginning of the decennial redistricting process when the states update their congressional and legislative district maps.

As Republicans focused on state legislative and governor races with an eye toward redistricting, Democrats marketed their national healthcare reforms in order to keep their majorities in Congress. After the Republicans' surprise win in a Massachusetts special Senate election held in January of 2010, Republicans expected to win seats in Congress in the midterms. Since the Franklin D. Roosevelt administration, nearly every first-term president has witnessed their party lose seats in Congress during the next midterm election, so a defeat at the polls for Democrats would have been hardly surprising.

Yet after the polls had closed and the votes were tallied, it was apparent that the Republicans had outperformed expectations. In the House, the Republicans managed to flip sixty-eight seats and won a comfortable majority. In the Senate, Republicans picked up an additional six seats and eroded Democrats' large majority. But it was at the state level where Republicans dominated. When the votes were counted, Republicans won twenty-nine of the thirty-seven governor contests and secured unified control over twenty-five state legislatures. In total, twenty state legislative chambers had flipped from Democratic to Republican control.

The Republican dominance in state-level races gave them a powerful advantage heading into 2011 redistricting. As we reported in *Gerrymandering in America* (McGann et al. 2016), state governments across the country redistricted to give Republicans a competitive advantage in congressional elections. In contrast to the 2001 cycle maps, which were only slightly biased to favor the Republicans, the 2011 maps tripled the level of pro-Republican bias nationwide and dramatically tilted the electoral geography of the US House to favor the GOP.

In McGann et al. (2016), we estimated that Democratic candidates would need to win about 54 percent of the nationwide two-party vote to have a fifty-fifty shot at winning control of the House. This is more or less what happened in 2018, when Democratic candidates won by slightly more than this and managed to win back a House majority.

Yet this is only part of the story of the 2011 redistricting. Though we know a great deal about the gerrymandering of the US House – indeed, many other studies have corroborated our findings – we know relatively little about gerrymandering of state government.

What were the consequences of the 2011 state legislative redistricting? Did the Republican legislatures gerrymander themselves, as they had done to Congress?

In this chapter, we assess state legislative redistricting maps approved by state governments in 2011 to answer these questions. We find results that are similar to our study of districting bias in Congress. On average, partisan bias increased after redistricting. State governments approved more than forty state legislative redistricting plans that gave one party an extreme electoral advantage. Although we find a few examples of Democratic gerrymanders with modest levels of bias, most of the extremely biased maps favor the Republican Party. In total, there are nearly two dozen maps that award Republicans 20 percent more of the seats than Democrats when the vote is close. These extreme partisan gerrymanders give Republicans a considerable structural advantage in state legislative elections. We estimate that, in the average state legislative assembly, Republican candidates can expect to win about 9 percent more seats than Democratic candidates would for a given share of the vote, between 45 percent and 55 percent of the vote.

Before presenting our results, we first discuss the concept of "gerrymandering." While there are many forms of gerrymandering, we limit this analysis to partisan gerrymandering – when the maps are drawn to advance the interests of a political party, or parties (Chapters 5 and 8 address racial gerrymandering and the effects of racial geography on partisan bias). Next, we identify a standard for measuring partisan gerrymandering in a district map, partisan symmetry, which is a scientifically valid and intuitive approach for comparing bias in state legislative maps that has been subject to decades of scrutiny in the scholarship. Then, we discuss our research design – how we estimate the partisan symmetry of state legislative maps, and how we collect data on the partisan composition of all state legislative districts nationwide, before and after 2011 redistricting. We conclude by reporting the findings of this investigation and analyzing some descriptive trends.

2.1 WHAT IS "GERRYMANDERING"?

"Gerrymandering" is a concept that means many things to many different people, but most commonly refers to the deliberate manipulation of legislative district boundaries in order to achieve some political or personal objective that serves the interests of those in power (or those who have been charged with drawing the lines). Gerrymandering occurs in electoral systems that assign seats in a legislative body to geographically localized constituencies.

Gerrymandering is a phenomenon that is typically associated with electoral systems that employ single-member districts, such as the

United States or the United Kingdom, and which have two parties. However, in principle, any electoral system that assigns representation based on the spatial demarcation of constituency boundaries may be vulnerable to some forms of gerrymandering.

The term "gerrymandering" borrows its name from an American politician, Elbridge Gerry, who used his power as governor of Massachusetts in 1812 to approve a state senate district plan that served the interests of his political party, the Democratic-Republicans. However, the practice of manipulating the geographic boundaries of electoral districts predates the founding of the United States. Early forms of gerrymandering can be traced to Great Britain, as early as the 1700s, when politicians would draw "rotten boroughs" for which a single neighborhood or city block – or even a single estate – would be drawn into one district, represented by a member of Parliament.

2.1.1 Malapportionment Gerrymanders

The practice of drawing "rotten boroughs" was a form of malapportionment, in which districts are manipulated so that legislators represent vastly different constituency population sizes (on the effects of malapportionment, see Bowen 2010; Frederick 2008; Keena 2019a; Lee and Oppenheimer 1999; Oliver 2000; Oppenheimer 1996). In this type of gerrymander, in which districts are created with unequally populated districts, the primary "harm" is the dilution of some citizens' votes relative to others, undermining political equality. In eighteenth- and nineteenth-century Great Britain (from 1801 the United Kingdom), before the passage of the Reform Act of 1832 which outlawed the practice, the malapportionment of rotten boroughs was advanced to serve the interests of wealthy landowners who used their influence over the districting geography to install their personal interests in Parliament, or to elect their friends or business associates.

Malapportionment also occurred in the United States, although for different objectives. For instance, as recently as the 1960s, state governments would allow urban districts to grow at exponentially faster rates than neighboring rural districts without redrawing the district lines to achieve population equity. Here, lawmakers were able to "gerrymander" simply by doing nothing. This had the effect of preserving and consolidating the power of rural districts, whose populations were in long-term decline, at the expense of diluting the influence of urban voters. In this regard, sometimes "gerrymandering" can occur without actually touching the maps, as was the case with "rural gerrymandering."

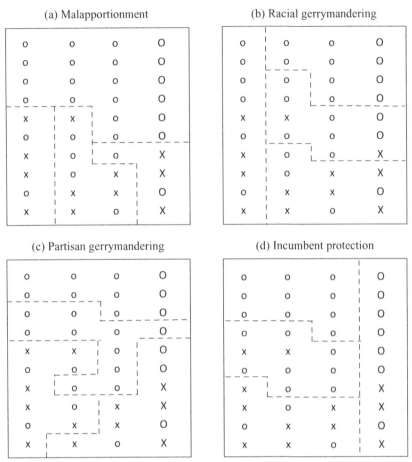

FIGURE 2.1. How gerrymandering is achieved through district shapes

Figure 2.1a illustrates how malapportionment works as a tactic for diluting the voting power of one party in order to expand the voting power of another. Because districting authorities are able to draw districts with unequally sized populations, it is relatively easy to give a minority party a majority of seats.

Although our discussion of historical (and hypothetical) examples of malapportionment pertain to representative democracies with two-party systems, in principle, it may also be possible to draw malapportionment gerrymanders in PR systems with more than two parties. This occurs, for example, in the Spanish Congress and Norwegian Storting, where election laws require a minimum allotment of seats to rural communities, resulting in a disproportional advantage for parties representing rural constituents.

2.1.2 Racial Gerrymandering

Another form of gerrymandering that was outlawed in the United States after the passage of the Voting Rights Act of 1965 is often called "racial gerrymandering," in which districts are drawn to dilute the power of racial or ethnic minorities, either through "cracking" (in which minority voters are distributed across multiple districts, thus preventing them from electing representatives of their choosing), or "packing" (in which minority voters are drawn into supermajority districts), or through the use of "winner-take-all," multimember districts that prevent small plurality populations from winning seats. As Figure 2.1b shows, racial gerrymandering can be achieved through "cracking," even when redistricting authorities must draw equal-sized districts, when the district lines prevent a minority group from gaining a majority in any single district.

As we discuss in Chapter 5, illegal racial gerrymandering was the pretext for the federal courts' invalidation of the 2011 Virginia House of Delegates map and the North Carolina house and senate maps. Because race and political party preference are highly correlated, it is often the case that Republican drafters are able achieve a partisan advantage through racial gerrymandering, insofar as the "packing" of African-American (or Latinx) voters has the effect of "wasting" the votes for Democratic candidates.

2.1.3 Partisan Gerrymandering

Today, one of the most prevalent types of gerrymandering in the United States is partisan, or "political" gerrymandering. Although malapportionment and racial gerrymandering were outlawed after the 1960s, the widespread practice of partisan gerrymandering is made possible due to advances in technology and information systems, such as the development of geographic information software in the 1980s, as well as Supreme Court decisions in the twenty-first century that prevents citizens from challenging politically biased district maps in the federal courts. The effect is that the gerrymanderers are permitted to draw district maps that systematically favor one party over the other, as long as they draw districts with approximately equal populations, do not illegally dilute the votes of minority citizens, and comply with state laws, which vary.

Figure 2.1c shows an example of how one party is able to gain an asymmetrical advantage in seat share. Districting authorities are able to comply with population equity and minority districting requirements, while drawing district lines in such a way that a party with only 30 percent of the vote is able to win a majority in two out of the four districts.

2.1.4 Incumbent Protection Gerrymanders

Another common, but conceptually distinct, type of gerrymandering is the "incumbent protection" gerrymander, in which districts are drawn to include "safe" seats for both parties through the "packing" of voters by party into separate districts. As with partisan gerrymandering, incumbent protection schemes serve the interests of the politicians who control redistricting. However, in contrast to partisan gerrymanders, which advance the interests of one party over another, incumbent protection gerrymanders serve the common interests of the two parties.

The effects of drawing "safe" districts are such that incumbent legislators are often easily reelected, and elections in general are uncompetitive and do not translate incremental shifts in two-party support by voters into changes in seat share.

Incumbent protection gerrymanders are achieved when districts are drawn with comfortable majorities for each party so that the members defending these districts will not face a serious threat to their power. As Figure 2.1d demonstrates, it is possible to achieve an incumbent protection gerrymander while satisfying population equity and minority representation by drawing districts with comfortable majorities for each party.

2.2 MEASURING PARTISAN GERRYMANDERING

We turn now to how we measure partisan bias. Bias means that the voting system gives one party an advantage over the other. We measure this by using the same partisan symmetry measure that we used in McGann et al. (2016), which is based on the approach of Gelman and King (Gelman and King 1990, 1994a, 1994b; Grofman and King 2007; Katz, King, and Rosenblatt 2020; see also Tufte 1973). However, we also introduce a far simpler way to calculate it. Partisan symmetry requires that the districting system does not advantage either party – that is, it has to give each party the same reward if it were to reach a certain share of the vote. So if the Republicans get seven seats out of ten when they win 60 percent of the vote, then the Democrats must also get seven seats out of ten, if they were to win 60 percent of the vote. Partisan symmetry is a measure of the degree to which this ideal is not achieved: how many more seats does Party A get for (say) 55 percent of the vote, compared to what Party B gets for 55 percent? Whereas calculating this involves some mathematics, the concept can be visualized very easily. Symmetry, after all, is a property that we can all recognize intuitively, whether in nature or art.

The use of partisan symmetry as our primary measure is not arbitrary. It is not simply a measure that has been made up because it is convenient or because it fits an intuition. Rather it follows logically from the principle that the electoral system should treat voters from both parties equally, which is surely a basic principle of electoral justice in a two-party system. This, in turn, can be derived directly from the majority rule principle (the requirement that the party that wins most votes should win most seats), which, in turn, is a logical consequence of the requirement that all votes should be counted equally in line with the principle of equal protection (see Katz, King, and Rosenblatt 2020; McGann et al. 2015, 2016).

It is important to recognize that partisan asymmetry is a direct result of asymmetry in the distribution of party support across districts. If the party support in the various districts is distributed symmetrically, it is impossible to create bias. This allows us to simplify things greatly. Calculating partisan symmetry in seat share requires us to run computer simulations to calculate a hypothetical seats–votes curve. However, demonstrating asymmetry in the distribution of districts can be done with a histogram in a spreadsheet program, or using some paper and pencil calculations. There are some advantages to calculating partisan symmetry from the seats–votes curve. For example, it allows you to calculate margins of error. For this reason, we will continue to use this method. However, simply looking at the distribution of districts has the advantage of simplicity and also addresses the requirement of Justice Kennedy in *Vieth v. Jubelirer* (2004) that measures not be based on hypothetical situations.[1] The key thing is to realize that the two forms of symmetry are two ways of looking at the same phenomenon (see also Wang 2016 on the use of histograms in evaluating partisan bias).

Some examples will make this point clearer. Figure 2.2 shows a districting plan where the districts are distributed symmetrically.

---

[1] We still hold that this position is unreasonable for the reason we gave in McGann et al. (2016), but calculating the asymmetry of the distribution of districts nevertheless addresses the objection.

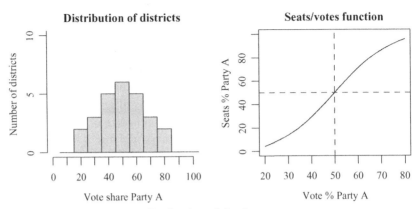

FIGURE 2.2. A symmetric distribution of districts

The symmetry is easy to see. There are six districts that are competitive, with Party A winning between 45 percent and 55 percent of the vote. On either side of this, there are five districts where Party A wins between 55 percent and 65 percent, and five districts where Party B wins 55–65 percent. Similarly, the three districts where Party A wins 65–75 percent are balanced by three districts where Party B wins 65–75 percent, and so on. This symmetric distribution of districts necessarily produces a symmetric seats–votes function, as shown in the panel on the right in Figure 2.2. Here we project how many seats each party would win for each level of statewide support, using the methodology in McGann et al. (2016).[2] It can be seen, for example, that if Party A wins 60 percent of the vote, it receives 71 percent of the seats, and also Party B receives 71 percent of the seats for 60 percent of the vote.

This distribution of districts in Figure 2.2 is centered on 50 percent. However, this is not necessary to produce a symmetric seats–votes function. Consider the distribution of districts in Figure 2.3. This is identical to the distribution in Figure 2.2, except it has been moved 20 percentage points to the right. The median district now has Party A winning 70 percent of the vote. However, this produces an identical seats–votes function.

---

[2] We assume that the swing in each district is approximately uniform across the state, in line with Gelman and King (1994b). That is, if Party A loses 5 percent of the vote statewide, it loses 5 percent in every district. However, we also include a random term to account for idiosyncratic, local factors. We simulate 1,000 elections and add a random term (mean 0, standard deviation 5) to each district at each election. We then plot the average seats won by Party A over the 1,000 simulated elections.

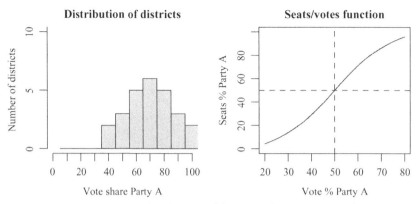

FIGURE 2.3. A symmetric distribution of districts where Party A is dominant

In the actual election, Party A would indeed win 70 percent of the vote and receive 87 percent of the seats, as the seats–votes function would predict. However, if there was a 20-point swing away from Party A so that it only won 50 percent of the vote in a hypothetical election, it would only win 50 percent of the seats. The seats–votes function depends on the shape of the distribution of seats, not where it is centered. Any symmetrical distribution will produce a symmetric seats–votes function that gives 50 percent of the seats for 50 percent of the vote.

All symmetric distributions of districts produce symmetric (and thus unbiased) seats–votes functions. However, by changing the distribution of districts we can still create very different levels of responsiveness. This can be seen in Figure 2.4, which gives two extreme examples. In the upper panels we have a distribution of districts that is symmetric, but makes all the districts extremely similar and competitive – Party A wins between 45 percent and 55 percent everywhere. This produces a seats–votes function that is extremely responsive, so that if a party wins 55 percent of the vote, it will win 80 percent of the seats (and probably 100 percent for 60 percent of the vote). The bottom panels, however, show a distribution where every district is either extremely safe for Party A, or extremely safe for Party B. We might characterize this as an "incumbent protection plan" – it is so unresponsive that each Party will retain its five safe seats unless one party is somehow able to win over 70 percent of the vote.

It is even possible to create a districting plan that produces a result that is proportional between the two parties, as shown in Figure 2.5. If the distribution of districts is uniformly flat, then if a party wins 60 percent of

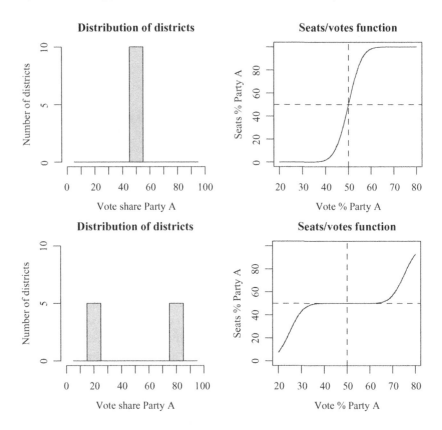

FIGURE 2.4. Symmetric distribution of districts with very high and very low responsiveness

the vote, it will win 60 percent of the seats, and so on. This is not actually proportional representation, of the type used in most countries of the world in some form. These rely on multimember districts and proportional distribution formulas.[3] However, it does produce a roughly proportional result. This, incidentally, demonstrates the difference between

---

[3] Proportional representation uses multimember districts so all parties receive seats roughly in proportion to their vote shares (there is a great deal of variation between countries as to how closely the results approximate true proportionality). A consequence of this is that it is easier for small parties to enter and compete, as they are not penalized by the electoral system (or at least are penalized less). The distribution of districts in Figure 2.5 produces proportionality in the result between the two main parties, but still makes it very difficult for third parties to compete.

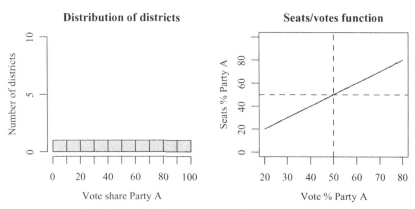

FIGURE 2.5. Distribution of districts that produce result that is proportional, as well as symmetric

symmetry and proportionality. A proportional seats–votes function is indeed symmetric. But, as we have seen, most symmetrical seats–votes functions are not proportional. It is quite possible to satisfy symmetry while giving a substantial "bonus" to the party that wins more votes, as is typically the case with single-member district elections. Symmetry only requires that we give the same "bonus" to whichever party happens to be largest.

We now turn to how to generate and detect partisan bias in districting plans. We already know that a symmetric distribution of seats will produce a symmetric, and thus unbiased, seats–votes function. Therefore, to create bias we need an asymmetric distribution of support across districts. Figure 2.6 shows a rather extreme example of this. This follows the strategy of packing your opponent's supporters into a small number of districts in order to use up their votes. This allows you to win a much larger number of districts by a smaller, but still comfortable margin. Thus, Party B wins two districts with 80 percent of the vote in each, while Party A wins eight districts with 57.5 percent of the vote. Party A wins eight districts out of ten, even though the two parties have an equal number of votes statewide. This naturally translates into an asymmetric seats–votes function that is biased in favor of Party A. The asymmetry – and thus bias – of this districting plan is plain to see simply by looking at the graphs.

Figure 2.6 shows a rather extreme example of a biased districting plan. If the asymmetry in the distribution of districts is moderate, then

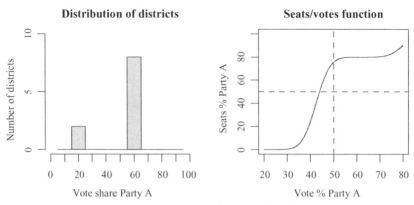

FIGURE 2.6. An asymmetric, biased distribution of districts

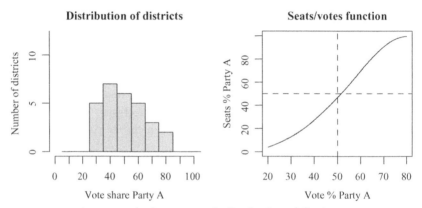

FIGURE 2.7. A very modestly asymmetric distribution of districts

the bias in the seats–votes will likewise be moderate. For example in Figure 2.7, the distribution of districts is only very slightly skewed in favor of Party B – some of Party A's supporters are packed in districts where they win by 80 percent, but Party B also has quite a few districts where it wastes votes by winning by 70 percent. This moderate skew produces only a very modest advantage for Party B. When both parties win 50 percent of the vote, Party A expects to win on average 48 percent of the seats.

We should note that there are many examples of districting plans in the United States where the level of skewness and bias is large. Figure 2.8 shows the distribution of support across the US House of Representatives

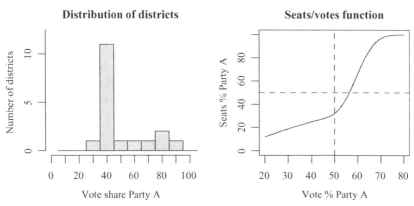

FIGURE 2.8. Distribution of districts in the US House of Representative for Pennsylvania 2012

districts in Pennsylvania in 2012.[4] The distribution of support across districts is strikingly asymmetric. No less than twelve out of the eighteen districts have Republican two-party vote share between 55 percent and 65 percent – that is, a comfortable, but not excessive margin of victory. This is balanced by three districts that the Democrats won by overwhelming margins. As a result, the Republicans took thirteen seats out of eighteen in 2012, even though the Democrats won 51 percent of the two-party vote. It turns out that the example of extreme gerrymandering in Figure 2.6 is not that different from the actual districts drawn in Pennsylvania following the 2010 Census.

2.2.1 Putting a Number on Bias and Responsiveness

As we have seen, asymmetry and bias are easy to see when we observe the graphs of both the distribution of districts and the seats–votes function. However, we would still like a numerical measure of bias. The main measure we use is partisan asymmetry. This is the same measure that we used in *Gerrymandering in America* (McGann et al., 2016) and is a simplification of the method in Gelman and King (1994b). This is based on the principle that in an unbiased districting system if one party gets a

---

[4] These districts were used in the elections of 2012, 2014, and 2016. However, following a decision by the Pennsylvania Supreme Court, they were replaced for the 2018 elections. The new districts gave less advantage to the Republicans, with the Democrats winning nine seats out of eighteen from 55 percent of the two-party statewide vote.

certain number of seats for a certain vote share, then if the other party manages to achieve that vote share, it is entitled to the same share of the seats. So, if winning 55 percent of the vote gets the Republicans 60 percent of the seats, then if the Democrats win 55 percent of the vote, they must also get 60 percent of the seats. This produces a symmetric seats–votes function. Our measure of partisan symmetry measures how much the actual districting system diverges from this. Figure 2.9 illustrates this.

The seats–votes function on the left is from an unbiased districting plan. If Party A gets 55 percent of the vote, it wins 61 percent of the seats. If party B wins 55 percent of the vote (so Party A gets 45 percent) then it also gets 61 percent of the seats. So, the difference between what Party A and Party B gets for winning 55 percent of the vote is zero. As a result the seats–votes function is symmetric. The seats–votes function on the right is clearly asymmetric and thus biased. If Party B wins 55 percent of the vote, it gets 73 percent of the seats, while Party A only gets 45 percent of the seats if it gets 55 percent of the vote. There is in fact a 28 percent difference between what Party B gets for 55 percent of the vote and what Party A gets for this level of support. Of course, we are not just interested in the advantage that Party B gets when both parties get 55 percent of the vote. We can also calculate the difference between what the two parties get when they both get 54 percent or 53 percent, and so forth. We calculate the difference between what two parties get between all levels of support between 45 percent and 55 percent and take the average. This is our measure of bias. The average difference of 33 percent is rather extreme – it reflects the fact that if both parties get 50 percent of the vote, Party B will get around 66 percent of the seats. However, as we showed in *Gerrymandering in America* (McGann et al., 2016) several districting plans for the US House of Representatives are this biased.

Our actual calculations of partisan symmetry are slightly more complex than this. We do not simply calculate the seat votes function by assuming uniform partisan swing (the assumption that if a party loses 5 percent of its vote statewide, it loses 5 percent of its vote in every district). Rather we add a random term to every district to account for idiosyncratic local factors. We run one thousand simulations, adding a random term (standard deviation 5 percent) to each district to account for the local factors. This adds to the complexity of our calculation somewhat, but there are two reasons we do it. First, it is more realistic. In reality there are likely to be many local factors that affect election outcomes. The effect of adding a substantial random term is to make our

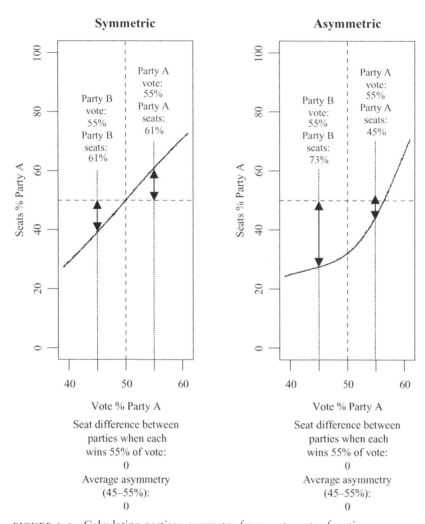

FIGURE 2.9. Calculating partisan symmetry from seats–votes function

estimates more conservative – the random noise to some degree drowns out the effect of the bias. As a result, our estimates of bias are lower than what we would have gotten without the random term. Secondly, it allows us to estimate margins of error. By doing a thousand simulations we can calculate not just the expected degree of bias, but how much we would expect that to vary due to random effects between elections. That is to say, we can say how confident we are that the bias we see is not just the result of random perturbations.

2.2.1.1 A Really Simple Measure of Bias/Asymmetry

We can provide a very simple, but effective measure of bias by measuring the asymmetry of the distribution of districts. We have already shown that asymmetry in the seats–votes function is a direct result of an asymmetric distribution of support across districts. Therefore we should be able to measure bias simply by looking at how skewed the distribution of districts is, without having to worry about projecting how many seats a party will win at different levels of support. In this section, we present a very simple measure that does just that. Even though it can be calculated from the election results with pencil and paper, it provides essentially the same information as the partisan symmetry measure. Indeed, we find that the two measures correlate very closely, with a correlation coefficient of around 0.95 when applied our state legislature data.

Having a really simple measure of bias has the obvious benefit of making partisan bias transparent to everyone. It also has benefits when bringing litigation concerning gerrymandered districts. Courts have been skeptical of arguments based on complex mathematical arguments – recall Chief Justice Roberts' comments about "sociological gobbledegook" during the oral arguments on *Gill* v. *Whitford* (2017). Indeed one of the justifications of the "efficiency gap" measure of Stephanopoulos and McGhee (2015) was that it answered the demand from Justice Kennedy for a simple measure that did not rely on hypothetical or simulated election results.[5] The efficiency gap is indeed simple to calculate and works well in some contexts (it was among the measures used by the plaintiffs in *Gill* v. *Whitford* (2017)). However, as we will argue subsequently, it can be very misleading in others, because it measures a combination of both bias and responsiveness. We provide a measure that is just as simple to calculate directly from the election results, but only measures bias.

The measure we propose simply involves taking the districts that are more than 5 percent above or below the statewide average and asking what proportion of them goes to the Democrats and what proportion goes to the Republican. The basic strategy for creating biased districting plans involves giving your opponents a few extremely safe seats to soak

---

[5] For a period of time measuring bias without having to project vote share was significant because of the opinion of Justice Kennedy in *Vieth* v. *Jubelirer* (2004). Justice Kennedy left open the possibility of finding a justiciable measure of bias, but rejected and standard based on hypothetical or projected election results. Although this was just an opinion of one Justice, it was important because Justice Kennedy was the swing vote in *Veith* and subsequent litigation. This consideration is less significant now that Justice Kennedy is no longer on the Supreme Court.

up their vote, allowing your party to win a much larger number of districts by a smaller (but still safe enough) margin. This measure captures precisely this logic. Formally the measure is:

Bias = (Proportion of seats with Democratic vote share 5% more than statewide average) – (Proportion of seats with Republican vote share 5% more than statewide average)

The measure has a clear intuition behind it – does the districting plan create more Democratic or more Republican leaning districts relative to the average level support the parties get in the state? We ignore districts that are within 5 percent of the statewide average, as these districts are close enough that they could go to either party if the vote is close to fifty–fifty at the statewide level. What we are interested in is how many districts does each party have where they have an entrenched advantage.

To give an example, let us consider again the distribution of the US House districts in Pennsylvania in 2012, in Figure 2.10. Here the Democrats have five districts where their vote is 5 percent more than the statewide average, which is 28 percent of the eighteen districts in the state. The Republicans have twelve districts where their vote is 5 percent more than the statewide average, which equals 67 percent of the districts. Thus, the Republican advantage is 67% – 28% = 39%. We can also validate this measure by comparing it with the results for the partisan symmetry measure we defined in the last section, which is based on the simulated seats–votes function.

The estimate of bias using the partisan symmetry method described in the previous section is a 36 percent Republican advantage. We would expect the two measures to produce similar results from theory. One is a measure of symmetry in the distribution of support, while the other measures symmetry in the seats–votes function, and we know that the two kinds of symmetry are two sides of the same process. We have tested this with the data on state House and State Senate results that we describe subsequently. We find that the correlation between the two measures lies between 0.92 and 0.98 depending on the year. Thus, we have a measure that can be calculated in minutes with pencil and paper, but which captures most of the information in the partisan symmetry measure.

2.2.2 Other Measures of Bias

We now turn to approaches to judging gerrymanders that do not rely on the concept of symmetry. These are the efficiency gap approach (Stephanopoulos and McGhee 2015), the three tests proposed by

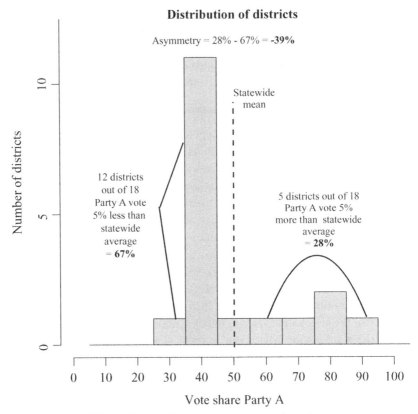

FIGURE 2.10. Calculating simple symmetry measure from histogram

Samuel Wang, and the use of computer-automated districting. All of these have been referred to in recent litigation before the US Supreme Court, including *Gill* v. *Whitford* (2018) and *Rucho* v. *Common Cause* (2019).

2.2.2.1 The Efficiency Gap

One measure of bias in districting that has gotten considerable attention in recent years is the efficiency gap, proposed by Stephanopoulos and McGhee (2015). They claim that this measure is simpler to calculate than partisan symmetry, and also addresses the objection of Justice Kennedy that a measure of bias should not use counterfactual reasoning (*LULAC* v. *Perry* 2006). It was one of the measures of bias used by the plaintiffs in *Gill* v. *Whitford* (2018), which challenged state-level districting in Wisconsin and was heard by the US Supreme Court.

However, we find that the efficiency gap is not a reliable measure of partisan gerrymandering. While it is simple to calculate, it can produce misleading results. We will show that it can both fail to detect bias when it clearly exists and can also find bias when there is none present. Although it seems to produce reasonable conclusions when the vote share of the parties is close to fifty–fifty, problems emerge when one party wins substantially more votes than the other (see also Veomett 2018). The basic cause of the problem is that the efficiency gap does not just measure bias. Instead it measures a mixture of bias and responsiveness. Furthermore, we now have other measures of bias that are just as simple to calculate, such as the simple symmetry measure we have proposed.

The efficiency gap measures the degree to which one party has more wasted votes that the other. Formally, it is defined as:

Efficiency gap = (Wasted votes Democrats – Wasted votes Republican) / (Total vote)

where a wasted vote is any vote cast for a party in a district it loses, and a "surplus vote" (a vote over 50 percent) in a district it wins (Stephanopoulos and McGhee 2015, p. 15).

Thus, for the efficiency gap to be zero, both parties have to have exactly the same number of wasted votes. In a two-party system with equal district population, the definition of the efficiency gap implies an even simpler formula:

Efficiency Gap = Seat Margin – (2 x Vote Margin),

where Seat Margin is the party's seat share minus 50 percent, and Vote Margin is the party's vote share minus 50 percent (Stephanopoulos and McGhee 2015, p. 17).

Suppose we want the efficiency gap to be zero, and thus for there to be no bias according to this measure. Then obviously if a party wins 50 percent of the vote, then it must get 50 percent of the seats. However, if that party wins an additional 1 percent of the vote, then it must get an extra 2 percent of the seats. Thus if the party gets 55 percent of the vote, it must get 60 percent of the seats, in order to keep the efficiency gap at zero. And if it gets 60 percent of the vote, it must get 70 percent of the seats. Similarly, if its vote falls to 40 percent of the vote, then it must get 30 percent of the seats. Another way of saying this is that for the efficiency gap to be zero across different levels of vote share, the responsiveness of the seats–votes function needs to be exactly two.

We can now look at the problems with the efficiency gap as a measure of bias. To get an efficiency gap of zero (no bias), both parties have to waste the same absolute number of votes. This requirement is reasonable when both parties have roughly the same vote share. However, it is not equitable when they have very different vote shares. Consider the case of Maryland US House districts in 2018. If we apply the efficiency gap methodology, we find that both parties waste a similar number of votes – the Democrats waste 527,713, while the Republicans waste 587,759. As a result, the efficiency gap is only 3 percent. However, the Democrats won 67 percent of the two-party vote. The 587,759 wasted Republican votes amount to 80 percent of the Republican total, while the Democrats only waste 35 percent of their vote! If we want to measure how efficiently each party's votes are being translated into seats, we should surely insist that each party waste the same percentage of their total (or waste the same number of votes per seat won). We should not require that the two parties waste the same absolute number of votes, when they win very different levels of votes and seats.

Equally concerning is the fact that the efficiency gap does not detect that the districts in Maryland are an egregious gerrymander in favor of the Democratic Party. When we calculate the efficiency gap in 2018, we get only 3 percent. Figure 2.11 provides the histogram and the seats–votes function calculated from the 2018 election, using the methodology described in this chapter. It is clear that the distribution of districts is highly skewed and that the estimated seats–votes function is biased to the benefit of the Democrats. We calculate that the asymmetry is 23 percent using the seats–votes function, and 25 percent from the simplified method using the histogram. We can see why the efficiency gap misses this gerrymander. The Democrats won 67 percent of the statewide vote. To have a zero efficiency gap, they would have to receive 84 percent of the seats. They actually received 87 percent (seven seats out of eight), which produces a 3 percent efficiency gap. The efficiency gap is low because in this one election, the seats awarded are close to what the efficiency gap says it should be. The problem is, with these districts the Democrats could have lost 10 percent of the vote, and still won seven seats out of eight. Unlike the partisan symmetry measure, the efficiency gap does not take this into account. Admittedly, if we calculated the efficiency gap for previous years when the Democratic vote was lower, the efficiency gap would be higher. However, it remains true that the efficiency gap for any given year may be quite misleading, and we cannot wait for several

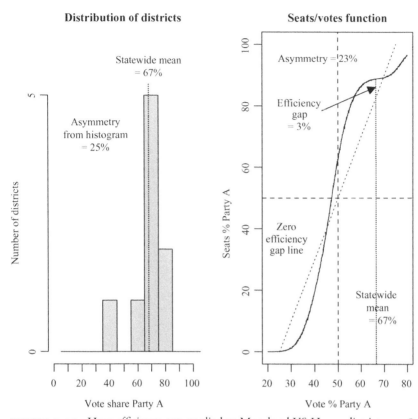

FIGURE 2.11. How efficiency gap applied to Maryland US House districts 2018

elections to get a selection of efficiency gaps at different vote level. By then it will be time for the next districting cycle.

We can also see how the efficiency gap measure can find bias when none, in fact, exists. Consider Figure 2.12. This gives three unbiased, symmetric seats–votes functions. The first is highly responsive, the second has low responsiveness, while the third is completely proportional. All three of these unbiased seats–votes functions produce sizeable efficiency gaps when we get away from a fifty–fifty vote split. The dotted line shows what seat share a party needs to get for each vote share in order to have a zero efficiency gap. As we have explained, for every 1 percent of the vote it wins above 50 percent, it needs to win 2 percent more seats (so it wins 70 percent of the seats for 60 percent of the vote, etc.) Thus, to satisfy the efficiency gap criterion across all vote levels, responsiveness needs to

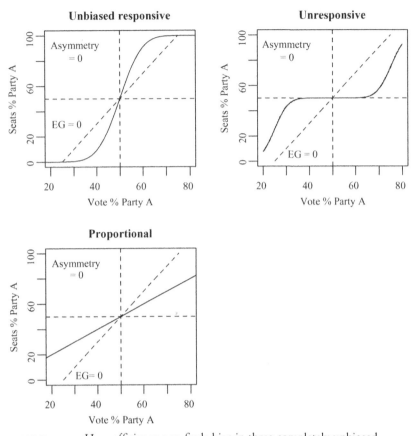

FIGURE 2.12. How efficiency gap finds bias in three completely unbiased districting plans

equal two. The first seats–votes function has a substantial efficiency gap away from the fifty–fifty point because it is too responsive for the efficiency gap criteria (responsiveness is greater than two). The second seats–votes function has an efficiency gap because it is not responsive enough. The third seats–votes function is proportional. However, even this generates an efficiency gap, because it has a responsiveness of one, not two. With the proportional seats–votes function, if a party wins 60 percent of the vote, it gets 60 percent of the seats. However, the efficiency gap criteria demand that it get 70 percent of the seats.

A great strength of the partisan symmetry approach to bias is that it makes no judgment as to what an appropriate level of responsiveness is.

Plans that have high responsiveness, low responsiveness, or something in between (such as proportionality) are all alright provided they treat both parties in the same way. The efficiency gap, on the other hand, requires that responsiveness equal two. The problem is, no one has to our knowledge given any coherent, normative justification of why the level of responsiveness should equal two. Thus, when we see a report of an election result producing an efficiency gap, we do not know whether this is really the result of bias, or the result of the (unjustified) requirement that responsiveness equals two.

Finally, we would note that the other advantages claimed for the efficiency gap no longer apply. There are measures of symmetry that are just as simple to calculate as the efficiency gap. These include histograms, the simple symmetry measure laid out in this chapter, and the mean–median difference advocated by Sam Wang (2016). Furthermore, the need to appeal to Justice Kennedy no longer exists. One of the justifications given by Stephanopoulos and McGhee (2015) was that Justice Kennedy in his opinion on *LULAC* v. *Perry* (2006) argued that a measure of partisan gerrymandering should not rely on counterfactual reasoning. As Justice Kennedy was the swing vote on the Supreme Court, there was a rationale for producing a measure that did not rely on counterfactual reasoning. With Justice Kennedy's retirement in 2018, that rationale no longer exists.[6]

2.2.2.2 Samuel Wang's Three Tests for Partisan Gerrymandering

Wang (2016) provides a number of simple tests for partisan gerrymandering, most of which can be done with a pocket calculator or even mental math. These tests have the advantage of being very simple to carry out, and also being quite intuitive. However, it is important to consider exactly what they are measuring and their limitations.

The first test is the "excess seats test." This starts by taking an average seats–votes function for the United States. You then take the vote share of one of the parties and calculate what seats it should get according to the seats–votes function. Then you compare this to the actual number of seats it won. If it won more seats than the seats–votes function predicts, then

---

[6] We argue in McGann et al. (2016) that the requirement that a measure of bias not use counterfactual reasoning makes no sense, legally or logically. To show that a contest is unfair, it is not sufficient to show that you lost. You need to show that you did not have a fair chance of winning, which requires counterfactual reasoning.

there is bias in its favor. Similar techniques have been previously used by Tufte (1973) and Goedert (2014b).

The limitations of this technique are very similar to that of the efficiency gap. The efficiency gap measures the seat share a party gets relative to straight line going through the fifty–fifty point with a slope (responsiveness) of 2. The excess seats test considers the number of seats a party gets compared to an average seats–votes function (divided by the standard deviation). Given that the slope (responsiveness) of the average seats–votes function for the United States will be close to 2, the efficiency gap and the excess seats test will give similar results. In particular, both tests will find bias in perfectly symmetric seats–votes functions because they are either too responsive or not responsive enough (as in the case of a proportional seats–votes function). They will also both sometimes fail to detect bias in clearly biased districting plans, such as in the Maryland US House map in 2018, because the seat share for that particular election is roughly what the seats–votes function predicts.

The second test is the "lopsided outcomes test." Here you calculate the average vote share of the Democrats in districts they win and the average Republican vote share in districts they win. Then you subtract one from the other. The intuition here is that the basic tactic of gerrymandering is to "pack" your opponents' supporters into a small number of districts that they win by an excessive margin. This test simply measures whether the Democratic average margin of victory is greater than the Republican margin of victory. The problem is that this test does not work very well if the statewide vote shares are not close to fifty–fifty. For example, in Maryland in 2018, the Republican vote share in the Republican district was 61.2 percent, while the average Democratic vote share in the Democratic districts was 70.8 percent. This would suggest a considerable bias in favor of the Republicans, while if you consider symmetry or the seats–votes function, there is clearly a strong bias toward the Democrats. The problem is that the lopsided outcomes test measures lopsided outcomes relative to a fifty–fifty vote share and not relative to the statewide vote share (which in Maryland 2018 was 67 percent in favor of the Democrats). A revised version of the lopsided outcomes test measured relative to the statewide vote share may work better.

The third test is the "reliable wins test." In the case of closely divided states, Wang measures this using the mean–median difference – simply the difference between the statewide mean for a party and its vote percentage in the median district. This measure has previously been used by Erikson (1972) and McDonald and Best (2015). It is extremely easy to calculate and is a measure of the asymmetry or skewness of the distribution of districts. However, it captures something rather different than the partisan symmetry measure we use. Suppose that there is a state with eleven districts and it has a mean–median difference of eight. Then the disadvantaged party would need to win 58 percent of the vote to capture the median district and hold six seats out of eleven. However, the mean–median difference tells us nothing about how severely the party is disadvantaged before it reaches 58 percent. It could be that when the vote is split fifty–fifty, the disadvantaged party gets five seats out of eleven – it is just the sixth seat that is really hard for it to take. On the other hand, it could be when it wins 50 percent of the vote it only wins two seats out of eleven. The mean–median difference does not tell us how many seats the gerrymander costs the disadvantaged party, but rather how many extra votes the disadvantaged party needs to overcome it. As Katz et al. (2020, 174) put it, it is an estimator of "vote denominated" partisan bias – "how much more one party must earn in votes than the other party to win a given seat proportion." It thus provides important information that supplements that provided by the partisan symmetry measure, but it is not the same.

2.2.2.3 *The Perils of Automated Districting as a Standard*
Another technique for testing for gerrymandering is to use computer-automated districting to construct a baseline, and then ask how much the actual districts vary from this (Cain et al. 2018; Chen and Rodden 2013a; Guest, Kanayet, and Love 2019; Krasno et al. 2019; Magleby and Mosseson 2018; Tam Cho and Liu 2016;). This methodology has become more common in recent years and has been referred to in recent litigation. It does not, strictly speaking, measure the degree of bias, and indeed it relies on already existing measures of bias. What it does is attempt to determine whether the bias we observe is the result of deliberate gerrymandering, or whether it has arisen accidentally because of factors such as geographic concentration. Unfortunately, the logic underlying this is fundamentally flawed, as we will explain subsequently. While computer-aided districting has tremendous potential for expanding our understanding of districting, it is simply logically impossible for it to show that a gerrymander is not intentional.

Of course, computer-automated districting has other purposes. Decades ago, Vickrey (1961), for example, advocated automated redistricting as a way of replacing biased human map drawers altogether, while Altman and McDonald (2011a) provide open source automated redistricting software (while at the same time providing important caveats about the approach). We, however, are concerned here with the use of computer-automated districting as a means of evaluating gerrymanders. Cirincione, Darling, and O'Rourke (2000) apply this technique to racial bias in districting, while the other authors listed in the previous paragraph apply it to partisan gerrymandering. The basic approach is to have a computer generate thousands of districting maps. As this process would not take into account political criteria, these maps would represent a neutral baseline – the lines that "would be drawn in the absence of partisan gerrymandering," as Cain et al. (2018, 8) put it. We could then compare the level of bias in the computer-generated plans to the amount of bias in the actual plan that was enacted. Cain et al. (2018, 11) suggest the following: does the plan produce "an expected seat/vote share or partisan bias score that occurs in only 5% or less of the machine generated maps?" If the plan is more bias than 95 percent of the plans generated by the computer, it is rejected as unacceptably biased.

There are two problems associated with this approach. The first is mathematical. If we are to judge whether a plan exceeds (say) 95 percent of all possible plans, we need to be confident that the computer is generating an unbiased sample of all possible plans. It turns out to be impossible to know whether this is true. The second and more fundamental problem is logical. Even if the technical problems could be overcome, the method would still not show that a gerrymander was unintentional.

We can start with the technical or statistical problem. In order to draw statistical inferences about whether the plan is more biased than 95 percent of all possible plans, we need our computer-generated plans to be a representative sample of all possible plans. The problem is, we cannot know this. As Altman and McDonald (2011b; 2015) argue, districting is the kind of problem mathematicians refer to as "NP-Complete." This means that as the number of districts increase beyond a trivially small number, the number of possible maps rise very quickly to an incomputably large number. That is to say, not just a larger number than we can currently compute, but a larger number than we think it will ever be theoretically possible to compute. As a result, it is impossible to enumerate all the possible district plans, and also impossible to know whether the sample of plans generated by the computer is random and unbiased. We might think that the computer is generating an unbiased selection of plans because it does not consider political variables, but we do not know this – there may be any number of hidden biases that we do not know about.

To make things worse, Altman and McDonald show that many computer-generated algorithms (including that of Chen and Rodden 2013a) fail to produce an unbiased sample of possible plans even in very simple "toy" problems where it is possible to write out all the possible plans. More recent work (Tam Cho and Liu 2016; 2018) address this and propose more powerful algorithms. Indeed Magleby and Mosseson (2018) show that their algorithm shows no sign of bias in a number of "toy" problems. Nevertheless, we still cannot be sure that these algorithms generate an unbiased sample of plans when they are applied to real-world examples, as there is no way to conceivably write out all the possible alternatives.

However, even if all these technical issues were overcome, it would still not be possible to ever conclude from computer-aided districting that a gerrymandering is unintentional. The second, logical problem would remain. Cain et al. (2018) and others argue that if the level of bias is higher than the amount found in 95 percent of computer-drawn plans, then we can conclude that it is deliberately gerrymandered. This is fair enough. However, if the level of bias is not greater than that in 95 percent of cases, we *cannot* conclude that there is no intentional gerrymander. We have simply failed to prove that there is an intentional gerrymander. From a logical point of view, failing to prove something is not the same thing at all as proving that something is *not* the case. In this case, the test based on computer-generated districting tells us literally nothing – the bias *may or may not* be result of intentional gerrymandering. Of course, you could argue (correctly) that there ought to be a presumption of innocence. But there may be plenty of other evidence of intent, and the inconclusive results from computer-aided districting can do nothing to negate this evidence.

Let us consider an example of this logic. Suppose I cheat at cards by intentionally dealing myself a winning hand. I am not very good at it, and people see me cheating. I, however, have a cunning defense. I hire a mathematician who uses precisely the same logic as is used to argue that gerrymandering is unintentional. My mathematician argues there is a slightly greater than 5 percent chance that an unbiased dealer would have dealt me cards at least as good as the ones I dealt myself. Therefore, I did not intentionally cheat. Of course, this defense is preposterous. The fact that it is just about plausible that an honest dealer could deal me cards as good as the ones I got is irrelevant. It does not prove that I did in fact get them honestly. My opponent's case does not depend on the cards I received being implausibly good, but on the fact that I was seen cheating.

The logic of the defense in the last paragraph is clearly ridiculous, but it is exactly the logic you would need to use to argue that partisan bias was unintentional using computer-aided districting. You would have to argue that because an unbiased process (computer-aided districting) could produce the same level of bias at least 5 percent of the time, then we should conclude that there is no intentional gerrymandering. The problem is the fact that an unbiased process plausibly *could have* produced the observed outcome does not prove that an unbiased process *did in fact* produce this outcome. There are, after all, plenty of reasons to believe the opposite. The state legislators who draw the districts have the power to choose any districts they like. They are partisans with every incentive to stack things in their favor. And they do indeed get to see the cards before they are dealt – they have access to modern geographic information systems (GIS) so they cannot credibly claim they do not know the partisan consequence of their choices. In short, they have the means, motive, and opportunity to stack things in their favor.

There are, in fact, far more direct ways than computer-automated districting to show that a gerrymander is intentional. If a state legislature (or other districting authority) has the option of drawing an unbiased districting plan, but chooses instead to draw a more biased plan, then it has made a (political) choice. Altman et al. (2015) refer to this as the method of revealed preference. If we can show that the authority knew about districting plans that are unbiased – or just one plan for that matter – and that meet all legal requirements, but nevertheless chose a more biased plan, we can infer that they made an intentional choice. It is also roughly the argument we made in McGann et al. (2016, 102), although the argument there was less rigorous and did not take into account that it is necessary to show not just that unbiased plans exist, but that the authority knew about them. The key is to show that the districting authority had access to less biased plans. The most straightforward way to do this is to consider plans "made public by any source through the districting process" (Altman et al. 2015, 33). The public redistricting programs of the kind organized by Altman and McDonald (2013, 2014, 2015) would be an excellent source of such plans. So might computer-aided districting exercises.

In addition to the logical and mathematical problems we have discussed, the various standards based on computer-aided districting appear rather favorable to state legislatures seeking partisan advantage. For example, the standard proposed in Cain et al. (2018) means that the party drawing the districts is essentially entitled to the advantage it would enjoy under a representative districting plan drawn without political data, even if it is completely possible to draw unbiased districts. Indeed, it is even more permissive than this – the standard suggested by Cain et al. (2018, 11) allows any plan that is within the 95 percent confidence limits of the distribution of computer-generated plans. The state legislature could take the distribution of plans, and then use political data to cherry-pick the one that gives greatest partisan advantage while not falling in the 5 percent tail. Thus, the way the Cain et al. proposed to use computer-automated districting would allow state legislatures a great degree of latitude to seek partisan advantage, particularly in states where one party is more concentrated than the other (see Chapter 4).

2.3 HOW WE COLLECTED OUR DATA

One of the appeals of the method for estimating partisan symmetry that we have outlined is that we are able to evaluate the performance of a district plan using the results of at least one single election cycle. Accordingly, in order to study the effectiveness of 2011 redistricting in the more than ninety state legislative chambers, we need at least two data points to assess the redistricting outcomes of a given plan: (1) the partisan composition of each individual district included in the "old" maps (those in place before 2011) and (2) the partisan composition of each individual district included in the "new" map (those approved in 2011).

Finding these data presents a number of challenges. The availability and accessibility of data on state legislative election outcomes varies widely between states, and the scale of districting at the state level complicates the data collection process. In the fifty states, there are a total of ninety-nine state legislative assemblies that employ ninety-nine districting maps, with a combined 7,000 legislative districts. At a minimum, this task requires us to find the results of more than 14,000 individual district-level elections.

One of the primary resources we relied upon, as a starting point, was the comprehensive State Legislative Election Results database published by Carl Klarner, which includes the vote returns for each candidate running in district-level state legislative elections going back to the 1970s (Klarner 2018). By aggregating candidate vote returns by district and election year, it is relatively simple to determine the voter turnout and the Democratic share of the two-party vote.

However, for most state legislative bodies, we were not able to rely on this data alone due to the sheer number of uncontested races in the typical state legislative election. In some state legislatures, well over 50 percent of the seats during a given election cycle were uncontested. Because states vary in how they report uncontested results, we had to find an alternative way of estimating district-level partisanship.

One solution, which we employed in McGann et al. (2016), is to use presidential election results, broken down by state legislative district, to estimate the partisan composition of those state legislative districts with missing election return data. Here, we are grateful to Stephen Wolf of the Daily Kos, who provided us access to his database on the 2008, 2012, and 2016 presidential election returns broken down by state legislative district.

By looking at the two-party presidential vote share at the precinct-level, we were able to estimate the level of support in state legislative districts where data was missing, due to uncontested races. We were able to impute the missing data by regressing the legislative Democratic two-party vote share against the presidential Democratic two-party vote share in the lower house, and apply these results to the uncontested districts in the lower house and upper house (which tend to be smaller). For most states this approach gave us one observation before 2011 (typically the elections held in 2008, but in a few instances, the elections in 2010 or 2007), as well as two observations post-2011 (most often, the elections in 2011–12 and 2015–16, but in a few instances 2014 and/or 2018).

We applied a similar fix when estimating partisanship in districts in state legislative assemblies (usually a state senate) that hold "staggered" election cycles, in which only half or a third of the body is up for reelection during a given election year. In these cases, we calculated the "swing" from one election cycle to the next, using the lower house elections. For example, in Tennessee, the lower house holds elections every two years during even-numbered years, while the upper house elects approximately half of the members every two years during even-numbered years. The lower house elections gave us a means of estimating the results of the state senate districts that were not up for election in 2012 or 2016. For example, in 2012 and in 2016, the sixteen even-numbered senate districts were elected, and the seventeen odd-numbered districts were elected in 2014. In order to estimate what the partisan composition of these odd-numbered districts would have been in 2012 and 2016, we regressed both the 2012 and 2016 state house results against the 2014 state house results, and applied these terms to the results of the 2014 senate elections (i.e., the seventeen odd-numbered districts). This gave us a way of estimating the partisan composition of the entire senate in both 2012 and 2016, while accounting for the two-party vote swings that occurred between the three election cycles.

In a few cases (i.e., Maryland and Michigan), states only elect their legislatures during off-year elections, while in other cases (i.e., Virginia), states held elections in odd years. In these instances, when there was not a concurrent presidential election, we applied the same approach – imputing the 2009 or 2010 lower house election results (for example) against the 2008 presidential election returns by district, the 2013 or 2014 results against the 2012 presidential data, or the 2018 results against the 2016 presidential data.

In general, the correlation between these state-level results and presidential results parsed by district were quite high, even in states with off- and odd-year elections. However, there were three notable outliers. In three states, we observed a relatively low correlation between partisan performance in state legislative lower house elections and in presidential elections. These states were Arkansas (r^2=0.38), Oklahoma (r^2=0.29), and West Virginia (r^2=0.25). Nevertheless, in most states, we observed a very high correlation (r^2>0.80) between state legislative and presidential results.

2.4 FINDINGS

In total, our dataset includes voter turnout and Democratic two-party vote share estimates for ninety-five state legislative chambers, for at least one election cycle before and after 2011. (We were unable to find complete, reliable data for the upper and lower houses in Alabama and Mississippi.) Using this data, we were able to estimate the partisan bias and responsiveness scores in forty-eight state legislatures, before and after 2011, using the methodology described earlier. With these estimates, we are able to evaluate the outcomes of redistricting in ninety-five state legislative bodies.

At the aggregate level, our estimates show that the 2011 districting maps have a bias in favor of the Republican Party of –9 percent on average. This means that, for a given level of support, Republicans would gain approximately 9 percent more seats than the Democrats would gain for that same level of support. In the previous districting round, based on our analysis the results of elections held between 2007 and 2010, the average symmetry score was about –6 percent, which indicates an increase of about 50 percent after redistricting. We find similar results when we use our alternative measure of bias, which measures the difference in the number of seats with a Democratic advantage and the number of seats with a Republican

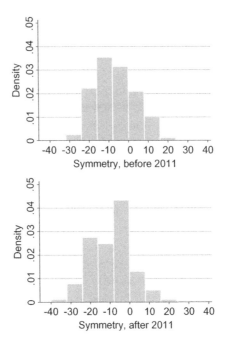

FIGURE 2.13. Distribution of symmetry scores, before and after 2011 redistricting

advantage. Here, we observe similarly that bias increased from an average of about –6.5 percent nationwide to –9.5 percent nationwide.

Figure 2.13 shows the distribution of all symmetry scores in the "old" maps used before 2011, as well as those enacted after 2011 redistricting. In most cases, we were able to estimate the post-2011 partisan symmetry scores for two separate election cycles. For maps with two observations, we report the average of both.

In the "old" maps, the distribution of all scores resembles a normal "bell curve" that is skewed right. There are many maps with extreme levels of bias that favor the Republicans, and a few that favor Democrats.

When we compare the new plans – those redistricted in 2011 – we find two different outcomes. Many maps became unbiased, and there is a sharp increase in the number of maps close to zero. But there were also increases in the number of maps with Republican bias in excess of 20–30 percent.

Table 2.1 reports the redistricting outcomes of the maps that were drawn in 2011 with the greatest levels of bias. This subsample includes

TABLE 2.1. *2011 state legislative redistricting plans with extreme partisan bias (+/– 10 percent)*

	Republican bias:	Democratic bias:
Biased maps that became *more* biased	AZ-L, FL-L, GA-L, GA-U, ID-U, IN-U, KY-U, MO-L, OH-L, OH-U, PA-L, PA-U, SC-U, TN-L, TN-U, TX-U, UT-U, VA-L Mean symmetry: –21.2 percent Mean change in symmetry: –6.1 percent	
Maps that preserved extreme bias	FL-U, KS-L, MI-U, MN-U, MO-U, NE-U, NY-U, OK-L, OK-U, SC-L, WY-L, WY-U Mean symmetry: –15.0 percent Mean change in symmetry: +3.1 percent	
Unbiased maps that became biased	ID-L, IN-L, LA-L, LA-U, MI-L, MN-L, NC-L, NC-U, TX-L, UT-L, WI-L, WI-U Mean symmetry: –18.3 percent Mean change in symmetry: –12.4 percent	HI-L, VT-U Mean symmetry: +13.2 percent Mean change in symmetry: +6.0 percent

forty-five separate district maps with "extreme partisan bias," which we define using the (somewhat arbitrary) threshold +/– 10 percent partisan symmetry. As is evident, in this subsample of maps, the bias overwhelmingly favors the Republicans. Of the forty-five maps, forty-three favor the Republicans, and only two favor the Democrats (the Vermont senate plan and the Hawaii house plan). The forty-three maps that were drawn with extreme Republican biased maps had an average symmetry score of about –18.5 percent representing an average increase of about –5.1 percent from the pre-2011 maps.

For most of the cases, the old maps were already substantially biased in favor of the Republicans. Here, redistricting authorities did not use decennial redistricting as an opportunity to mitigate districting bias. Rather, in most cases they drew more bias into a plan that was already extremely biased. Second, many states drew substantial increases into maps that had previously been neutral. If the ostensible purpose of redistricting is to redress malapportionment – which tends to harm Democrats more so than Republicans – then the simplest explanation for this increase in Republican bias is that the districting authorities had intended to gerrymander the maps to create a partisan advantage that had not previously existed.

We see a similar story when we look at the outcomes of redistricting in the two maps drawn with extreme Democratic bias. Before redistricting, the bias in the Vermont senate map (9.4 percent) and Hawaii house map (5.1 percent) were minimal. After redistricting, the level of pro-Democratic bias increased markedly in the Hawaii house plan (16.1 percent), but only marginally in the Vermont senate map (10.6 percent). However, it is easier for Democrats to explain the increase in bias as the by-product of reconfiguring district lines to achieve population equity.

2.5 CONCLUSION

In this chapter, we have investigated partisan bias in state legislative maps in order to assess the outcomes of state legislative redistricting in 2011. We first identified the concept of "gerrymandering" and discussed the unique harms posed by the type of gerrymandering we are primarily interested in, partisan gerrymandering. We then identified partisan symmetry as an intuitive and scientific standard for quantifying violations of democratic norms – in particular, violations of political equality. Partisan symmetry allows us to quantify the degree to which the voters of one party are harmed by a district map, under competitive statewide conditions. This gives us a basis for comparing the extent of gerrymandering in state legislative bodies.

Our findings demonstrate that the results of 2011 state legislative redistricting are comparable to what we observed when we investigated congressional districting. On average, state redistricting authorities gave Republicans an advantage in state legislative elections. We find that the average state legislative symmetry increased from about −6 percent before 2011 to about −9 percent after 2011. This increase was driven by several dozen state legislative maps that were drawn with extreme Republican bias. Indeed, the most extremely partisan gerrymandered maps are almost exclusively Republican. Of the forty-five maps that include asymmetries of 10 percent or more, only two favor the Democratic Party.

The findings of this chapter add an additional perspective to the story of 2011. The available evidence suggests that the voters who participated in the 2010 midterm elections were focused primarily on national politics and did not appreciate the consequences of these elections on control over 2011 redistricting. As we reported in McGann et al. (2016), many of the state governments elected in 2010 went on to aggressively gerrymander the US House maps. The findings of our investigation in this chapter provide a definitive answer to the question of whether the "Great Gerrymander of 2012" also occurred at the level of state government. It clearly did, and there is good reason to believe that the increase in bias in several state legislatures was deliberate.

In subsequent chapters, we investigate the political, institutional, and geographic determinants of the bias that we observe in 2011 redistricting. In the next chapter, we investigate whether this bias varies by redistricting institutions and political control. In Chapter 4, we analyze the role of political geography in shaping this bias.

3

When Politicians Draw the Maps

In this chapter, we investigate the role of politics in determining districting outcomes. As we saw in Chapter 2, there was wide variation in the maps produced by state governments during 2011 redistricting. In many of the plans, we saw large increases in bias favoring the GOP in states where previous plans were already biased toward the Republican Party. We also observe that, while bias favoring the Democratic Party increased in a few states, the resulting asymmetries are much smaller in scope and scale. If we average the bias in all ninety-five maps in our sample, we observed that, after 2011 redistricting the pro-Republican advantage in the plans increased such that, on average, Republican candidates win about 9 percent more seats than Democrats do for a similar share of the statewide vote. To understand this variation in districting bias, we take a systematic look at the processes that states use to regulate the drawing of the lines. We pay particular attention to one key variable: whether the maps were drawn by politicians.

Despite the intuitive appeal of political control of redistricting as a determinant of districting outcomes, political scientists have been debating the effects of political control for more than three decades. Scholarship dating back to the 1970s has sought to link political districting with electoral advantages. While some studies in the 1990s and 2000s suggest that political control of redistricting affects democratic politics in fundamental ways (Butler and Cain 1992; Engstrom 2006; Gelman and King 1994a), others have found that the electoral benefits associated with one-party controlled redistricting are modest (e.g., Lyons and Galderisi 1995; Niemi and Abramowitz 1994; Niemi and Jackman 1991). More recently, studies show examples of political parties gaining an electoral advantage through redistricting control (Chen 2017; Chen and Rodden 2015; Cottrell 2019; Powell, Clark, and Dube 2020), while other studies suggest that political districting does not decrease competition in the aggregate or argue that the effects of electoral impact of redistricting are minimal (Friedman and Holden 2009; Goedert 2014a; McGhee 2014; Seabrook 2017). In our investigation of congressional districting (McGann et al. 2016), we followed the framework advanced by Butler and Cain (1992) – that partisan gerrymandering occurs when actors have the "motive" and "opportunity" to draw bias – and found that the vast majority of the most biased maps occurred in states where one party controlled redistricting and had an incentive to use this control to gain an electoral advantage.

In this chapter, we use this framework to investigate the effects of political control of redistricting on outcomes through case studies and empirical analyses of redistricting outcomes. As a starting point, we assert that the human beings tasked with redistricting tend to make decisions with regard to their own interests to the extent that they are able to do so while conforming to legal districting criteria. Although states vary in terms of the rules they impose on districting authorities (rules that include population equity requirements and district contiguity, as well as district compactness, the promotion of political competition, and political community or boundary preservation) in practice, these rules represent obstacles, not barriers. They do not prevent motivated authorities from advancing political goals. We also assume that districting decisions are informed by political context. The maps are not made in a historical vacuum – rather, they are revised from the status quo, which may or may not already advance their political interests.

Despite the variation among states in terms of rules, constraints, and historical context, the one common thread is that when politicians draw the maps, they draw them to benefit their political party (see Owen and Grofman 1988). This can mean drawing partisan bias into a plan that provides a partisan advantage in vote–seat translation, as well as colluding with the other party to draw maps that are favorable to both parties, such as incumbent protection schemes that solidify the balance of power status quo through the drawing of "safe districts." In short, we assert that when politicians draw the maps, they exploit the process to advance their political interests.

The findings of our investigation into 2011 redistricting suggest that politics is indeed a powerful predictor of redistricting bias. We find that the most biased maps occur in competitive states where politicians from a single party were able to draw the maps without having to work with the minority party. Our examination of the effects of bipartisan districting yields inconclusive results. In some cases, when the redistricting process requires two parties to work together to pass a plan, redistricting authorities draw the maps with low levels of seat–vote responsiveness, presumably as a result of the drawing of "safe seats" that benefits incumbents from both parties. However, in other cases, we do not see this outcome. We do find that, on average, bipartisan districting leads to a preservation of the status quo. In the states where two parties worked together to draw the maps, the level of bias in the post-2011 plans deviated little from the pre-2011 plans.

3.1 HOW THE STATES DELEGATE REDISTRICTING AUTHORITY

In the fifty states, there is wide variation in the processes that govern state legislative redistricting. While a majority delegate the task to "political" bodies of elected officials, others empower nonpolitical actors, such as independent redistricting commissions, to redraw the maps insulated from direct political influence. Moreover, most state laws delegate the authority to contingency actors if the primary authority is unable to draw the lines, while others give third-party actors a veto power over maps that are drawn.

In order to investigate the links between redistricting processes and their outcomes, our first challenge is to investigate this variation in districting control. How do the fifty states redistrict their state legislative boundaries? To answer this question, we sought a variety of sources, ranging from state constitutions and statutes, to scholarship, to blogs and news reports, so that we could provide a comprehensive yet generalizable dataset on how each state governs the process. A crucial and invaluable source was Justin Levitt's website on redistricting, "All About Redistricting" (redistricting.lls.edu), which documents on a state-by-state basis how the state legislative redistricting was governed during the 2011 cycle and provides links to state laws and constitutional provisions that govern redistricting. Similarly, Michael McDonald's (2004) work comparing state redistricting institutions is an authoritative source on redistricting outcomes in 2001. Using these data, we are able to make generalizations about the methods and processes of the fifty states.

First, many states have legal requirements for passing legislative maps that are separate and distinct from congressional maps. This makes it somewhat confusing, because much of the popular and scholarly

TABLE 3.1. *State legislative districting authorities (2011 cycle)*

State	Primary Authority	Veto Players	Backup Authority
Alabama	State Legislature	Governor, DOJ	
Connecticut	State Legislature		Politician Commission, Court
Delaware	State Legislature	Governor	
Florida	State Legislature	State Court, DOJ	
Georgia	State Legislature	Governor, DOJ	
Illinois	State Legislature	Governor	Politician Commission
Indiana	State Legislature	Governor	Politician Commission
Kansas	State Legislature	Governor	State Court
Kentucky	State Legislature	Governor	
Louisiana	State Legislature	Governor, DOJ	State Court
Maine	State Legislature[a]	Governor	State Court
Maryland	State Legislature		Governor[a]
Massachusetts	State Legislature	Governor	
Michigan	State Legislature	Governor, DOJ	
Minnesota	State Legislature	Governor	
Mississippi	State Legislature	DOJ	Politician Commission
Nebraska	State Legislature	Governor	
Nevada	State Legislature	Governor	
New Hampshire	State Legislature	Governor, DOJ	
New Mexico	State Legislature	Governor	
New York	State Legislature[a]	Governor, DOJ	
North Carolina	State Legislature	DOJ	
North Dakota	State Legislature	Governor	
Oklahoma	State Legislature	Governor	Politician Commission
Oregon	State Legislature	Governor	Secretary of State
Rhode Island	State Legislature[a]	Governor	
South Carolina	State Legislature	Governor, DOJ	
South Dakota	State Legislature	Governor, DOJ	
Tennessee	State Legislature	Governor	
Texas	State Legislature	Governor, DOJ	Politician Commission

(*continued*)

TABLE 3.1. (*continued*)

State	Primary Authority	Veto Players	Backup Authority
Utah	State Legislature	Governor	
Vermont	State Legislature[a]	Governor	
Virginia	State Legislature[a]	Governor, DOJ	
West Virginia	State Legislature	Governor	
Wisconsin	State Legislature	Governor	
Wyoming	State Legislature	Governor	
Arkansas	Politician Commission		
Colorado	Politician Commission	State Court	
Hawaii	Politician Commission		
Missouri	Politician Commission		State Court
New Jersey	Politician Commission		
Ohio	Politician Commission[a]		
Pennsylvania	Politician Commission		
Alaska	Citizen Commission	DOJ	
Arizona	Citizen Commission	DOJ	
California	Citizen Commission	DOJ	State Court
Idaho	Citizen Commission		
Iowa	Citizen Commission[a]	State Legislature	State Court
Montana	Citizen Commission		
Washington	Citizen Commission	State Legislature	

[a] Redistricting authority is aided by an advisory commission

discussions of redistricting refer to congressional districting. However, there is considerably more variation and more complexity at the state level, insofar as many states articulate distinct processes for the drawing of state legislative lines and involve third-party actors that play no role in the redistricting of congressional maps.

Second, in every state, the process of redistricting state legislative lines is governed by statute, or through state constitutional provisions, which vary on a state-by-state basis. Other than population equity and minority representation requirements required by the US Constitution and the Voting Rights Act of 1965 and its subsequent amendments, there is no federal authority over the processes. Each state effectively governs itself. This means that the federal government plays a limited, almost inconsequential role, in maintaining uniform standards, which is perhaps not surprising given how federalism is structured and implemented in the states. That said, as we discuss subsequently, there are many instances in which federal courts weigh in on federal legal challenges to state legislative maps.

Third, although there is wide variation in terms of how state laws govern redistricting, each state specifies a primary districting authority that is the "first mover" and that is authorized to take a first attempt at drawing the lines, often within a given time frame. We can group these primary authorities into three types of institutions: (1) a state legislature; (2) a politician commission; and (3) an independent commission. As Table 3.1 shows, the most common institution that is granted primary authority is the state legislature, which typically passes the redistricting bill as it would any other bill, through the normal legislative process, or through a joint resolution. For the states that do not grant primary authority to the legislature, redistricting control is delegated to a commission, either made up of elected officials or politicians, or of citizens (with varying rules about party affiliation), or judges. Following others, we refer to redistricting commissions that are staffed by elected officials (such as the governor), political party officials, and other public officials as "Politician Commissions." For those commissions that bar elected officials, lobbyists, and politicians from membership, we classify them as "Citizen Commissions." Note that Iowa presents a special case, because state law tasks a nonpartisan government entity with the drawing of the lines. However, because it is advised by a five-person advisory commission (in which elected officials, political party officeholders, and relatives of sitting legislatures and members of Congress are barred from serving) we classify it as a citizen commission.

Most states grant an external actor with veto power over the maps approved by the primary authority. Among the states that grant primary authority to the state legislature, most grant the governor the power to veto plans. However, in Connecticut, Florida, Maryland, Mississippi, and North Carolina the governor does not have veto power over state legislative plans, and redistricting maps can be enacted through joint resolution by the legislature. In a few states, maps enacted by a primary authority are subject to automatic judicial review. This is the case with Florida (which uses the legislature) and Colorado (which uses a politician commission). Relatedly, at the time of redistricting in 2011, many of the states were subject to mandatory preclearance requirements of Section 5 of the Voting Rights Act, which meant that any redistricting plans had to be approved by either the US Department of Justice or in other cases a Federal Court. However, the formula governing preclearance was invalidated in *Shelby* v. *Holder* (2013) and, as of this writing, going forward states must be "opted-in" to the preclearance requirements in 2021.

In other cases, state law grants the legislature with the power to reject redistricting maps of which it does not approve. This is the case in Iowa and Washington, where primary authority is vested in an independent commission. In Iowa, the state legislature has two opportunities to reject the commissions' redistricting plan proposed before it can make its own amendments; In Washington, the legislature can make revisions to a plan with a two-thirds supermajority vote.

In addition to primary authorities and veto players, many states specify contingency options in cases when the primary authority is deadlocked or fails to enact a plan before a legally mandated deadline. These "backup" authorities vary by state, but they tend to delegate the responsibility to political commissions, elected officials, and state courts. One unique case is Maryland, where the governor first proposes a plan with the consultation of an advisory commission, after which the legislature has forty-five days to enact its own plan by joint resolution. If it fails to do so, the governor's plan is adopted.

3.2 WHO ACTUALLY DREW THE MAPS?

Ideally, the redistricting processes outlined are orderly, predictable, and result in maps being approved in a timely matter in advance of the state elections that follow reappointment. In reality, however, the process tends to be messy and often results in contingency actors drawing maps, or federal courts stepping in to mandate revisions or to issue remedial maps, and outcomes often fall beyond the boundaries of the "normal" process. As such, it is important to distinguish between the "normal process," as outlined in state law, and the realized outcomes. Indeed, our close study of the redistricting outcomes in all fifty states underscores the wide gulf that exists between how the redistricting process *should* unfold and how it actually happens. For our purposes, the more important question going forward is, who *actually* drew the maps?

To answer this question, we studied the processes that governed the redrawing of each state legislative maps that were eventually adopted by referencing news reports, legal documents, such as case briefings and court opinions, as well as the redistricting website maintained by Justin Levitt at Loyola Law School. In our investigation of case-by-case redistricting outcomes, we have identified and coded the body (or bodies) that were primarily responsible for drawing a map. In some cases, this task was fairly simple, as the original districting plans were submitted, approved, and implemented without drama, through the "normal" processes. In other cases, answering the question of "who drew the map" is complicated, because multiple entities influenced the final drawing of the lines.

In Florida, for example, the state Supreme Court rejected the legislature's original state senate map, and approved a second plan, modified from the original, in time for the 2012 state elections. However, a few years later, facing a state-level partisan gerrymandering legal challenge, the legislature voluntarily withdrew the plan and approved a third map, which was implemented for the 2016 elections. Who had more influence over the drawing of the second and third maps? While the legislature was the primary author of the plans, the state Supreme Court succeeded in stopping the first plan from being implemented, while the threat of judicial intervention resulted in the legislature adopting the third plan. According to the symmetry estimations we report in Chapter 2, the 2016 plan appears to be less asymmetrical than the previous plan, and resulted in a 35 percent decrease in pro-Republican bias, relative to the previous cycle plans. The effect of the threat of court intervention was a net reduction in bias. However, the legislature still managed to draw considerable bias into the plan (about −12 percent), which perhaps highlights the limits of the courts in preventing partisan bias.

Similarly, in Texas, the state legislature's House and Senate plans were denied by a federal court during mandatory VRA preclearance. That court subsequently enacted interim maps for the 2012 state legislative elections, based largely upon the original plans, which the Republican legislature ultimately approved for subsequent election cycles. However, the federal court's revisions were limited. In the state house plan, its revisions affected the boundaries of 14 districts, leaving the remaining 136 untouched. In contrast to the Florida example, in the case of Texas the federal court's intervention did little to curb partisan bias, in either the House or Senate map. Compared to the map implemented in 2010, the interim plan that was later signed into law resulted in sharp reductions in symmetry, to the benefit of the Republicans.

As these cases illustrate, multiple bodies may impact the final legislative boundaries, and each of these actors may have distinct (and perhaps limited) motivations in their decisions. Although a court can influence the decision-making calculus of a redistricting body in important ways, either through the threat of judicial intervention and the issuing of a

TABLE 3.2. *Who drew the plans? How redistricting institutions shaped outcomes*

Asymmetry (distance from zero)				
Institution	Old Plans (2008–10)		New Plans (2011–16)	
	Mean	S.D.	Mean	S.D.
Legislature (*n*=53)	10.8	6.31	12.5	8.72
Commission (*n*=34)	8.75	6.99	9.72	7.71
Court (*n*=8)	8.22	4.82	5.81	4.77

Responsiveness				
Institution	Old Plans (2008–10)		New Plans (2011–16)	
	Mean	S.D.	Mean	S.D.
Legislature (*n*=52)	2.48	.967	2.40	.793
Commission (*n*=33)	2.43	.793	2.27	.791
Court (*n*=8)	2.22	.474	2.29	.326

remedial map, or (the worst case scenario for a legislature) appointing a special master to redistrict the previous cycle lines, it typically takes a minimalistic approach that privileges the status quo and defers to the redistricting authorities enshrined in state law, particularly when they are elected bodies.

3.3 DOES INSTITUTIONAL CONTROL MATTER?

We grouped every redistricting plan into one of three categories, based upon who was primarily responsible for the maps that were eventually enacted: the state legislature; a commission (including elected officials); or a court. In cases like that of Texas and Florida, where the final map was a negotiation among multiple actors, we made a judgment call based on the unique circumstances of each case. (In both cases, we concluded that the maps were drawn primarily by the state legislature.) This approach gives us a window into the relationship between the types of institutional bodies that control redistricting and districting outcomes.

Table 3.2 reports summary statistics for partisan bias and responsiveness for each of the three types of institutions that drew the state legislative maps. Because our partisan symmetry estimates include both positive (pro-Democratic) and negative (pro-Republican) values, we took the absolute value of these measures (the distance from 0, which represents perfect symmetry) as a way of comparing partisan asymmetries between the groups. As evident, among the "new" plans, state legislatures produced, on average, the least symmetrical maps, a difference that is statistically significant (p = 0.028) compared to the other two groups. However, the magnitude of this difference is small, and we see no meaningful differences in responsiveness between the types of controlling institutions.

Another way to grasp the impact of institution on outcomes is to look at how the outcomes *changed*, relative to the maps used during the previous cycle. Here, we find rather intuitive results. The maps passed by legislatures tend to become *less* symmetrical, while maps drawn by courts appear to reduce asymmetries and maps drawn by commissions are relatively unchanged. However, looking at controlling institutions divorced from their political contexts tells us little about how the maps were drawn, or how the processes affected the outcomes.

3.4 HOW POLITICS SHAPES REDISTRICTING OUTCOMES

In addition to categorizing the adopted plans by institution, we classified the maps in terms of the political parties that drew them. Here, we recognize three distinct possibilities: (1) one party, either the Republicans or Democrats, controlled the process and drew the maps without input from the other; (2) two parties worked together to draw the maps; and (3) some independent body, such as a court or a commission, staffed by nonpolitician actors drew the maps. Note that we use the term "independent" rather loosely here. We do not mean to claim that "independent" actors are necessarily nonpolitical. Although judicial actors may make decisions with impartiality as a goal, many of the commissions that we code and refer to as "independent" are either appointed by politicians, or they are staffed by nonpolitician and/or unelected citizens who affiliate with one of the major parties. In other cases, an "independent" citizen commission may also be staffed with unaffiliated citizens, or judges, who are in fact impartial. The key difference in our decision to treat these commissions as "independent" is that they are not staffed by elected officials, lobbyists, or politicians, which we expect insulates them from types of partisan factors that affect how politicians behave.

Table 3.3 reports the findings for each map that was implemented for the ninety-nine state legislative chambers and their controlling bodies during the range of our analysis, which includes all new plans that were implemented for at least one election cycle, from 2011 to 2017, as well as

TABLE 3.3. *Who actually drew the maps?*

Republicans	Democrats	Both Parties	Independent Body
State Legislature	*State Legislature*	*State Legislature*	*Citizen Commission*
Alabama	Delaware House	Nebraska	Alaska House I[*]
House[§]	Delaware Senate	Legislature	Alaska Senate I[*]
Alabama	Illinois House	New York House	Alaska House II[*]
Senate[§]	Illinois Senate	New York Senate	Alaska Senate II[*]
Florida House	Kentucky	Oregon House	Arizona House
Florida Senate	House[*]	Oregon Senate	Arizona Senate
I[*], II[*]	Massachusetts	Virginia Senate[†]	California House
Georgia House	House	*Politician*	California Senate
Georgia Senate	Massachusetts	*Commission*	Idaho House[*]
Indiana House	Senate	Colorado House[*]	Idaho Senate[*]
Indiana Senate	Rhode Island	Colorado Senate[*]	Iowa House
Kentucky	House	Connecticut	Iowa Senate
Senate[*]	Rhode Island	House	Montana House
Louisiana	Senate	Connecticut	Montana Senate
House	Vermont House	Senate	Washington House[‡]
Louisiana	Vermont Senate	Hawaii House[*]	Washington Senate[‡]
Senate	West Virginia	Hawaii Senate[*]	*Court*
Michigan House	House	Maine House	Kansas House
Michigan Senate	West Virginia	Maine Senate	Kansas Senate
New Hampshire	Senate	Missouri House	Minnesota House
House	*Politician*	Missouri Senate	Minnesota Senate
New Hampshire	*Commission*	New Jersey	Nevada Assembly
Senate	Arkansas House	General	Nevada Senate
North Carolina	Arkansas Senate	Assembly	New Mexico
House I	Maryland	New Jersey Senate	House[§]
North Carolina	House	Pennsylvania	New Mexico Senate
Senate I	Maryland	House	North Carolina
North Dakota	Senate	Pennsylvania	House II
House		Senate	North Carolina
North Dakota			Senate II
Senate			Virginia House II
Oklahoma			
House			
Oklahoma			
Senate			
South Carolina			
House			
South Carolina			
Senate			
South Dakota			
House			

Republicans	Democrats	Both Parties	Independent Body
South Dakota Senate			
Tennessee House			
Tennessee Senate			
Texas House*			
Texas Senate*			
Utah House			
Utah Senate			
Virginia House I			
Wisconsin Assembly*			
Wisconsin Senate*			
Wyoming House			
Wyoming Senate			
Politician Commission			
Ohio House			
Ohio Senate			

* *Map was enacted with revisions mandated by a court;*
† *Final map was drawn after gubernatorial veto;*
‡ *Legislature made minor revisions to plan;*
§ *Map was enacted with revisions mandated by a higher court*

remedial, court-drawn plans in North Carolina, which were in place for the 2018 elections, and in Virginia for the 2019 elections.

As is evident, we observe a great deal of variation in outcomes. While most of the maps were drawn by a single-party (mostly Republicans), many others were drawn by members of both parties, or by independent actors. How precisely did these actors draw the maps? In the next section, we consider a few cases in order to derive hypotheses about how politics affects outcomes.

3.5 HOW POLITICIANS DRAW PLANS WHEN ONE PARTY HAS CONTROL

What happens when politicians from one political party draw the maps without input from their opponents? Here there are two possibilities: first, a party with a majority (or supermajority) in both houses of a legislature has control of the redistricting process along with the governorship (if there is a veto) and therefore does not need to work with the opposition party to pass a map; or second, members from one party outvote the other on a politician commission. Redistricting in Wisconsin is a textbook example of the former. After big wins in 2010, Republicans controlled both houses of the legislature along with the governorship for the first time since the mid-1990s. The redistricting process was tightly controlled by Republican leadership in the Legislature, which saw redistricting as a unique opportunity to ensure Republican control of the state house for the next decade.

Although politicians tend to be less than forthright when discussing redistricting, the process as it unfolded came under scrutiny after a group of Democrats challenged the State Assembly and Senate maps as an unconstitutional partisan gerrymander. Although the maps were struck down in federal district court, the decision was later vacated and remanded by the Supreme Court in *Whitford* v. *Gill* (2018) because the plaintiffs had failed to demonstrate standing. Notwithstanding, the lower court's initial ruling provides key insights into the deliberations of party leadership as they exploited control of redistricting to draw an aggressive Republican gerrymander in both the State Assembly and Senate maps.

First, after the delivery of Census data, the Republican leadership hired expert consultants to provide a variety of different plans, using the old maps as a baseline, that met the legal standards of population equity, contiguity, municipal boundary preservation, and compactness. Then, Republican leadership had the drafters revise the plans to maximize incumbent safety and partisan performance statewide.

The process was shrouded in secrecy throughout. Not only were Democrats left out of the deliberations, but leadership also kept their own members in the dark until they decided upon a final set of plans that suited their interests, which increased the number of both Republican-leaning districts and Republican "safe districts." Tad Ottman, an aide to Senate Majority Leader Scott Fitzgerald, pitched the final plans to the Republican Caucus, telling the members that they had "an opportunity and an obligation to draw these maps that Republicans haven't had in decades" and assuring the caucus that the maps would "determine who's here 10 years from now" (quoted in *Whitford* v. *Gill* , No. 15-cv-421-bbc, 2016 WL 6837229 (W.D. Wis. Nov. 21, 2016 Whip. pg. 15)). Thus, as the federal court concluded, "a focal point of the drafters' efforts was a map that would solidify Republican control" (*Whitford* v. *Gill* , No. 15-cv-421-bbc, 2016 WL 6837229 (W.D. Wis. Nov. 21, 2016), page 64).

As our symmetry estimates from Chapter 2 suggest, these efforts were largely successful. In contrast to the old maps used during the 2010 elections, which were symmetrical in the translation of statewide vote share to seat share, the new plans implemented in 2012 were highly asymmetrical to the benefit of the Republicans, such that Republican candidates in the Assembly and Senate can expect to yield about 20 percent more seats than the Democrats would, for a given share of the statewide vote between 45 percent and 55 percent. In addition, the drafters succeeded in drawing a map that maximized both partisan advantage and incumbent protection. During the 2018 state elections, although Democrats dominated at the state level, winning the popular vote by more than 8 percent in the State Assembly and 5 percent in the State Senate, Republicans maintained a nearly 2–1 seat majority in the Assembly and even gained a seat in the Senate.

Wisconsin provides an example of how a single party with a legislative majority can control the redistricting process to advance political goals. Similar outcomes occur when politicians from one party control redistricting through a commission that is made up of politicians or elected officials. This is the case in Ohio, which delegates authority to a politician committee called the Ohio Apportionment Board, staffed with the Governor, State Auditor, Secretary of State, and one delegate each appointed by Republicans and Democrats in the legislature. In principle, the design of the commission serves to balance the influence of executive branch officials, who are popularly elected by voters, with the legislative branch. In practice, however, the commission design guarantees one-party control of redistricting.

In 2011, four of the five commissioners were Republicans: Governor John Kasich, Auditor David Yost, and Secretary of State Jon Husted, along with state senator Tom Niehaus, who was chosen to represent the Republicans in the legislature, and state representative Armond Budish, who represented the Democrats. Though we know less about the internal deliberations of the Ohio Apportionment Board than we do of the Republican leadership in Wisconsin, the effects of one-party control were evidently the same. The 2011 plans, which were approved along party lines, dramatically increased pro-Republican bias relative to the old maps, which had already favored the Republicans.

A similar model governed redistricting in Arkansas, where a three-member commission, called The Arkansas Board of Apportionment, comprised of the governor, secretary of state, and attorney general, redrew the legislative maps. In 2011, the Board included two Democrats, Governor Mike Beebe and Attorney General Dustin Daniel, and one Republican, Secretary of State Mark Martin. The design of the Board of Apportionment is such that two members of one party – in this case, the Democrats – are able to enact a plan without input of a member of the other party – in this case, the Republicans. In 2011, the effect of Democratic control was that the plans saw a marked decrease in what was previously an asymmetrical map that favored the Republicans. However, the end result was a set of plans that was symmetrical in its treatment of both parties. In this regard, the outcome diverged from that of Ohio, despite similar institutional models.

Why did the Arkansas commission, controlled by Democrats, fail to enact a pro-Democratic gerrymander? There are two possible explanations. First, political geography makes it difficult (though not impossible) for Democrats to draw maps that give their party an asymmetrical advantage. Although we investigate the effect of political geography on bias in greater detail in the next chapter, it is clear that because urban areas are disproportionately populated by Democratic voters, it is far easier to produce a Republican gerrymander than a Democratic one in states with large urban populations. However, because Arkansas is among the least urbanized states, this explanation for the absence of pro-Democratic bias is unlikely. A second, more compelling explanation is the nature of two-party competition in Arkansas. Until the 2012 elections, the Arkansas legislature had been dominated by Democratic Party, and there was little reason to expect that the Republican Party posed a viable threat to the Democratic Party's control of both houses of the General Assembly. In this context, there was no clear incentive to draw an aggressive gerrymander that gave the controlling party a seat-share advantage when the statewide vote is close. Indeed, as Nicholas Goedert has argued (2014a; 2020), in noncompetitive states the controlling party instead manipulates the district boundaries to solidify an advantage under normal conditions, when the vote share *is not* close. Thus, it seems reasonable to assume that this mindset influenced the Democrats' decision-making in adopting their redistricting plans in 2011. Of course, one might argue that the Democrats in Arkansas misplayed their hand and underestimated their opponent's strength. Indeed, after 2012, the Republicans swept into power to control the General Assembly, and in 2014 won unified control of state government for the first time in a generation, which, as of 2021, they have yet to give up. In all likelihood, the Democrats could have prevented these gains if they had had a better grasp of their party's changing political fortunes in state politics.

3.6 MOTIVE, OPPORTUNITY, AND BIAS

What lessons do the cases of Wisconsin, Ohio, and Arkansas hold for understanding how and when redistricting institutions lead to gerrymandered maps? They underscore the links between political control of redistricting and politically biased outcomes. In the cases of Wisconsin and Ohio, because state law delegates redistricting authority to elected bodies, this means that districting maps are vulnerable to political manipulation. Indeed, in the case of Wisconsin, court documents show that the Republican leadership had no trouble drawing substantial asymmetries into the state legislative maps while conforming to legal redistricting criteria, such as population equity, contiguity, community preservation, and district compactness. Moreover, because the Republican Party controlled the State Assembly, Senate, and Governorship, Republican leaders were able to exclude Democrats from participating in the process, as well as many within their own caucus, because they were able to convince their members that secrecy was in the best interest of the party.

As in Wisconsin, the politician commission authorized to redistrict the state legislative maps in Ohio was dominated by Republicans, who were able to pass district plans that solidified a long-term Republican advantage over the objection of the lone Democrat on the Apportionment Board. However, in contrast to Ohio and Wisconsin, Arkansas enacted district maps that were largely free of bias and treated both parties symmetrically. Here, we suspect that a key intermediating variable is the lack of a competitive minority party, in this case, the Republicans. Accordingly, in cases when one party historically has controlled the legislature and the minority party poses no viable threat against this control, partisan districting authorities have little incentive to draw plans that give their party a competitive advantage when the two-party statewide vote is close.

Thus, as argued by Butler and Cain (1992), and demonstrated empirically by McGann et al. (2016), we expect to see bias when a party has both the "opportunity" to draw bias and the "motive" to do so. In other words, asymmetrical maps are most likely to occur when two conditions are met: (a) one party drew the maps without input from the other and (b) the controlling party has the motivation to draw maps to help it win the two-party vote is close. While condition (a) was present in all three cases, condition (b) was present only in the cases of Wisconsin and Ohio.

How does this framework fare when we account for the outcomes that occurred in the remaining maps? Using the partisan symmetry scores that we estimated in Chapter 2, we grouped states based on the level of partisan bias in their post-2011 district plans, as well as the degree of competition in state legislative elections. We considered the state legislature to be competitive if, during the decade that preceded redistricting, two parties shared power in the state legislature at any point. We considered a plan "biased" if the symmetry score exceeded +/– 10 percent. As Table 3.4 demonstrates, we see that most of the asymmetrical plans were drawn in states where both the "motive" and opportunity" conditions were met – that is, in states where both parties have a viable chance to take control of the state legislature, and where a single party was able to draw the maps without having to work with the other. By contrast, we see far fewer biased plans when one or both of these conditions are not met.

In order to assess the relative impact of each of our independent variables on partisan symmetry, we conducted OLS regression analysis and included the following independent variables in our model: (1) the symmetry scores from the previous cycle (the baseline from which mapmakers started drawing the new plans); (2) a dummy variable indicating whether or not the maps were drawn by Republican politicians; (3) our competition variable; and (4) an interaction term (*Republican*Competitive*). The model as a whole explains well over 60 percent of the variation in symmetry scores in the newly enacted plans. When the symmetry scores from the previous cycle are removed from the model, the model loses about a third of its predictive power. When the *Republican* variable is omitted from the model, the model loses about a quarter of its predictive power, and the omission of the *Competitive* variables decreases the performance of the model by about a tenth. Thus, the two most important variables for predicting the level of bias after redistricting are the level of bias in the old plans and whether or not Republicans controlled the process. In short, solving the puzzle of partisan bias is rather simple: partisan bias occurs when one party controls redistricting. When one party controls redistricting and revises a plan that was already biased in this favor, the maps become even less symmetrical. And when it has an incentive to draw itself a partisan advantage when the statewide vote is close, bias increases even more.

TABLE 3.4. *Motive, opportunity, and partisan bias*

	Motive – Competitive State Legislature	No Motive – Noncompetitive State Legislature
Opportunity – Single-Party Control of Redistricting	Biased Map: GA-L; GA-U; IN-L; IN-U; KY-U; LA-L; LA-U; MI-U; MI-L; NC-U; NC-L; OH-L; OH-U; OK-U; OK-L; SC-U; SC-L; TN-L; TN-U; TX-U; TX-L; VT-U; VA-L; WI-L; WI-U	Biased Map: FL-U; FL-L; RI-U; UT-U; UT-L; WY-U; WY-L
	Unbiased Map: DE-L; DE-U; IL-U; IL-L; KY-L; NH-L; NH-U; VT-L;	Unbiased Map: AR-L; AR-U; MA-L; MA-U; MD-L; MD-U; ND-U; ND-L; RI-L; SD-U; SD-L; WV-U; WV-L
No Opportunity – Two-Party/ Independent Control of Redistricting	Biased Map: AZ-L; MN-L; MN-U; MO-U; MO-L; NY-U; PA-L; PA-U	Biased Map: HI-L; ID-U; ID-L; KS-L; NE-U
	Unbiased Map: AK-L; AK-U; AZ-U; CO-L; CO-U; IA-U; IA-L; ME-U; ME-L; MT-U; MT-L; NJ-L; NJ-U; NV-L; NV-U; NY-L; OR-U; OR-L; VA-U; WA-U; WA-L	Unbiased Map CA-L; CA-U; CT-U; CT-L; HI-U; KS-U; NM-L; NM-U

3.7 HOW POLITICIANS DRAW PLANS WHEN TWO PARTIES SHARE POWER

Our findings in the previous section suggest a simple and intuitive rule for predicting the occurrence of partisan bias in redistricting: when politicians do not need to consult their opponents during redistricting, they draw plans that help their party win. However, in many other cases, two parties must work together to pass new district maps. When politicians from both parties must share power – either in divided government, or in a commission is staffed by an equal number of politicians from both parties – the decision-making calculus changes.

In our case studies of redistricting in 2011, we find that split party control of the districting process can lead to a number of distinct outcomes, depending on the balance of power between the parties and the degree of cooperation. First, in states that delegate redistricting authority to the state legislature with gubernatorial veto via the normal political processes, "divided government" (when control of the governorship and legislature is split between two parties) often means that a dominant party must make concessions to the minority party in order to successfully pass a districting plan. In principle, this may also occur when one party controls state government, but state law requires a supermajority to approve a districting plan.

Sometimes, when the two parties are not able to agree on a set of maps, divided government results in deadlock, and the legislature forfeits control of redistricting to a contingency authority. This was the case in New Mexico, when a state court stepped in to draw the maps after the Republican governor vetoed the plans that were passed by the legislature, which was controlled by Democrats. A similar process occurred in Connecticut, where state law requires a two-thirds majority approval of the legislature to approve a plan. Because the legislature did not approve a plan by the legally imposed deadline of September 15, 2011, the task fell to a politician commission.

However, when a divided legislature does successfully pass a map, it can take a couple of distinct forms. One possibility is that, if two parties control different branches of the legislature, they "collude" with one another by letting the other party draw the plans for the legislative house it controls. In this regard, both parties get to draw a plan without having to work directly with the other. This occurred in both Kentucky and Virginia, where different parties controlled the upper and lower houses of the state legislature. In Kentucky, for example, Democrats were in a dominant position of controlling both the House of Representatives and the governorship, while Republicans controlled the Senate. This meant that both parties effectively held veto power: Republicans in the Senate could prevent a Democrat-drawn House map from reaching the governor's desk, while Democrats in the House could withhold support of a Republican-drawn Senate plan. Consequently, the two parties struck an agreement that the Democrats would draw the House plans and Republicans would draw the Senate maps. Although the original House and Senate maps were passed by the General Assembly in 2012 in advance of November elections, they were subsequently invalidated by a state court for violating population equality and for failing to "preserve county integrity" (*Fischer* v. *Grimes*, No. 2012-SC-000092-T (Ky. Sup. Ct.)). However, a few months later, the General Assembly passed a revised redistricting bill, which was signed into law by Governor Steve Beshear and implemented in advance of the 2014 elections. The effect of the bargain struck by the two parties in the General Assembly was that each map reflected the controlling party's interests: in the Senate, bias increased dramatically in favor of the Republicans, shifting from a symmetry score of −11 to −28, while in the House, Democrats managed to reduce pro-Republican bias from a symmetry score of −9 under the old maps to −4, while responsiveness in both plans was reduced by 15 percent and 30 percent, respectively. In a nutshell, both parties got something they wanted, and the consequence was that the new plans were made to be less responsive to shifts in voters' support than the plans in the previous round.

A similar scenario unfolded in Virginia, with Republicans controlling the House of Delegates and governorship, and Democrats controlling the State Senate. In 2011, the General Assembly ignored the recommendations of the state's independent redistricting advisory commission and enacted a set of plans that was authored by the party leadership from each chamber. The original agreement between the House and Senate appears to have been that each chamber would respect the maps produced by the other. Although a redistricting bill was passed by both chambers in April of 2011, Republican Governor Bob McDonnell vetoed the original Senate plan, asserting that the map (drawn by the Democrats) amounted to a partisan gerrymander. Thus, the Democrats' position meant that they confronted two veto players – the Republican leadership in the House of Delegates and a Republican governor. Despite the agreement made with the first veto player, Republican House leader Kirk Cox, they were forced to revise the Senate plans to accommodate the Republican Governor Bob McDonnell's unforeseen demands. By contrast, after the governor's veto the House plan remained largely unchanged, despite assertions from the independent advisory committee that it too was a partisan gerrymander. In the House plan that was eventually signed by the governor, the Republicans were able to preserve an asymmetrical advantage (a symmetry score of −12), in part by packing Black voters in Richmond and Petersburg into majority–minority districts, which had the effect of reducing the responsiveness of the plan, relative to the previous cycle plan, by about 10 percent. In 2018, a Federal Court invalidated the plan as an unconstitutional racial gerrymander and appointed a special master to redraw the maps for the 2019 state legislative elections in a decision that the Supreme Court upheld in *Bethune Hill* v. *Virginia State Board of Elections* (2019). By contrast, the revised Senate plan signed into law by the governor only modestly benefited the Democrats in the Senate (a symmetry score of 3). Here, the most consequential change was a roughly 20 percent reduction in responsiveness in seat share to statewide two-party vote swings.

In sum, although Republicans in the House were able to draw a map with a substantial partisan advantage, the Democrats were prevented from drawing an aggressive partisan gerrymander. Although the processes in Kentucky and in Virginia were largely similar insofar as one party held a dominant position of controlling one house along with a gubernatorial veto, the key difference was that in Virginia the Republican governor appears not to have been privy to the agreement reached between Democratic leadership in the Senate and Republican leadership in the House and was much more assertive in preventing the Democrats from getting what they wanted by vetoing the first plan. This had the effect of a bipartisan compromise between the Senate Democrats and the Republican governor. By contrast, in Kentucky the Democratic Governor appeared much more accommodating to the agreement made between the Democratic leadership in the House and Republican leadership in the Senate, and declined to veto the bill, over objections to some members of his party.

While Kentucky and Virginia suggest that a "look-the-other-way" approach can be an effective form of compromise when a dominant party must grant concessions to an opposition party with veto power, in other cases two parties must work together to enact a plan because neither party is in a dominant position. In such cases, rather than seeking to maximize partisan advantage and consolidate party control of the legislative chamber through the maps, the two parties must agree on a common set of goals. Often, this means drawing "safe" districts that are unresponsive to vote swings, in order to protect incumbents of both parties from defeat.

This often is the outcome when state redistricting procedures grant authority to a "bipartisan" politician commission, staffed by an equal number of politicians from both parties. In New Jersey, for example, a commission made up of five Republicans and five Democrats, who are appointed by the chairs of the state Democratic and Republican parties, draws the state legislative maps. If the commission fails to approve a plan, the state Supreme Court appoints a eleventh member, to act as tiebreaker (a similar model is in place in Hawaii). In 2011, the commission was able to approve plans that maintained pre-2011 levels of partisan symmetry, but which ultimately decreased in responsiveness. The two parties were able to collude by drawing "fair" maps that gave neither party a vote–seat advantage, but had the effect of insulating both parties from statewide vote swings. Thus, the outcome was essentially a preservation of the status quo.

A similar scenario played out in Maine, where the maps were drawn by members of a bipartisan commission. Although the Maine Legislature is granted formal authority over redistricting, the constitution requires a supermajority rule to approve plans. Because the Republicans, who controlled both houses of the Legislature as well as the governorship, were short of a two-thirds majority in both chambers, they needed the support of Democrats to enact a plan before the deadline imposed by the state constitution, after which redistricting authority moves to the state Supreme Court. Ultimately, the Legislature adopted the plan drafted by the bipartisan advisory commission, staffed by members who were appointed by the majority and minority parties in both houses of the legislature. Like New Jersey, because the process required cooperation by both parties, the plan that was eventually enacted was largely free of partisan bias and treated both parties symmetrically in terms of vote–seat translation. However, because both parties had a common interest in protecting their incumbents, the new plans decreased in responsiveness by approximately 20 percent in the Senate and 10 percent in the House.

3.8 BIPARTISAN REDISTRICTING, COMPETITION, AND RESPONSIVENESS

Although bipartisan control over districting changes the calculus insofar as it prevents a dominant party from extracting huge gains in the form of partisan bias, it does not necessarily mean that the plans are "fair." While the cases outlined earlier illustrate that one common outcome of bipartisan-drawn plans is that they are drawn symmetrically to give neither party a huge seat-share advantage, the end result can be an incumbent protection scheme that decreases responsiveness. This makes sense insofar as both parties share a common interest in protecting their own legislators from defeat.

Of course, here competition also plays an important variable. When states are competitive – that is, when both parties have a reasonable chance of taking control of the legislature at some point in the future – then they have a shared incentive to reduce competition when the vote

TABLE 3.5. *Mean responsiveness in state legislative plans adopted after 2011*

Who Drew the Maps?	Competition for Control of Statehouse	No Competition for Control of Statehouse
One Party/Independent Body	2.17 (*n*=47)	2.64 (*n*=28)
Two Parties	2.10 (*n*=15)	3.19 (*n*=5)

share is close. This is the case in both New Jersey and Maine, as well as in Kentucky and Virginia. However, when state government is not competitive, and one party has historically dominated state legislative elections, then there is little reason to expect that bipartisan cooperation will reduce responsiveness when elections are close. Instead, we expect the map-makers to draw the maps to be unresponsive when the vote share is not close, in order to preserve the status quo.

Table 3.5 reports the average responsiveness of all plans, grouped by the motive and opportunity categories discussed earlier. As we expect, we observe that the least-responsive plans were drawn in states where the two parties worked together to draw the maps, and where both the parties compete for control over the state legislature. By contrast, the most responsive maps appear to occur when the "bipartisanship" condition is present, but where one party holds a dominant position in state politics. Here, it would appear that the dominant party is willing to draw plans that are more responsive to vote shifts if the two-party statewide vote is close, because under normal circumstances, the two-party vote share is not close. Here, a highly responsive plan poses little risk to the dominant party (see Goedert 2020). However, the difference in responsiveness scores between the plans drawn by two parties and the rest of plans included in the "competition" group is small and statistically insignificant.

We also modeled the effects of bipartisan control and two-party competitiveness in states using OLS regression. We regressed the post-2011 responsiveness scores against the pre-2011 responsiveness scores, along with dummy variables indicating two-party control of redistricting and competitiveness and an interaction term. While the model estimates that responsiveness is lowest in competitive states where two parties shared control of redistricting, the results fall outside of statistical significance. In addition, the performance of the model (r^2=0.49) is driven primarily by the pre-2011 responsiveness scores; the inclusion of variables for two-party control, competitiveness and the interaction term improve the "fitness" of the model by less than 10 percent.

Ultimately, we cannot reject the possibility that two-party control of redistricting has no meaningful impact on the seat–vote responsiveness of a district map. For example, while maps drawn by two parties working together in New Jersey, New York, and Oregon produced maps with very low responsiveness scores (as predicted), we also observe plans drawn with relatively high responsiveness scores in Colorado and Maine, contrary to our predictions. Thus, the evidence is mixed that bipartisan redistricting processes undermine electoral competition.

For policymakers considering whether or not to adopt redistricting reforms, these results matter. For example, consider the debate over redistricting reform that unfolded in Virginia in 2020. Opponents of the reforms ostensibly opposed the design of the commission in part because it requires half of the sixteen commissioners to be legislators representing the two parties, presumably leading to "incumbent protection" gerrymanders. However, as we have shown here, there is simply not enough evidence to conclude that a decrease in seat–vote responsiveness is a probable outcome of bipartisan districting. Moreover, as we have shown, when the redistricting process is not dominated by a single party, the maps are generally free of bias. Accordingly, our evidence suggests that the reforms debated in Virginia are very likely to succeed at preventing extreme partisan gerrymandering and that this benefit probably outweighs the small risk that the bipartisan design of the commission would lead to "incumbent protection" gerrymandering (i.e., a marked reduction in seat–vote responsiveness).

3.9 HOW THE STATUS QUO SHAPES REDISTRICTING OUTCOMES

Our results thus far have shown that one of the most powerful determinants of redistricting outcomes is the status quo – that is, the level of bias present in the previous maps. Indeed, redistricting authorities do not draw the maps from scratch. Rather, they make deviations from the maps used in the previous cycle, using the old maps as a starting point. This is particularly true of state legislative redistricting, where redistricting authorities must often contend with dozens or even hundreds of districts, as opposed to congressional redistricting, which can involve as few as two or three districts in a small state. When a mapmaker is tasked with redistricting a map with more than 100 districts represented by dozens of incumbent lawmakers, it simply is not feasible to start the districting processes with a clean slate, nor is it desirable when dozens of incumbents hope to remain in their districts. Instead, redistricting actors will make alterations based upon the previous map. In this way, the status quo is crucially important for understanding outcomes in districting.

In the previous sections, we found that the "old" maps shaped redistricting outcomes in important ways. When we modeled the effects of one-party (Republican) control on the level of partisan symmetry drawn in the new maps, we saw that the level of bias in the old maps accounted for more than half of the model's predictive power. Similarly, in our model of post-2011 responsiveness scores, we saw that responsiveness scores in the pre-2011 map contributed to more than 90 percent of the predictive power of the model.

In addition, we can gain critical insight into the motives and intent of mapmakers by observing the direction and scope of changes in redistricting outcomes. To illustrate this point, Figure 3.1 plots the symmetry scores of the old maps against the symmetry scores of the new maps as a way of showing how outcomes changed after redistricting. We grouped each map in terms of "who" drew the plans – whether they were drawn by Democrats, Republicans, members of both parties, or independent actors (i.e., courts and citizen commissions). We then plotted the pre-2011 asymmetry (X-axis) against the post-2011 asymmetry (Y-axis). This gives us a baseline (i.e., the old maps) with which to compare the newly enacted maps.

In the maps drawn by members of both parties, we observe very little change to symmetry, insofar as the partisan symmetry scores in the new maps tend to mirror the scores of the old maps. Here, the slope of the trendline (which illustrates the correlation between the post-2011 and pre-2011 plans) is nearly identical to the dashed line, which represents the equation $y=x$. This suggests that these mapmakers sought to preserve the status quo in their decision-making. This makes sense when we consider the cases of New Jersey and Maine, where neither party had a numerical advantage during redistricting. In both cases, bipartisan politician commissions appear to have prioritized preservation of the existing balance of power. The old maps were free of extreme bias, and the new maps were also drawn free of extreme bias. In addition, in Pennsylvania and Missouri, where the two parties worked together to draw the maps, we similarly observe a commitment to the status quo. Because in both cases the old maps were already biased in favor of the Republicans, drawing an unbiased map would have represented a substantial shift to the Democratic advantage. Accordingly, the best outcome either party could have hoped for was a preservation of existing norms. Unfortunately

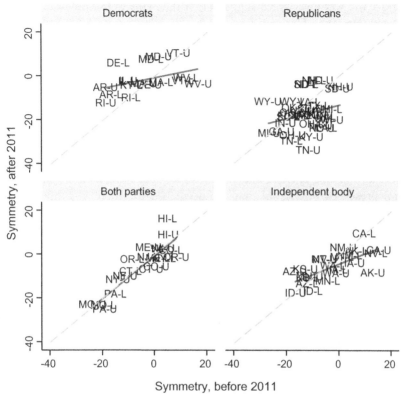

FIGURE 3.1. Partisan control and change in partisan symmetry after redistricting

for the Democrats, this meant maintaining a considerable pro-Republican advantage.

Like the maps drawn by members of both parties, when we observe the plans drawn by independent bodies, we see many maps that are free of extreme bias. However, one notable difference is that the nonpartisan plans tend to deviate more from the old plans, presumably, because their drafters prioritized partisan neutrality over status quo preservation. In cases when an independent body draws the maps, there is evidently less of a commitment to minimalism in redistricting changes.

We see the most change in maps drawn by a single party. Here the post-2011 maps deviate substantially from the pre-2011 maps. Among plans drawn by Republicans, the new maps cluster well below the y=x line, which shows that asymmetry generally increased in favor of the Republican Party. Among the Democratic-drawn plans, we see clustering above the $y=x$ line, which suggests that the plans were drawn to increase Democratic bias. However, it is notable that Democrats did not succeed in drawing plans with high symmetry scores. Rather, many of the increases in pro-Democratic bias occur in plans that were previously pro-Republican and were "corrected" by Democratic mapmakers to reduce bias. (One possible explanation that we assess in the next chapter is that political geography limits the ability of Democrats to draw pro-Democratic bias into their plans.) However, in both the Democratic- and Republican-drawn plans, there is much less fidelity to the previous maps. Here, it is obvious that politicians discounted the status quo in their decision-making and did not shy away from deviating from the asymmetries preserved in the old maps. Indeed, because there was no need to consult with the minority party in order to enact a plan, the controlling party had little incentive to solidify the preexisting balance of power between the two parties.

3.10 CONCLUSION

In this chapter, we have investigated the political and institutional determinants of partisan bias in districting. Although there is wide variation in how the states delegate redistricting authority, in most states the maps were drawn by one of three types of actors: (1) a state legislature; (2) a commission; or (3) a state court.

We also observe variation in the role of politicians in shaping districting outcomes. Most state legislatures that redistricted in 2011 were controlled by a single party – most commonly the Republicans – while a minority were jointly controlled by two parties. In addition, many redistricting commissions were controlled by politicians, from one or two parties jointly. In other cases, when a map was drawn by a court or commission, politicians did not draw the maps that were ultimately approved.

We then evaluated the effects of institutional and partisan control on redistricting outcomes. We find little evidence that the type of redistricting institution affects districting bias in a significant way. Although state courts appear to draw plans with less bias, there is little difference between the bias in the maps drawn by legislatures and commissions. Instead, our results show that partisan bias is driven by the influence of politicians.

Our findings boil down to a simple rule: partisan bias occurs when politicians from one party are able to control redistricting by themselves –

either through a legislature or a commission. When two parties must work together, either through a commission or legislature, we tend to see less bias. When independent actors, such as a court or a commission comprised of citizens, are tasked with redistricting, we do not see significant levels of partisan bias.

Our analysis also underscores another important variable driving districting outcomes that is often missing from assessments of gerrymandering: the status quo. Redistricting actors start from the status quo, and they redistrict based on the maps that are currently in place. Accordingly, in order to evaluate redistricting outcomes, it is necessary to compare the new maps with the old maps.

When Republicans and Democrats draw the lines, they tend to draw plans that benefit their party – even if the old map was unbiased, or even biased to favor the other party. When members of two parties work together to draw maps, we tend to see very little change to bias. The level of bias in the new plan tends to mirror the level of bias that was in the old plan. This suggests that the two parties find common ground in preserving the status quo. When courts or citizen commissions draw the maps, the maps tend to become less biased and there is relatively less adherence to the status quo, particularly if the previous maps were biased.

Our findings show that it is possible to predict the level of partisan bias in a redistricting plan with relative accuracy, using only two pieces of information: (1) the level of bias in the old map and (2) whether or not the controlling actor is Republican. These two variables alone explain more than 50 percent of the variation in redistricting bias that we observed in the 2011 maps. When we add a third variable – whether or not the two parties in the legislature compete for power – our simple model predicts more than 60 percent of the variation in partisan symmetry scores.

In sum, understanding the determinants of partisan gerrymandering is not rocket science, but political science: Politicians exploit redistricting to advance their interests, when they are free to do so. When nonpolitical actors draw the maps, they do not have an incentive to draw partisan gerrymanders. Therefore, we do not see bias.

Our results in this chapter suggest that the increased Republican bias after 2011 state legislative redistricting that we observed in the Chapter 2 is no accident. That the most biased plans were passed in the states where Republicans controlled redistricting provides strong evidence that legislatures have been using their power to gerrymander themselves, and will continue to do so into the foreseeable future.

Yet it is clear that politics alone does not fully explain redistricting outcomes. Indeed, although most state legislatures that redistricted were controlled by Republicans, there were a few that were controlled entirely by Democrats. However, the magnitude of the bias drawn in Democratic gerrymanders does not compare to that of Republican gerrymanders. Why did Republican districting authorities draw more aggressive gerrymanders than Democratic redistricting authorities? In the next chapter, we investigate a likely solution to this puzzle: political geography.

4

How Political Geography Affects Bias

So far, we have found that, during 2011 redistricting, many state governments implemented state legislative district plans that favored the Republican Party. When we look at the state legislative plans that were redrawn after the 2010 Census, we find that the average legislative map has a 9 percent pro-Republican bias, which represents an increase of more than one-third compared to the plans used in the previous cycle.

In the previous chapter, we found compelling evidence that politics is behind this increase. Indeed, we observe the most bias in states where one party controlled the districting process without input from the other, and where two-party competition in state politics tends to be competitive, giving the controlling party a motive to manipulate the district maps to solidify an advantage.

Most of the maps with substantial partisan bias were drawn by Republicans. Indeed, Republicans fared very well at the state level in the 2010 elections, which gave them control of most of the state legislatures at a key moment. However, the Democrats also controlled several state governments during redistricting. In many of these states, Democrats appear to have had both a motive and the opportunity to draw partisan gerrymanders, yet our results show only a few examples of district maps drawn with a substantial pro-Democratic bias. For example, we did not observe bias in the maps drawn in Delaware and Illinois, despite the fact that in both states the Democrats controlled redistricting and had an incentive to draw partisan gerrymanders. Thus, while the Republicans appear to have succeeded in drawing aggressive partisan gerrymanders in states where they had both the motive and opportunity to do so, Democrats did not. Why?

In this chapter, we illuminate the role that political geography plays in determining districting outcomes. We find that the political geographic features of a state population limit the types of maps that districting authorities are able to draw. When Democrats are highly segregated – for example, in populous urban areas – it is easier for Republicans to draw very efficient gerrymanders and difficult for Democrats to draw plans that give Democrats an advantage. However, this does not mean that geography necessarily leads to biased outcomes that favor the GOP.

When we analyze the links between Democratic clustering in cities and Republican bias, we only see a correlation in the maps that were drawn by Republicans. The link between Democratic clustering in cities and Republican bias does not occur in maps drawn by Democrats, or by independent actors such as courts and citizen commissions. In these cases, redistricting authorities somehow managed to draw unbiased, or even Democrat-biased maps, despite having more urbanized populations on average. In sum, political geography only seems to lead to a Republican advantage when Republicans are drawing the lines.

This underscores an obvious truth about redistricting: *the maps do not draw themselves.* Rather, humans choose the maps that best serve their personal and political interests. Geography may constrain the types of outcomes achievable – for example, it may prevent Democratic mapmakers from drawing aggressive partisan gerrymanders. However, it does not determine which maps are ultimately selected. When geography favors one party – for example, the Republicans – partisan redistricting authorities will use this advantage to draw more efficient gerrymanders. To the contrary, when geography presents a disadvantage to a party, then the politicians drawing the maps will select the map that minimizes that disadvantage. In the context of Democrats drawing district maps, it is often the case that the best they can get is a fair map that treats both parties symmetrically.

We show that districting decisions are driven primarily by politics, rather than geography. And that the demographic features of a state ultimately determine the necessity of drawing irregularly shaped district lines in order to draw biased (or neutral) maps. In this light, we evaluate the impact of district compactness laws and how they affect districting outcomes.

4.1 IS DISTRICTING BIAS "UNINTENTIONAL"?

It is frequently argued that at least some of the advantage that Republicans have in congressional and state legislative elections stems from "unintentional" gerrymandering as a result of the geographical concentration of Democratic voters in urban areas (Chen and Cottrell 2016; Chen and Rodden 2013a; Goedert 2014b; Rodden 2019). The idea that the geographical concentration of Democratic voters (particularly minorities) in urban areas disadvantages the Democrats has a long history (Erikson 1972; Hirsch 2003).

While it is clear that the American electorate has polarized geographically (Johnston et al. 2020; Rhola et al. 2018), we have argued vigorously that the urban concentration of Democrats cannot explain *away* political gerrymandering (McGann et al. 2016). After all, as we show in Chapter 2, partisan bias increased substantially after redistricting. However, this fact cannot be explained by Democrats suddenly moving to urban areas after 2002. Nevertheless, it is clear that geographical concentration does have an effect on districting, in that it has a role in determining what kind of districting plans are possible, and how easy or difficult it is to advantage one party or the other.

As we argue in McGann et al. (2016), geographical factors can help explain the patterns of partisan gerrymandering we observe, but cannot explain it away. It is necessary to distinguish between these two senses of the word "explain."

When we talk about explaining away gerrymandering, we are talking about explanation in a strong sense. Here when we say that some factor (say the urban concentration of Democratic voters) explains partisan bias, we mean that this factor forces states to adopt biased districting plans, whether they want to or not. If we want to argue that partisan bias is not a matter of political choice, but rather the result of, say, demographic factors, we need an explanation in this sense. We need to argue that demographic factors make it impossible not to draw biased districts, given other constraints. That is to say, we have to argue that even if the other party had drawn the districts, they would have been forced to draw districts just as biased.

Districting is not a random process where bias emerges at the end as a result of a variety of factors. Rather districting plans are chosen by the districting authorities (most commonly state legislatures with the approval of the governor, as we showed in Chapter 3). Furthermore, with modern geographical information systems technology, districting authorities will be quite aware of the partisan implications of their choices. Therefore, if we wish to absolve districting authorities from responsibility for biased districts – or even argue that the bias was unintentional – we need to argue that the partisan bias was unavoidable, and thus that the districting authorities had no choice but to create biased districts.

We can contrast this with a weaker sense of the word "explanation." Here when we say that urban concentration explains partisan bias, we mean that urban concentration was a contributing factor that made it easier for districting authorities to district in a biased way. That is to say, if districting authorities wish to create partisan bias, urban concentration may increase the opportunity for them to do this. Suppose we have a state where the party controlling the districting process wishes to district for partisan advantage in both the 2000 and 2010 districting cycles. We might explain the increase in partisan bias between 2000 and 2010 in terms of the growing urban concentration of Democrats. The reason, we might claim, that partisan bias has increased is that increasing urban concentration has increased the potential for drawing biased districts. This kind of explanation does not absolve the districting authorities from responsibility – there is a biased plan because the districting authorities chose to adopt it. Rather, what has increased is the *ability* of the districting authorities to get the districting outcomes it wants.

4.2 GEOGRAPHY CANNOT *EXPLAIN AWAY* DISTRICTING BIAS

Let us consider first the strong sense of "explanation." There is one clear way to show when demographic or geographic factors cannot *explain away* partisan bias. We simply have to show that unbiased districting was, in fact, possible. Suppose we can show that it is relatively straightforward to produce a districting plan that is unbiased, in spite of geographical concentration and other constraints. Then the districting authorities cannot argue that they were forced by these constraints to produce a biased plan – unbiased plans were available, but they chose not to adopt them. In such cases, adopting a biased plan was a choice the districting authorities made (and likely a politically motivated choice). There are at least two ways we can show that unbiased districting plans were possible. First, we can demonstrate that there are states that manage to avoid partisan bias in spite of the presence of, say, large urban concentrations of Democratic voters. Second, in states where biased plans were adopted, we can use alternative districting plans to demonstrate that unbiased districting was possible.

First, we can show that it is possible to draw unbiased districts in precisely those states with the largest urban concentrations – California, New York, Illinois, and New Jersey. If partisan bias were the inevitable result of the geographic concentration of Democratic voters in urban centers, then we would expect to see evidence of bias in the state with the largest urban centers. These, as McDonald (2013) argues, are the places where it is simply not possible to draw maps that blend urban areas with suburban and rural precincts to prevent heavy (and electorally inefficient) concentrations of Democratic voters.

The problem is when we look at the states that contain the largest metropolitan areas, we do not find evidence of partisan bias toward the Republicans, in spite of the fact that the urban areas listed account for at least 35 percent of the population of each state. If we turn to the symmetry measures we report in Chapter 2, we find that the districting plans in New Jersey and Illinois are virtually unbiased (symmetry scores of −1.3 percent and 2.5 percent in the New Jersey Assembly and Senate maps; −2.3 percent and −2.5 percent in the Illinois House and Senate maps). In California, there is minor bias in favor of the Democrats (9.5 percent in the Assembly and 2.0 percent in the Senate), while in New York there is bias in favor of the Republicans in the Senate (−12 percent), but not in the Assembly (−2.1 percent). It is also notable that we find that the 2002 California State Assembly and State Senate maps were significantly biased in favor of the Democrats. Evidently, large urban concentrations do not make unbiased districts – or even districts biased in favor of the Democrats in some cases – impossible.

When we look at our entire sample of district plans, we do not see a correlation between a states' urban geography and partisan bias in its maps. The US Census Bureau keeps records of two relatively straightforward statistical measures of urbanization at the state level: the urban population percentage and urban population density. The urban population percentage reflects the proportion of the states' total population that resides in cities, as defined by "urban areas" (populations of over 50,000) and "urban clusters" (above 2,500 but less than 50,000). According to the 2010 census, the states with the most urbanized population are California, New Jersey, and Nevada, each of which have in excess of 94 percent of the state population living in cities. At the bottom of the list are Maine, Vermont, and Arizona, which have less than 50 percent of their populations living in cities. When we examine the correlation between urban population percentage and partisan bias, the most urbanized states are no different than the least urbanized states in terms of the bias in their state legislative maps ($r = 0.072$).

A second measure that the Census Bureau tracks is urban population density, which measures the number of inhabitants per square mile in designated urban areas and urban clusters. High urban density means that the populations in cities are tightly clustered in space. Based on the

2010 census, the states with the least dense cities are South Carolina and New Hampshire, both of which have less than 1,300 residents per square mile in their cities. At the top of the list are California and New York, which exceed 4,000 inhabitants per square mile in their cities. When we look at the correlation between state urban population density and symmetry scores, we find the two variables are moderately correlated ($r = 0.34$). A simple regression analysis estimates that urban population variable explains about 12 percent of the variation in symmetry scores. However, the effect of population density on symmetry is in the *opposite* direction, meaning that the states with the most densely populated cities tend to have *more* Democratic bias – not less. Apparently, the most urbanized states had no trouble avoiding maps that we expect would give Republicans an advantage – indeed, many have managed to succeed in drawing Democratic bias.

Of course, these observations are hardly surprising when we recognize that districting outcomes reflect political choices. Divorced from political context, it may seem odd and perhaps counterintuitive that the most densely urbanized states tend to draw maps that advantage the Democrats, rather than the Republicans. However, when we consider politics – that is, who controlled districting – this result is to be expected because the states with the most densely populated cities – such as California, New York, New Jersey, and Illinois – tend to prefer Democrats and are thus less likely to grant redistricting power to Republicans. Indeed, a simple probit analysis suggests the odds of having Republicans in control of redistricting in 2011 diminish as the state urban population density increases. The key here is that large and densely clustered urban populations do not make Republican bias an inevitable outcome of districting. Therefore, it is not accurate to say that geography can *explain away* the Republican bias we see in many of the maps.

A second way to show that demographic or geographic factors cannot *explain away* partisan bias is to show that it is possible to draw unbiased (or almost unbiased) districting plans in other states, including those that adopted the most biased plans. The definitive way to show that it was possible to draw districts that were relatively unbiased is to produce such districting plans. Modern web-based redistricting tools make it possible for ordinary citizens to draw their own districts (Altman, MacDonald, and McDonald 2005; Bradlee 2014; The Public Mapping Project et al. 2014). McGann et al. (2016) summarize various redistricting exercises. Altman and McDonald (2013, 2014, 2015) have done this for three states with considerable partisan bias in their congressional maps (Virginia,

Ohio, and Florida). There is also an alternative districting plan for Pennsylvania that produces approximately unbiased results (Perkins 2014). Chen and Rodden's (2013b) expert testimony in *Romo* v. *Detzner* (2014) shows that computer-generated districting in Florida often produce unbiased congressional districts. Furthermore, in the case of several southern states in the 2001 districting round, Democratic controlled state legislatures drew plans that were notably biased toward the Democrats (North Carolina, Tennessee, Texas). Texas redistricted in 2003, replacing a plan that was strongly biased toward the Democrats with a plan more favorable to the Republicans.

Consider one of the most biased set of maps in our sample – the Wisconsin State Assembly and Senate maps approved by the Republican legislature in 2011. Here, there is strong evidence that districting authorities deliberately rejected a politically neutral plan that met the legally mandated districting criteria and instead selected a plan that maximized Republican advantage. According to the findings of the district court in *Whitford* v. *Gill* , "the drafters produced a document comparing the partisan performance of the Current Map to two early draft maps: Joe's Basemap Basic and Joe's Basemap Assertive," which gave Republicans a majority in fifty-two and fifty-six districts in the General Assembly, respectively (No. 15-cv-421-bbc, 2016 WL 6837229, 11). Leadership subsequently "evaluated the partisan performance of at least another six statewide alternative maps ...". Each of these "improved upon the anticipated pro-Republican advantage generated in the initial two draft plans" (ibid., 12).

In terms of its political geography, Wisconsin falls in the middle of the pack. About 70 percent of the state's population lives in cities, which have an average population density of 2,000 persons per square mile. Moreover, there is a great deal of urban clustering in and around Milwaukee, which accounts for roughly a quarter of the state population. Presumably, this makes it difficult to draw pro-Democratic gerrymanders. However, do the geographic features of Wisconsin absolve the Legislature of responsibility for enacting an asymmetrical plan that favors the Republicans? Clearly, the answer is no. Court documents show that, from the outset of the redistricting process, politically neutral maps were presented to the Republican Party leadership, but leadership dismissed these plans, opting instead to support maps that gave their party an asymmetrical advantage. In this regard, unbiased plans were possible, but these were deliberately rejected in order to advance political goals.

4.3 DISTRICTING IS A POLITICAL CHOICE, BUT GEOGRAPHY CONSTRAINS OUTCOMES

It is clear that geographical considerations such as the urban concentration of Democrats cannot *explain away* partisan gerrymandering. There is strong evidence that it is indeed possible to draw unbiased (or almost unbiased) districting plans, even in states with large and densely clustered city dwellers. Given modern GIS technology, state governments are well aware of the partisan effects of districting plans. If they choose to adopt a biased plan when an unbiased plan is possible, then they have made a political choice. However, this is not to say that geographical constraints are not important in understanding the districting process. While districting is a political choice, geographical considerations determine the set of plans that state governments can choose from.

We can gain an understanding of precisely how geography constrains districting decisions by bringing politics back into the equation. As we saw in Chapter 3, "who" controls districting matters; when politicians are in charge, they manage to draw plans that serve their interests, while satisfying legally mandated districting criteria. Thus, we expect that the political geography of a state determines the universe of choices available to districting authorities. When one party is geographically concentrated relative to another, we expect that this determines whether it is possible to draw highly efficient gerrymanders that "pack" an opposing party into a small number of districts in order to waste their votes. To this end, we expect that the geographic concentration of Democrats helps Republicans draw highly efficient gerrymanders when they are in charge of districting. However, when Democrats draw the maps, the geographic concentration of Democrats limits their opportunity to draw maps that "crack" and "pack" the Republican opposition.

4.3.1 Democratic Concentration and Bias

In the previous section, we used very basic measures of political geography recorded by the Census Bureau. However, these measures do not directly measure political geography; they rely on the assumption that cities are predominantly populated by Democratic voters. This may or may not necessarily be the case. Here, we consider a more direct measure of Democratic clustering so that we can provide a more precise estimate of the links between geography, politics, and bias. In measuring the geographic clustering of Democrats by state, we rely on the index of dissimilarity formula, which was originally conceived as a way to measure racial segregation in cities (see Massey and Denton 1988). Although we provide a more detailed account of the intuition behind this metric in the next chapter, in which we focus on race and redistricting, here we find that it also provides an intuitive way of measuring how spatially segregated Democrats are relative to Republicans.

In order to measure the index of dissimilarity between voters associated with different parties, we use vote tallies from the 2004–16 presidential elections. Here we are faced with the challenge of finding a suitable analytical scale. One option is that we can analyze Democratic and Republican election returns on a countywide level. That is, we can measure the statewide concentration of Democrats by looking at how the two-party vote is unevenly distributed across counties. However, the size of a county varies widely by state. In some states, like California, counties are very big, which means that we do not gain much of a fine-grained perspective. By contrast, in states like Alabama and Georgia, counties are comparably smaller. An alternate approach that we take here is to measure political dissimilarity in a state by focusing on precinct-level election results. However, the problem is that precinct-by-precinct results are not yet available for all fifty states for any one presidential election year. But thanks to publicly available datasets provided by the MIT Election Data and Science Lab,[1] the Florida Election Science Team,[2] and the Harvard Election Data Archive,[3] we are able to compile precinct-level presidential election returns for each state for at least two different presidential elections, between 2004 and 2016. This gave us at least two data points in each state, for which we could calculate partisan dissimilarity. Using these data, we calculated the two-party dissimilarity index (PDI) by state each election cycle for which we have precinct-level returns, using the following formula:

$$PDI = \frac{1}{2} \sum_{i=1}^{n} \left| \frac{d_i}{D} - \frac{r_i}{R} \right|$$

where:

d_i = the votes cast for the Democratic presidential candidates in precinct i

[1] MIT Election Data and Science Lab, 2018, State Precinct-Level Returns 2016, https://doi.org/10.7910/DVN/GSZG1O, Harvard Dataverse, V10.
[2] Florida Election Science Team, 2018, 2016 Precinct-Level Election Results, https://doi.org/10.7910/DVN/NH5S2I, Harvard Dataverse, V13.
[3] Ansolabehere, Stephen, Palmer, Maxwell, and Lee, Amanda, 2014, Precinct-Level Election Data, https://doi.org/10.7910/DVN/YN4TLR, Harvard Dataverse, V1.

D = the total statewide votes cast for the Democratic presidential candidate

r_i = the votes cast for the Republican presidential candidates in precinct i

R = the total statewide votes cast for the Republican presidential candidate

In general, when we look at the different PDI scores estimated for a given state, we observe very little change from one election cycle to the next. However, because we wanted to estimate what the PDI would have been in 2010, for each state we imputed the 2010 PDI by fitting the available presidential year PDI calculations onto a regression line.

This measure gives us an accurate and intuitive measure of the relative clustering of Democrats in geographic space by state. The mean 2010 PDI we observe is about 0.27, which means that 27 percent of the Democrats statewide would have to move to a new precinct in order to achieve a distribution of Republicans and Democrats at the precinct level that reflects the statewide distribution. Therefore, a lower score reflects a more even concentration of Democrats and Republicans, while a higher score suggests that Democrats are more segregated in space, presumably affecting the type of districting bias that is achievable. The highest value we observe – the most politically segregated state – is Louisiana, where about 49 percent of the Democrats in the state would have to move to a new precinct in order to achieve a perfectly even distribution of Democrats and Republicans. The least politically segregated state is Hawaii, with a score of less than 14 percent.

In order to understand precisely how Democratic clustering affects districting bias, we use regression analysis to model the symmetry scores of the plans enacted after 2011. Our model includes four independent variables: the partisan symmetry score from the pre-2011 maps; a dummy variable indicating whether Republicans drew the maps; the political dissimilarity score; and a variable interacting the dissimilarity score with the *republican* variable. The results of this model are reported in Table 4.1.

As is evident, the model performs well in predicting post-2011 symmetry scores. As we noted in Chapter 3, the first two variables (*symmetry score, pre-2011* and *republican*) account for most of the variation in symmetry scores in the post-redistricting maps. When the PDI variable is omitted from the model, the r^2 value drops to 56 percent. Thus, the PDI variable and interaction term account for an additional 6–7 percent of the

TABLE 4.1. *Predicting the effects of political geography on bias after redistricting*

Symmetry score, pre-2011	0.491[*]	(.0748)
Republican	8.59	(5.28)
Partisan dissimilarity index	8.49	(12.9)
Republican[*]partisan dissimilarity index	−59.1[*]	(18.2)
Constant	−4.98	(3.37)
N	95	
R^2	0.625	

[*] $p < 0.05$

variance in post-2011 symmetry scores. The model also lends context to the precise effects of geography on bias. Consistent with our expectations, the clustering of Democrats appears to reduce symmetry scores (to the benefit of the Republicans), but this effect is conditional on Republican control of the maps. In other words, when Republicans have drawn the maps, they are able to draw more bias when Democrats are geographically segregated. When Republicans have not drawn the maps, we do not observe a meaningful association between geography and bias.

Figure 4.1 plots the marginal effects of the partisan dissimilarity index variable when it is interacted with the *republican* variable. While there is a strong correlation between geography and bias in the plans that Republicans have drawn, there is no correlation between the two variables among the maps *not* drawn by Republicans. We find similar results when we use a *democrat* dummy variable (signifying Democratic control of redistricting) in place of the *republican* variable. Although the slope of the effect is considerably smaller, Democrats manage to draw more Democratic bias into plans as the level of Democratic clustering increases, despite unfavorable geography.

4.4 WHAT DISTRICT SHAPES CAN EXPLAIN ABOUT GERRYMANDERING

We have argued that geography cannot *explain away* partisan bias and political gerrymandering. Nevertheless, geography clearly does have an effect on what districting plans are possible. As we show in the previous section, the geographic segregation of Democrats in a state can lead to extreme bias, when Republicans are in charge of redistricting. But we do not see bias when Democrats, both parties, or independent bodies draw the maps.

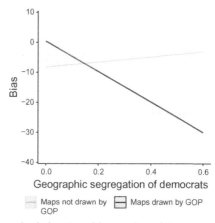

FIGURE 4.1. Geography helps Republicans draw bias

We can think of the process of districting in two stages. First, geographical and demographic factors define what kinds of districting plans it is possible to draw. Then state governments choose what districting plan to enact from this choice set. In states with highly segregated and geographically concentrated populations of Democratic voters, it is possible to draw maps that favor the Republicans by "packing" Democrats into a small number of districts, in order to "waste" their votes. However, it may not be possible to draw a map with Democratic bias, and the best that Democrats may be able to get is an unbiased map. Thus, the geographical concentration of party support can make it harder or easier for state governments to draw districts that favor one party or another, depending on who is in charge and the extent of geographic sorting.

Here it is helpful to consider the shape of state legislative districts in terms of their compactness. Compactness is useful for a number of reasons. First, it is intuitively appealing. Discussions of gerrymandering in the press often point to oddly shaped districts as evidence of wrong-doing (consider Ingraham 2014). When people see a district map that looks like an exercise in abstract art, it is easy to imagine that something is amiss.

Indeed, in our investigation of congressional districting (McGann et al. 2016), we assumed that there would be a simple relationship between partisan bias and compactness. When politicians engaged in gerrymandering to produce political advantage, they drew districts that had odd, noncompact shapes. After all, why else would they draw strangely shaped districts that exposed them to ridicule? Yet we found that there was only a weak correlation between bias and compactness.

There is no logical link between compactness and partisan bias. There is no reason why districts that are biased should not be compact, and vice versa. It is quite possible to create partisan bias in compact districts (Alexeev and Mixon 2018). As we have seen, the way you create partisan bias is to "pack" your opponents' supporters in a few districts, allowing you to win the rest. Ideally, you would like your opponents to win districts with 80 percent of the vote or more. If there are large areas where your opponent is very strong, it may be possible to achieve this goal without needing to draw oddly shaped, noncompact districts. (We would resist calling these "naturally occurring gerrymanders," because district lines are intrinsically human-made, and the claim to "naturalness" too easily becomes a defense.) Conversely, it is possible to have very oddly shaped, noncompact districts without partisan bias. Indeed, this has frequently occurred when state legislatures have drawn districts to create "incumbent protection" gerrymanders. Here there are violations of compactness, but not partisan bias.

However, compactness has at times been used as an indicator or as evidence of gerrymandering. For example, Justice Stevens in his concurring opinion on *Karcher* v. *Daggett* (1983, 755, 758) argued that "substantial divergences from a mathematical standard of compactness may be symptoms of illegitimate gerrymandering"; and that "drastic departures from compactness are a signal that something may be amiss" (1983, 755, 758).

The concept of compactness is useful to us as a measure of stress. It serves to show how hard those drawing state legislative districts are trying to achieve a certain aim. It is straightforward to draw compact districts. Drawing highly irregular districts takes a great deal of effort. It seems reasonable to ask for what this effort was expended.

We would expect there to be a trade-off between partisan bias and compactness. This trade-off will depend on the relative concentration of the support of the two parties. Suppose that the support of the two parties was concentrated about equally. If a party wanted to draw unbiased districts, this goal could be achieved with relatively compact district boundaries (see Nagle 2019). If it wished to advantage one party over the other, then it would have to draw oddly shaped districts. The way we advantage one party over another is by concentrating a great deal of one party's supporters into a few districts. The party then wastes votes winning those districts by a far larger margin than necessary, leaving the other party to win more districts by narrower (but still sufficient) margins. If neither party's supporters are geographically more concentrated than others, artificially concentrating the supporters of one party will require drawing some very specific district lines, which will often violate compactness.

However, the relationship will be very different if one party's support is geographically far more concentrated than the other. Suppose that Democratic voters are concentrated in a few urban areas. It is now possible to draw districts that advantage the Republicans. You simply have to draw a few lines around the areas of Democratic concentration. The resulting districts will be compact, but will lead to the Democrats winning a few districts by inefficiently large margins. By drawing irregularly shaped districts, it might be possible to advantage the Republicans even more. However, in order to draw districts that do not disadvantage the Democrats, you will need to violate compactness. You may need to draw districts that snake into the areas of Democratic concentration and then blend into the surrounding areas, in order to break up the Democratic concentration and use this support to win a larger number of geographically dispersed districts. Furthermore, it is likely to be impossible to draw districts that positively advantage the Democrats – you need to draw highly irregular districts just to break even.

This, of course, in no way detracts from the fact that state legislatures or other authorities choose districting plans. Indeed, we would still expect partisans to choose the districting plans that most advantage their party. The effect of geographical concentration is simply to change the set of plans that are feasible for politicians to choose between.

4.5 THE TRADE-OFF BETWEEN BIAS AND COMPACTNESS

There are a variety of different ways to measure the compactness of legislative districts. We calculate compactness based on the ratio of district area over the convex hull (minimum bounding polygon) of the district. The shape of the convex hull conforms to the particular boundaries of a district (like a rubber band), reflecting the extent to which a district bypasses some geographic areas for others. As a result, a skinny "I"-shaped district may reflect high compactness, while "C"- or "S"-shaped districts will receive much lower scores as a result of their concave shapes. For each map, we then take the average of the convex hull compactness measure of all its districts.

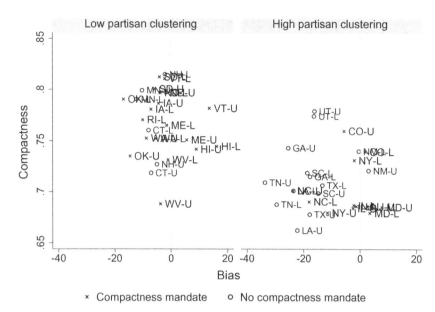

FIGURE 4.2. How Democratic clustering impacts bias and compactness

We plotted the average district compactness (*y*-axis) against the level of bias in a map (*x*-axis), and we separated the maps based on the partisan dissimilarity index of the state. Figure 4.2 shows the maps drawn in states with the lowest PDI scores (the bottom quartile) on the left, and the states with the highest PDI scores (the top quartile) in the right. It also includes separate label markers indicating whether districting authorities were legally required to draw compact districts.

Here, a clear pattern emerges. Among the low clustering states, many of the maps that are unbiased are also very compact. Because Democrats and Republicans are evenly distributed across the state's precincts, it is very easy to draw neutral maps. In this context, districting authorities can achieve unbiased maps simply by drawing compact districts. However, the even distribution of Democrats and Republicans also seems to have prevented aggressive gerrymanders that benefited the Republicans in a number of states. Each of the maps enacted in Oklahoma, South Dakota, North Dakota, and New Hampshire were drawn by Republicans. While these districting authorities succeeded in drawing Republican bias, the level of bias was constrained, possibly because state law mandated the drawing of compact districts.

By contrast, when we considered the high clustering states, it becomes more difficult to draw unbiased districts and less difficult to draw Republican bias into districts. In some states, such as Tennessee, the high geographic clustering of Democrats provides an opportunity to draw highly efficient gerrymanders. However, in many other states, districting authorities must draw less compact district lines in order to achieve unbiased maps. And notably, in this group of states, there are no maps drawn with meaningful levels of pro-Democratic bias. In Illinois, for example, Democrats controlled the districting process entirely, yet they were unable to draw aggregative partisan bias into the maps because the geographic clustering of Democrats into the Chicago metropolitan area made this effectively impossible. In the states where Republicans drew the maps, we see far more bias. Republican legislatures in Utah, Georgia, South Carolina, and Tennessee managed to draw plans with extreme bias, while maintaining relatively compact district boundaries.

In sum, introducing compactness into the equation lends insight into how political geography determines the spectrum choices that districting authorities confront. When one party is inefficiently distributed across the state, it becomes difficult to draw unbiased maps without drawing irregularly shaped districts. And when the geographically disadvantaged party happens to control the districting process, it is often the case that the best they can hope for is a neutral map that gives neither party an advantage.

4.6 CONCLUSION

The question of whether partisan advantage is the result of intentional political gerrymandering or the geographical concentration of Democratic voters rests on a fundamental misunderstanding. Geography does not draw legislative districts' maps – human beings do. However, geographical considerations do affect the set of possible plans available. Geographical considerations may make it easier or harder to advantage one party or the other.

We can reject the idea that the geographical concentration of Democratic voters can in any way "explain away" partisan gerrymandering. There is strong evidence that it is nearly always possible to draw districts that are approximately unbiased. With modern GIS technology there is simply no way that those who draw the districts can claim to be ignorant of their political effects. If a state legislature knowingly draws biased districts when it could have drawn unbiased districts, then it has made a political choice. The fact that someone can run a regression that shows that bias is more likely when there are geographical concentrations of the supporters of one party is utterly irrelevant to the question of whether there was an intentional choice.

However, it would be equally ridiculous to claim that geographical constraints do not have an effect on what districts are adopted. Some outcomes will not happen because they are probably impossible. For example, in states where the Democrats are highly concentrated geographically, it may be impossible to draw a districting plan that creates a strong bias in favor of the Democrats. We find that a model where partisans choose the districting plans that most advantage their party, given what the geographical constraints make possible, fits the available data well.

In this chapter, we shed light on the interrelationship between political geography, partisanship, and political bias. In the next chapter, we investigate the role of racial geography as a determinant of bias. In particular, we investigate whether voting rights-era reforms require districting authorities to draw bias.

5

Racial Geography, the Voting Rights Act, and Bias

So far, we have found that partisan bias increased after the 2011 state legislative redistricting. Bias is most pronounced in the maps drawn by one party, and as we found in our study of congressional redistricting (McGann et al. 2016), the most biased maps overwhelmingly favor the Republican Party.

In the previous chapter, we found that political geography can lend insight into how and why Republicans are able to draw very efficient gerrymanders while Democrats are not. From the perspective of Republicans drawing the maps, the tendency of urbanites to vote for Democrats makes it possible to draw aggressive partisan gerrymanders without having to resort to irregularly shaped district lines. In some cases, Republican gerrymanderers can draw bias simply by drawing relatively compact districts around urban areas, where Democratic populations are geographically concentrated, thereby "wasting" Democratic votes. For this very reason, it can be difficult for Democrats to draw partisan gerrymanders that "waste" Republican votes. In states like Illinois, where much of the Democratic support is clustered in and around Chicago, it is simply not possible to draw an extreme Democratic gerrymander; the best Democrats can hope for is an unbiased map.

In this chapter, we focus specifically on the role of race and redistricting reforms on bias. The Voting Rights Act of 1965 (VRA) and its subsequent amendments mandated that states with sizable communities of minority voters draw majority-minority districts. It also outlawed the use of race as a predominant factor in redistricting decisions. As Lublin (1997) argues, the effect of federal law is that redistricting authorities must maintain a fragile balance by drawing majority-minority districts that expand descriptive representation of minority communities, without drawing these districts in a way that serves to dilute the voting power of historically disenfranchised groups.

Because Black and Latinx voters increasingly tilt in favor of the Democratic Party, it is possible that the drawing of majority-minority districts leads to partisan bias in some states. However, our findings in this chapter suggest that Republican bias is not an unavoidable outcome of minority districting. While majority-minority districting rules can make it easier or more difficult for districting authorities to draw an unbiased map, they do not make bias inevitable. When Republicans are in charge, we often find more bias in states with large and geographically segregated Black and Latinx populations. In this regard, Republican gerrymanderers appear to use majority-minority districting as a tool for creating partisan advantage, much like we see with the geographic clustering of Democrats. But we do not see the same outcomes when Democrats, both parties, or independent actors are in charge. Even in states with large populations of Black and Latinx voters, they still manage to draw unbiased plans that advance minority representation. This underscores our findings from previous chapters that bias in districting is the outcome of deliberate political considerations.

We also assess a civil rights-era reform that is often forgotten: the elimination of multimember districts. Once widespread, "winner-take-all" multimember districts were often deployed as a way to disenfranchise Black voters in state and local politics (Grofman and Davidson 1992). From the 1960s through the 1980s, dozens of states rewrote their state constitutions to end the use of multimember districts, opting instead to establish single-member districts. In principle, the near-universal use of single-member districting in state legislatures has made it possible for partisan districting authorities to increase efficiency in their gerrymanders by maximizing the wasted votes of their opponents. We find that, among the handful of states that still use multimember districts to elect state legislators, the average district magnitude in a state legislature imposes a ceiling on the level of bias achievable. However, when partisans are not in charge, multimember districts do not appear to limit partisan bias. Once again, the key variable in predicting the occurrence of bias in districting is whether or not politicians are in charge.

5.1 THE VOTING RIGHTS ACT AND MAJORITY-MINORITY DISTRICTING

The VRA has had profound consequences for racial representation in state legislatures. Before the passage of the VRA, state governments across the country, and in particular the South, designed their election laws to prevent participation by African-Americans citizens. The VRA banned once-common practices that prevailed during Jim Crow, such as literacy tests, that served to prevent Black citizens from accessing the polls, but it also includes broad language that effectively prevents state and local governments from using redistricting laws as a way to dilute the right to vote based on the basis of race or color. Specifically, Section 2 of the VRA holds that, "No voting qualification or prerequisite to voting, or standard, practice, or procedure shall be imposed or applied by any State or political subdivision to deny or abridge the right of any citizen of the United States to vote on account of race or color."

In addition to the 1965 Act, a number of amendments to the VRA were passed by Congress in the 1970s and 1980s that expanded the scope of the voting rights protections and compelled state governments to draw majority-minority districts into their state legislatures. In 1975, the VRA was amended to include language-banning discrimination against non-English speakers. In 1982, Congress passed an amendment in response to a Supreme Court decision in *Mobile* v. *Bolden* (1980) in order to make it easier for voters to challenge discriminatory election laws. In the *Bolden* case, Black residents of Mobile, Alabama, challenged the city's use of "at-large" districts as an illegal form of vote dilution that functioned to prevent Black candidates from winning municipal office. A plurality of the Court, led by Justice Potter Steward, held that the VRA "prohibits only purposefully discriminatory denial or abridgment by government of the freedom to vote" on the basis of race, and thus does not "entail the right to have [Black] candidates elected" (446 US 65). In response to the controversial ruling, Congress passed an amendment to the VRA that bolstered the language in Section 2 of the Act to explicitly prohibit district maps with discriminatory effects. This effectively made it easier to challenge discriminatory election laws, as plaintiffs no longer needed to show that lawmakers acted deliberately in passing discriminatory election laws.

A few years later, in *Thornburg* v. *Gingles* (1986), the Court established a three-prong test for determining whether and when Section 2 required state governments to draw a majority-minority district. In cases when a minority group is "sufficiently numerous and compact to form a majority in a single-member district," and is "politically cohesive," and the "majority votes sufficiently as a bloc to enable it ... usually to defeat the minority's preferred candidate," a state would be required to draw a majority-minority district.

Combined with the law's Section 5 "preclearance" requirements that gave the Justice Department the power to review changes in the voting laws of several states, the new standards in Section 2 compelled state governments to expand minority representation through redistricting in order to avoid potential legal challenges. As Grofman and Handley (1991) demonstrate, enforcement of the VRA and the success of Section 2 challenges in the Courts contributed to an increase in the number of Black legislators across the country. It also consequently led to many states ending the use of multimember districts in their state legislatures and adopting single-member districts. However, conflicting signals by the Court in the 1990s served to limit the expansion of majority-minority districts after the 2001 redistricting cycle (see Lublin 1997; McGann et al. 2016).

In recent years, two landmark Supreme Court decisions have changed the way the VRA is enforced. As we note in Chapter 3, during 2011 redistricting several states were subject to Section 5 mandatory preclearance requirements. However, the Supreme Court's ruling in *Shelby* v. *Holder* (2013) has effectively removed this requirement, with the Court finding that the formula governing preclearance, outlined in Section 4, is an unconstitutional overreach by the federal government on states' rights to administer their own elections. Although aggrieved citizens can still pursue VRA challenges to state districting laws in the federal courts, changes to redistricting laws are no longer sent to the Justice Department (or a federal court) for automatic review. This will likely have profound consequences during the 2021 redistricting cycle, and it will mean that potentially unlawful racial gerrymanders may survive multiple election cycles as litigation advances through the federal court system.

However, despite weakening federal enforcement of the VRA, the federal courts appear to be adopting a stricter standard in evaluating racial gerrymandering claims. In *Alabama Legislative Black Caucus* v. *Alabama* (2015), the Supreme Court vacated a lower court's ruling that rejected a racial gerrymandering challenge to Alabama's state legislative maps. The challenge, brought by the state legislature's Black caucus, charged that the state had improperly sought to preserve districts with large majorities of Black voters during redistricting. In some cases, district lines were revised to maintain majorities of Black voters exceeding 75 percent of the district population. The district court found that such means were "narrowly tailored" to advance the goal of minority representation, and that the plaintiffs failed to demonstrate that race was a predominant factor in the state's decisions. The Supreme Court rejected the lower court's treatment of the racial gerrymandering claim, holding that the VRA did not require that minority districts maintain a certain numerical percentage of minority residents – only that the state ensures a minority group's ability to elect their preferred candidate. In practice, this decision means that, in order to comply with Section 2, states must maintain "minority influence" districts rather than districts with an absolute majority of minority voters.

The Court affirmed its decision in *Alabama Legislative Black Caucus* in another racial gerrymander challenge of the Virginia House of Delegates map in which it upheld a lower court's ruling that had rejected eleven state house districts with 55 percent Black majorities as an unlawful racial gerrymander (*Bethune-Hill* v. *Virginia Board of Elections* 2019). The lower court appointed a special master to revise the House of Delegates map in advance of the 2019 state legislative elections.

5.2 DOES MINORITY DISTRICTING CAUSE REPUBLICAN BIAS?

The Voting Rights Act and its amendments have been a powerful tool for compelling state governments to expand minority representation. However, it is possible that the expansion of majority-minority districts has led to systematic districting bias in states with large populations of minority groups. One common claim holds that, because Black and Latinx voters tend to favor the Democratic Party, the drawing of majority-minority districts serves to pack Democratic supporters into inefficiently large majorities, resulting in bias that helps the Republican Party (see Nakao 2011).

In the 1990s and 2000s, there was a great deal of scholarly interest on the political effects of majority-minority districting, with the consensus that racial representation hurts the Democrats. In a study of the 1990–92 congressional elections, Hill (1995) argues that "several previously uncompetitive Democratically held districts were made competitive by the creation of majority black districts" and attributes four of the nine seats taken by Republicans in 1992 to the creation of new majority-Black districts. Similarly, in a study of southern state legislators, Lublin and Voss (2000) find that the creation of new majority-minority districts "systematically harms the party chosen by most black voters" and "cost the Democratic party legislative seats" across the South during the 1990s, although they note that the effect of majority-minority districts was dwarfed by the "strong shift toward the Republicans among white voters" (p. 793), a conclusion that is also shared by Petrocik and Desposato (1998). Similarly, Whitby has found that the drawing of Black congressional districts in the South after 1991 redistricting resulted in the "bleaching" of surrounding districts that "may lead to a shift in partisan control" (Whitby 2000, 131–32), while Overby and Cosgrove (1996) find similarly that white incumbents who lost Black constituents "became less sensitive" to Black voters (540).

More recently, Steven Hill has argued that the VRA is a "great ally" to the Republican Party that has "helped the party win a great number of legislative races" (2013). In addition, because low turnout can serve to increase partisan bias in districting (Grofman, Koetzle, and Brunell 1997), low turnout among Latinx voters may exacerbate the effects of minority districting on Republican bias (Fraga 2016). Others have identified several democratic benefits of "majority-minority" districting, in contrast to claims that minority districting harms minority interests (Canon 1999; Clayton 2004; Hayes and McKee 2012; Lublin 1999; Washington 2012).

Does minority districting lead to asymmetrical districting outcomes? It is important to make the distinction between the claim that minority districting has hurt the Democratic Party and the claim that minority districting leads to districting bias. The loss of a few Democratically held seats may have been a temporary, one-off event that was partly attributable to other trends, such as the realignment of the Democratic South. That many states stopped expanding the number of majority-minority districts after 2001 may mean that the long-term political consequences of minority districting have stabilized. Indeed, if states stopped drawing new majority-minority districts after the 1990s, then districting authorities would have had the opportunity to "correct" any systemic biases in the maps when they were redistricted in 2001 and 2011.

In order to assess the links between minority representation and bias, the first challenge is to find a valid measure to compare the scale of minority districting across states. As a starting point, we can compare the relative size of the Black and Latinx populations across states.[1] After all, states with the most sizable minority communities will be required to draw more majority-minority districts in their state legislatures, or else risk racial gerrymandering challenges to their maps. And if the logic holds that minority districts "waste" Democratic votes and thus lead to

---

[1] It should be noted that in at least two states, California and Hawaii, there are sizable Asian-American populations that are represented by majority-minority districts.

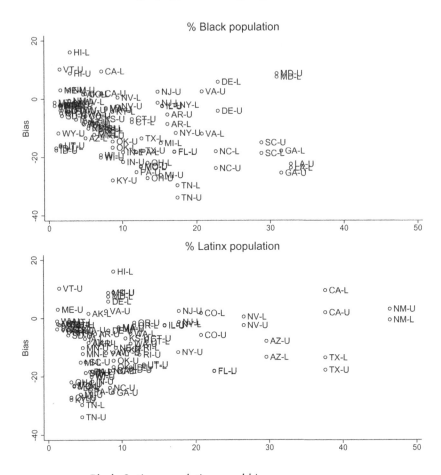

FIGURE 5.1. Black, Latinx populations, and bias

Republican bias, we should observe more bias in states with larger groups of minority residents.

Figure 5.1 plots the relationship between statewide Black and Latinx populations (based upon the 2010 census) and districting bias. When we look at the proportion of Black residents living in a state, we find that this metric is moderately correlated with bias ($r = -0.31$). At face value, this suggests that the states with the largest proportion of Black voters tend to produce maps that favor the Republicans. Indeed, among the states with the largest Black populations in our sample, Louisiana, Georgia, South Carolina, and North Carolina all produced maps with substantial

Republican bias. However, there are also notable outliers. Maryland, Delaware, and Virginia all managed to adopt districting plans that are biased in favor of the Democrats, despite having some of the largest proportions of Black residents in the country.

When we consider the statewide Latinx populations, we observe a correlation in the *opposite* direction ($r = 0.20$). Here, it would seem that states with the largest proportions of Latinx residents tend to produce plans that do not favor the Republican Party. Indeed, this is the case in California, New Mexico, Colorado, Nevada, New York, and New Jersey, where districting authorities drew approximately unbiased plans. However, this was not the case in Texas, Florida, and Arizona, which drew plans with substantial Republican bias. Thus, from this vantage, there is little evidence that Republican bias is an unavoidable outcome of minority representation, as the relationship between minority communities and redistricting bias is weak.

One possible explanation for the absence of a strong correlation between minority populations and districting outcomes is that there is variation among states in the geographic distribution of their Black and Latinx populations. As we discussed in Chapter 5, geography can be a powerful force in determining the types of maps that are available to districting authorities. Accordingly, it is possible that we see Republican bias in states like Texas and Florida (with large Latinx populations) and Louisiana and Georgia (with large Black populations) due to racial and ethnic segregation. In principle, high segregation along race and ethnic lines would mean that districting authorities would be required to draw majority-minority districts that inadvertently waste Democratic votes by large margins. By contrast, if a state with a large Black or Latinx population had less geographic segregation along race or ethnic lines, districting authorities would be able to respect minority districting requirements without having to draw districts that end up wasting Democratic votes.

5.2.1 Measuring Minority Segregation

Quantifying racial segregation is not a straightforward task. "Segregation" is a broad concept that can encompass many distinct phenomena. Massey and Denton (1988) identify five conceptually distinct "dimensions" of racial segregation, which we summarize on Table 5.1. While this literature addresses the problem of racial segregation in urban areas, these insights are applicable for conceptualizing segregation at the

TABLE 5.1. *The five "dimensions" of segregation, according to Massey and Denton (1988)*

Evenness	"the differential distribution of two social groups among areal units in a city" (p. 283)
Exposure	"the degree of potential contact, or the possibility of interaction, between minority and majority group members within geographic areas of a city" (p. 287)
Concentration	"the relative amount of physical space occupied by a minority group in the urban environment" (p. 289)
Centralization	"the degree to which a group is spatially located near the center of an urban area." (p. 291)
Clustering	"the extent to which areal units inhabited by minority members adjoin one another, or cluster, in space" – "the checkerboard problem" (p. 293)

State A

W	W	B	B
W	W	B	B
W	W	W	W
W	W	W	W

State B

B	W	W	W
W	B	W	W
W	W	B	W
B	W	W	B

FIGURE 5.2. Hypothetical distribution of Black and white voters

statewide level. For our purposes, we have identified the first dimension – "evenness" – as the one standard that is both relevant for understanding districting outcomes and feasible in terms of operationalizing, although the authors note that many of these measures are highly correlated.

Figure 5.2 illustrates how the relative "evenness" in the distribution of a state's population can lead to districting bias. Consider two states, with populations of white (W) and Black (B) citizens, distributed across its geographic territory. In State A the white and Black populations are unevenly distributed, insofar as the Black and white populations occupy distinct geographic areas. Assuming that districting authorities are required to draw four, equally populated districts, districts that represent sizable minority groups, and compact districts, the likely outcome would be one district in which Black residents comprise a majority. If we make additional assumption that political party affiliation in State A is racially polarized, the consequence would mean districting bias that disadvantages the party favored by Black voters.

By contrast, Black and white residents in State B are much more evenly distributed. Assuming the same districting requirements as State A, districting authorities would likely be required to draw two minority districts, each with approximately equal populations of white and Black voters. The result would be a district plan that is relatively unbiased, with respect to the party favored by Black voters.

As Figure 5.2 illustrates, the concept of "evenness" with respect to the distribution of Black and Latinx populations relative to white populations provides an alternative approach to assessing the links between minority districting and districting bias. A simple way to measure evenness is the index of dissimilarity, which estimates the proportion of a minority group's population (i.e., Black citizens) that would need to move to a different geographic subunit (i.e., a census tract) in order to achieve a distribution at the subunit level that matched that of the larger geographic unit (i.e., a state).

We measured the Black, Latinx, and white populations at the level of the census tract, using data on race published in the 2010 census. We calculated the dissimilarity index for Black-white and Latinx–white state populations using the following formula:

$$DI = \frac{1}{2} \sum_{i=1}^{n} \left| \frac{b_i}{B} - \frac{w_i}{W} \right|$$

where:

b_i = the number of Black/Latinx residents living in census tract i
B = the total statewide Black/Latinx population
w_i = the number of white residents living in census tract i
W = the total statewide white population

5.2.2 Racial Segregation and Bias

Although the dissimilarity index does not directly measure the number of majority-minority districts in a state, we expect that high geographic segregation of minority communities would mean that a state would be required to draw less efficient majority-minority districts. When we look at the relationship between a state's Black–white dissimilarity index and bias in its districting maps, we observe a moderate, negative correlation

(r = -0.38). This suggests that districting authorities produce maps with more Republican bias when the geographic segregation between white and Black residents is high. We see a similar relationship when we look at the correlation of Latinx–white dissimilarity and bias. As with Black–white segregation, we observe a moderate correlation between the Latinx–white dissimilarity and bias (r = -0.27), which suggests that states with high Latinx segregation tend to produce maps that favor the Republicans. However, does the presence of a correlation between Black–white segregation and Republican bias mean that drawing biased plans is unavoidable when minority groups are highly segregated?

Once again, politics provides important context to the relationship between minority communities and districting outcomes. When we look at the correlation between Black–white dissimilarity and bias broken down by who controlled redistricting, the outcomes diverge in important ways. Among the maps drawn by Republicans, we observe a strong negative correlation between bias and Black segregation (r = -0.65), as well as bias and Latinx segregation (r = -0.62). In these maps the geographic distribution of a state's Black and Latinx populations relative to its white population is a powerful variable at predicting the level of symmetry (r^2 = 0.42 and 0.38, respectively).

However, we observe markedly different outcomes when Republicans are not in control. The correlation between a state's Black–white dissimilarity index and bias is much weaker in the maps drawn by Democrats (r = -0.25) and nonexistent in the maps drawn by courts and citizen commissions (r = 0.058). What's more, there are several notable outliers: New York, New Jersey, Maryland, Arkansas, and Illinois are among the most racially segregated states in our sample, yet districting authorities in each state managed to draw plans without bias. That Democrats drew the maps in Maryland, Arkansas, and Illinois, and both parties drew the maps in New York and New Jersey, suggests that when a districting authority is motivated enough, they somehow manage to draw unbiased plans despite highly racially segregated populations. Likewise, many of the states with the most Latinx–white segregation managed to draw plans free of bias. Of the eight states with Latinx–white dissimilarity indices that exceeded 0.50, seven of them drew maps that were approximately unbiased.

Here, it is telling to consider the compactness of the districts. Using the average convex hull measure that we calculated for each map (see Chapter 4), we compared the compactness of the districts drawn in the most highly segregated states. In this sample, there are twelve states with

Black–white dissimilarity scores that exceeded 0.60 in 2010. Republicans drew the maps in five of these states (WI, MI, TN, IN, OH), while Democrats drew the maps in three of these states (MD, AR, IL). In the maps drawn by Republicans, the average symmetry score was −23.6. However, Republican districting authorities were able to achieve this bias while drawing relatively compact districts (with an average convex hull of 0.75). Because the Black populations in these states are highly segregated relative to the white population, districting authorities were able to comply with minority districting requirements while "wasting" Democratic votes. In this regard, the VRA requirements aided Republican redistricting authorities' efforts to draw highly efficient gerrymanders, without resorting to irregularly shaped district lines. By contrast, in the maps drawn by Democrats, there was practically no bias drawn (−1.31). However, because Black voters across the state were highly segregated, Democrats had to draw districts that were less compact (a convex hull of 0.69 on average) in order to achieve unbiased plans.

A similar pattern emerges in the states with high Latinx–white segregation. Among the maps passed in the most segregated states (those in top 25 percent of Latinx–white dissimilarity indices), political control is an important variable in understanding how segregation affects districting bias. Of these, the maps drawn by Republicans are highly asymmetrical (−20.0 symmetry on average), yet relatively compact (average convex hull of 0.77). By contrast, the maps drawn by Democrats in this group were at once markedly less biased (−2.70 average symmetry) and less compact (0.71 average convex hull). As with Black–white segregation, here we see the trade-offs that partisan districting authorities make when confronted with the racial geography of their state and minority districting mandates. For Republicans, complying with the VRA by drawing majority–Latinx districts provides an opportunity to draw districts that end up wasting Democratic votes. For Democrats, in order to comply with the VRA and draw unbiased maps, they must necessarily draw irregularly shaped districts.

In this way, both the Republican and Democratic mapmakers confronted similar geographic constraints: a highly racially segregated state population along with minority districting requirements. However, because districting authorities have free will over the shapes of their district lines, the two parties dealt with these constraints in markedly different ways. Democrats were able to draw the lines in a way that allowed them to comply with federal law, while neutralizing a geographic disadvantage. Republicans were able to meet federal minority districting requirements, while exploiting a geographic advantage in order to draw severe bias without having to resort to irregularly shaped district boundaries. Thus, the racial distribution of the state does not determine the level of bias or make bias inevitable or "natural." However, it clearly imposes limits on the universe of options that are available to partisan districting authorities.

To estimate precisely how single party control affects the relationship between minority segregation and bias, for each map we regressed the post-2011 symmetry scores against the pre-2011 symmetry scores, along with the Black–white dissimilarity indices, a *republican* dummy variable, and an interaction term. We then plotted the marginal effects of Black–white dissimilarity on post-2011 symmetry when Republicans controlled the districting process and when Republicans did not control the process. We ran an additional model with Latinx–white dissimilarity indices.

As Figure 5.3 illustrates, the nature of the relationship between racial geography and partisan bias in districting depends on whether or not Republicans control redistricting. Among the maps drawn by Republicans, we see a steep decline in symmetry scores when racial segregation increases. This suggests that Republicans were able to exploit minority districting laws to their advantage by wasting Democratic votes in the process, as others have argued (Waymer and Heath 2016). By contrast, among the maps not drawn by Republicans, this did not occur.

5.2.2.1 Minority Representation, Republicans, and Bias

Does achieving minority representation make bias unavoidable? It would be wrong to claim that districting bias is an inevitable consequence of expanding representation to minority communities. We have demonstrated that the many of the states with the largest Latinx and Black populations have no trouble drawing unbiased plans. Further, when we look at the states with the most racial segregation, we find similarly that many have succeeded in drawing maps without Republican bias. Thus, the states that contain the most "numerous and compact" communities of Black and Latinx voters are not doomed to produce bias plans.

When we do see bias, however, it is when Republicans were in charge of redistricting. When we control politics accordingly, we begin to understand how racial geography actually effects bias. When Republicans are in charge, they exploit racial geography to maximize bias to help their party win. In states with racially segregated populations, this makes it possible to draw districts that waste Democratic votes, leading to

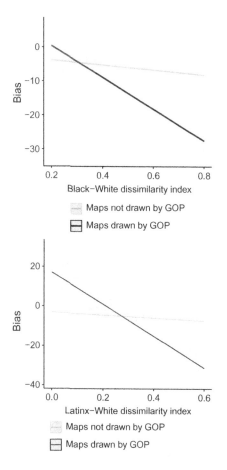

FIGURE 5.3. Marginal effects of racial segregation on districting bias

Republican bias in a districting plan. However, when Democrats are in control, they succeed in neutralizing the effects of this geography. They are able to draw district boundaries so that minority communities do not lead to the inefficient distribution of Democratic votes across districts.

These observations underscore the key role that politics play in districting. The decision to choose a biased map over an unbiased one is deliberate, and reflects the interest of mapmakers. While geography may constrain the possible outcomes that can be achieved through districting – as in the case of Democrats, it forecloses the possibility of a map with Democratic bias – it does not make biased plans inevitable. For political parties, the prevailing interest is winning.

5.3 THE DECLINE OF MULTIMEMBER DISTRICTS

In addition to the rise of minority districting, one of the many consequences of the VRA was the decline of multimember districts, which were widespread in state legislatures as recently as the 1950s (Klain 1955). Although this trend began in state legislatures as early as the 1960s, the number of states that used multimember districts sharply declined after Congress passed the Section 2 amendment to the VRA in response to the *Bolden* (1980) case. In *Bolden* the Court had sided with the city of Mobile, Alabama, in its use of "at-large" districts for municipal elections. Congress responded by mandating an "effects-based" standard for challenging racially discriminatory election laws, which the Court would later clarify in *Gingles* (1986).

The *Bolden* case drew scrutiny to the dubious effects of "at-large" district schemes, once widespread in the South, that serve to dilute the voting power of racial minorities. When a white majority holds racially discriminatory views, as in the 1960s South (Derfner 1972), Black candidates running in "at-large" races have no reasonable chance to win office, and Black citizens are consequently denied political representation. In state legislatures, the practice of using multimember districts produced similar effects due to their "winner-take-all" design. Multimember districts can serve to prevent Black and Latinx candidates from winning office when they give voters the opportunity to cast n votes for n seats being contested (in contrast to a typical PR system where voters are given a single vote for a party or candidate of their preference) and "crack" Black and Latinx populations to prevent a voting majority (see Gerber et al. 1998).

Accordingly, the abandonment of multimember districting practices and the shift to single-member districts in state legislatures has been instrumental in the election of minority legislators over the past four decades. However, one possible unforeseen consequence of the shift to single-member districting is that it has made it easier for districting authorities to draw partisan bias. Early studies of the transition to single-member districts suggest that the transition resulted in the election of more minority and women candidates, but also benefited Republicans (Bullock and Gaddie 1993; Pritchard 1992). We expect that single-member districts (compared to multimember districts) are more efficient in wasting the votes of an opposition party, making it easier to draw efficient partisan gerrymanders. If this is valid, then the adoption of single-member districting has given gerrymanderers new opportunities to maximize partisan bias.

We can consider the average district magnitude, M, as existing on a continuum, where the minimum value of M is 1 seat and the maximum is equal to the total number of seats in a legislature. Assuming a mapmaker has the motive to create partisan bias through districting, the ideal value of M is 1, because it maximizes the "wasted votes" for the opposition. However, at the other extreme, when M equals the total number of seats in a legislature, it becomes impossible to create partisan bias through districting (because the entire legislature is treated as a single district). In this case, there are no district lines to draw.

Of course, with a "winner-take-all" decision mechanism whereby voters cast n votes for n seats up for grabs, it is conceivable that the majority party voters could wind up winning all the seats, but this isn't always the case, particularly when M *is* very large. For example, consider the New Hampshire House of Representatives, which includes several multimember districts. In the Hillsborough 21 district, which includes eight seats, Republican and Democratic candidates managed to take four seats apiece in the 2018 election, despite the fact that voters were given the opportunity to cast up to eight votes.

Ultimately, the success of a majority party in a multimember district with a "winner-take-all" rule hinges on the ability of the majority party voters to coordinate their choices effectively. In his study of the evolution of single-member districting in Congress, J. K. Dow (2017) offers several historical examples of "at-large" US House elections gone wrong for the majority party, due to the failure of major party voters to coordinate their choices of candidates. We expect that the ability of voters and parties to coordinate diminishes with the number of seats up for grabs and the number of candidates running.

Thus, we expect that the logical effect of M is that it reduces the potential for maximum bias when a motivated actor has control of redistricting. As illustrated in Figure 5.4, districting bias falls to zero when M is equal to the size of an assembly. In this case, no partisan bias is achievable, because the entire "state" becomes a single at-large district, which means that the seat allocation is responsive to the majority vote. By contrast, the potential for bias is maximized when $M = 1$ (i.e., a single-member district), which represents the most efficient district magnitude for wasting votes. Accordingly, we expect that M should have a negative impact on bias when partisans are controlling the process. Conversely, we

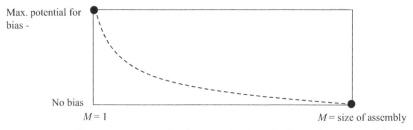

FIGURE 5.4. How the average district magnitude (*M*) affects the potential for redistricting bias

do not expect to see any relationship between bias and *M* when a single party does not control the districting process.

5.3.1 Multimember Districts and Bias: Results

Although the majority of state legislatures use single-member districts in their elections, there still exist a handful of states that retain the practice of multimember districts. This amounts to thirteen state legislative chambers in ten states. In this sample, the average district magnitude ranges from 1.49 (the West Virginia House) to 3.0 (the Maryland House). Although this sample represents only a small subset of the ninety-nine state legislatures, it can still provide some insight into how the transition to single-member districts a generation ago might have impacted the ability of districting authorities to draw extreme bias into their plans.

When we look at the correlation between *M* and asymmetry in a map (as measured by the absolute value of the post-2011 symmetry score), we observe a weak, negative correlation ($r = -0.19$). However, when we isolate those maps drawn by a single party, the correlation is stronger ($r = -0.38$). In total, there are four maps drawn with multimember districts in states where districting authorities had both the motivation and opportunity to draw bias, according to our assessment in Chapter 3. These are: the New Hampshire House and Senate plans, and the Vermont House and Senate plans. The maps drawn in New Hampshire were unbiased, and both violated our expectations (see Table 3.4) that a map drawn by one party in a state with a competitive state legislature will be drawn with partisan bias. Likewise, this was also the case with the Vermont House map, which was unbiased, although the Vermont Senate map was indeed drawn with Democratic bias (13.6).

TABLE 5.2. *Predicting asymmetry in newly enacted plans*

Asymmetry, old plan	0.495[*]
	(.113)
M (average district magnitude)	3.40
	(3.28)
Drawn by one party	15.3[*]
	(4.81)
M^* Drawn by one party	-10.3[*]
	(3.98)
Constant	-0.0847
	(4.00)
N	95
R^2	0.343
Adjusted R^2	0.314

[*] $p < 0.05$

In order to model the effects of average district magnitude (M) on bias, we regressed the folded post-2011 symmetry scores against the folded pre-2011 symmetry scores, along with variables for M, a dummy variable for signifying one-party control, and an interaction term for the two. As Table 5.2 reports, the effect of M on bias is conditional on one-party control. When a single party does not control the process, there is no meaningful relationship between M and bias. When partisans do control districting, increasing M reduces asymmetry substantially. This is not surprising, given our findings in Chapters 3, which illuminate the links between one-party control of redistricting and partisan bias. Indeed, when one party has the opportunity to monopolize the districting process, the result is often maps that are heavily tilted to favor the controlling party. However, when one party does not control redistricting, we do not see partisan bias in districting outcomes.

How should we interpret these results? One possibility is that multi-member districts impose a ceiling that effectively limits the magnitude of the partisan bias that can be drawn into a plan. The model estimates that each additional seat assigned to a district reduces partisan asymmetry by about 10 points, but only when the process is controlled by politicians from a single party.

Notwithstanding, it is important to note that there are several limitations in this approach to estimating the long-term effects of the switch to single-member districts. First, many of the states that switched to SMDs did so because the state governments had a history of denying racial and ethnic minorities the right to vote through the design of their electoral systems. Accordingly, it is possible that our sample of states is prone to selection bias. That is, those states that still use multimember districts in their state legislatures happen to be those that did not systemically disenfranchise minority voters. Second, because the sample of states that use multimember districts is very small, we cannot make definitive conclusions about the switch to multimember districts based on the available data. Third, we cannot dismiss the possibility that the relationship we observe between district magnitude and bias is spurious because many of the state legislatures with the highest average district magnitude were redistricted by Democrats, who are often unable to draw extreme bias in their maps due to political geography (see Chapter 4).

Despite these limitations in our empirical assessment of multimember districts, both the logic and the balance of evidence suggests that the movement away from multimember districts in favor of single-member districts has given districting authorities an opportunity to draw more aggressive gerrymanders than they otherwise would have. If this is valid, it is clear that politics matters in a fundamental way. The result of our analysis of states that still use multimember district shows that, when politicians are not in control, there is no clear link between single-member districting and bias. Rather, partisans use the tools they have at hand to draw districts in a way that helps their party win. In this case, single-member districting is a tool that, under conditions of racially polarized voting, can be used to discriminate against minority voters, whether they are geographically concentrated or not.

Yet it is difficult to argue that the "costs" of transitioning to single-member districts, in terms of more efficient gerrymanders, outweigh the benefits of expanding racial and ethnic representation to minority groups. Indeed, the design and functioning of plurality multimember districts served to prevent Black and Latinx voters from effectively influencing state politics, while preventing non-white candidates from winning office. But this does not mean that multimember districts necessarily punish minority candidates and dilute minority votes. Rather, it was the so-called winner-take-all decision-making mechanism whereby voters cast n number of votes for n number of contested seats combined with multimember districting that perpetuated racial disparities associated with "at-large" and multimember district schemes. The electoral formula that converts votes into seats – not the district magnitude – is the discriminatory mechanism. Multimember districts that provide a more proportional formula in place of "winner-take-all" should be less susceptible to partisan manipulation.

5.4 CONCLUSION

Achieving minority representation and unbiased districting are not mutually exclusive goals. The VRA and its amendments have helped expand racial representation in Congress as well as in state legislatures. Among the many changes caused by the VRA, the law required states to draw majority-minority districts, and it forced many states to transition from multimember "winner-take-all" state districts to single-member districts in their state legislatures. The evidence we presented in this chapter shows that politicians have been able to exploit these requirements in order to draw aggressive partisan gerrymanders.

Yet this does not mean that bias is inevitable or unavoidable. Indeed, we have shown many examples of states that drew unbiased maps and achieved minority representation, despite electorates that are segregated along racial and ethnic lines. We only see a link between segregation and bias when Republicans are in charge, which tells us something about how politics determines districting outcomes when a political party controls redistricting.

We also studied the effects of multimember districts on bias in order to evaluate the long-term consequences of the shift to single-member districts. Although multimember districts constrain the ability of gerrymanderers to draw bias into the maps, this does not mean that single-member districting makes bias inevitable. Indeed, there are many states with unbiased plans and single-member districts. And while we do observe a clear reduction in bias in states with multimember districts and where one party drew the maps, the apparent benefits of multimember districts on reducing bias disappear when one party does not control the mapmaking process.

Politicians use the tools they have available to help their party win. With the abolition of most multimember districts, political parties have focused on the boundaries of single-seat districts and restrictive (or expansive) election laws. Indeed, while many voting rights organizations have focused on doing away with multimember districts as a remedy against vote dilution, it is the plurality electoral formula, rather than the district magnitude, that operates to dilute the voting strength of electoral minorities.

More recently, electoral reform advocates have successfully enacted changes to electoral formulas for single-seat systems, moving from plurality or runoff to instant-runoff ranked choice voting (RCV) in a number of cities (Fairvote 2019). Under RCV, voters rank all candidates in order of preference, and if no candidate meets the electoral threshold (50 percent +1 of first-place choices in a single-seat district), the least favored candidate is eliminated and second-choice preferences are reallocated to the remaining candidates, until seats are filled. Several states allow overseas and military personal to rank order candidate preferences for congressional runoffs, nineteen local jurisdictions have adopted RCV in district elections, and in 2018 Maine became the first state to adopt RCV for all Congressional and most statewide elections. In 2019, New York City became the largest jurisdiction in the nation to adopt RCV for primary elections, and Eastpointe, Michigan, used RCV in a multiseat district election, commonly known as the single transferable vote (STV), as the result of a Voting Rights Act settlement. Other more proportional formulas, including approval and cumulative voting, were used in cities during the 2020 general election.

We see the capacity to enhance minority representation through the use of more proportional electoral formulas as an important advancement in voting rights law and election science in the United States. While there is a substantial research history of domestic alternatives to single-seat districts (Donnovan 2017; Grofman 1981; Santucci 2017; Trounstine and Valdini 2008; Welch and Studlar 1990), more research needs to be done to substantiate the quality of proportional formulas in the context of contemporary US politics. Racially polarized voting is increasing in magnitude, especially in many of the areas previously covered under Section 5 of the Voting Rights Act (Ansolabehere, Persily, and Stewart III et al. 2013). Conjoined racial and partisan polarization further complicates court attempts to treat racial and partisan vote dilution as independent, unrelated problems (Hasen 2018).

Given the incentive to gerrymander with the adoption of single-member districts, multimember proportional districting should be considered more broadly as a remedy for partisan and racial bias in US elections. However, even within the scope of single-member district planning, our research shows that there are effective solutions to reduce bias.

6

The Policy and Social Consequences of State Legislative Gerrymandering

We have shown that state legislatures gerrymandered their own districting plans in 2011 in order to entrench governing parties in power and deny the other party seats. Districting outcomes are a political choice. We showed that political considerations shape redistricting outcomes, and that partisan motive and opportunity largely explain the level of partisan bias observed in state legislatures.

In many cases, partisan redistricting authorities took advantage of their state's racial and political geographies to draw highly efficient partisan gerrymanders by diluting votes. In the states where Republicans controlled redistricting, mapmakers were able to draw more extreme partisan bias when Democrats statewide were geographically concentrated in urban areas. Similarly, in Chapter 5, we showed that because race and partisanship are highly correlated in the United States, Republican mapmakers took advantage of voting rights laws that mandate minority districting in order to waste the votes of Democrats. The Republican Party had a dominant position in 2011 redistricting, in part, due to their performance in the 2010 state legislative elections, which determined which party would control state government during redistricting.

In this chapter, we extend our analysis to consider some of the political and social consequences of the 2010 election and the gerrymandering that followed. We show that many of the governing parties that implemented extremely biased maps also enacted greater restrictions on voter eligibility and ballot access prior to the 2016 presidential election. Furthermore, we find evidence that the level of partisan bias present in state legislatures influenced policy outcomes, distinct from partisan control of the legislatures. Many state legislatures, including those in crucial swing states, have effectively insulated themselves from public accountability at the same time that their constituents face growing public health challenges.

6.1 WHAT DID VOTERS WANT IN 2010?

In spite of the extraordinary consequences of the 2010 midterm elections, there is little evidence that voters in state-level races across the country understood the full weight of their decisions and the implications for national politics. Indeed, voters in these elections were ostensibly casting votes in individual state-level races that were waged over state-level issues. Although no simple narrative captures the dynamics of state-level races across the country, Republican candidates seized upon economic anxieties, as well as anti-establishment sentiment and distrust of government to win (Rosentiel 2010; Weeks 2010).

Some Republican gubernatorial candidates emphasized their qualifications in business and private industry experiences as evidence of their ability to manage the economy and create jobs. In Wisconsin, the gubernatorial race featured Republican Scott Walker, the Milwaukee County Executive, and Democrat Tom Barrett, the mayor of Milwaukee. Walker managed to win narrowly by harnessing anger at the economic conditions and rising unemployment. Promising to bring business mindedness to the governorship, he declared that Wisconsin was "open for business" (Spicuzza and Hall 2010). The Republican capture of the governorship was matched with a takeover of both chambers of the state legislature.

In Ohio, which also featured a governor's race, incumbent Democrat Ted Strickland faced Republican John Kasich. Although Strickland had won in 2006 by more than a 20 percent margin of victory, he was in the uncomfortable position of having to defend his record after the state had lost 400,000 jobs the previous year. Although Strickland painted Kasich as a Wall Street insider, Kasich's campaign strategy embraced his experience in business, and he promised to govern with a "free-market, business-first mindset he learned in the private sector" in order to bring jobs to the state (Fields 2010). Kasich managed to win narrowly by a margin of 80,000 votes. The result was a statewide sweep for the Republican Party, giving them control of the governorship and both houses of the General Assembly.

As in Ohio and Wisconsin, the state-level races that played out across the country in 2010 largely reflected the economic anxieties amid steep job losses stemming from the Great Recession, as well as anti-incumbent sentiment. These conditions favored Republican candidates in state-level races across the country who promised to apply conservative policies to economic problems.

The political rhetoric of these campaigns matches theoretical expectations of party organization. Whether theories of US political parties prioritize the role of policy-seeking politicians (Aldrich 1995) or "groups of organized policy demanders" (Bawn et al. 2012), control over legislative policymaking is understood to be a central goal of political parties and the coalitions of voters that they represent. In particular, the Republican Party's overarching ideological principles regarding a limited role of government should be anticipated in policy outcomes, even if those policies diverge from majority preferences (M. Grossman and Hopkins 2016).

However, political parties are not merely conduits for the demands of policy activists. Parties have their own internal logic and structure. Leaders of state party organizations have a stake in the legislative strength of the party distinct from the demands of interest groups and activists (Mayhew 2014; Schattschneider 1975). In other words, party leaders have incentive to attend to the institutional structures that shape how voters, activists, and interest groups are represented. As the broader topic of the book already suggests, changing electoral rules is a viable survival strategy, especially in a "winner-take-all" two-party system, when the benefits to a threatened governing majority outweigh the costs of altering the institutional framework.

6.2 PARTISAN BIAS AND POLARIZATION OF THE COST OF VOTING

In this section, we show how the ideological commitments of the Republican Party aligned with the incentive to maximize partisan electoral advantage, resulting in greater restrictions on voter participation in the most gerrymandered states. Most research on the manipulation of electoral rules comes from developing democracies outside the United States (Kovalov 2014; Tan and Grofman 2018), as it is thought that older democracies have evolved constraints over time to prevent manipulation (Kaminski and Nalepa 2004). However, established democracies exhibit considerable rule manipulation, at least at the micro-level of administrative regulations (McElwain 2018). Erik Engstrom (2013) has shown that, at least historically, partisan manipulation of electoral rules was the norm in the United States prior to the professionalization of the party system. Indeed, both historical and contemporary research suggest that electoral rule manipulation beyond gerrymandering has been a highly partisan, racialized, and regular affair in the United States (Bentele and O'Brien 2013; Epperly et al. 2019).

The substantial shift in partisan control after 2010 and subsequent legislative victories by Republicans prior to the 2016 presidential election enabled party leaders to erect barriers to voting that worked to the advantage of their older, more affluent, whiter voters. Restrictive election laws have consistently been shown to depress turnout (Leighley and Nagler 2013; Schlozman, Brady, and Verba 2018; Schlozman, Verba, and Brady 2012; Wolfinger and Rosenstone 1980). Resource-based models of participation imply that erecting barriers to voter eligibility and ballot access increases the difficulty of casting a ballot, especially for those who possess fewer resources like time, education, and affluence. The likelihood of voting depends not only on the politically relevant resources that one possesses, but also the degree to which people are embedded in resource-rich environments that facilitate recruitment into political action. Both the economic and legal ecosystems can exert a cumulative suppressive effect on voter participation due to a scarcity of organizational and institutional opportunities to engage or be recruited into politics by others.

After the 2011–12 legislative session (when most of the new gerrymanders were being drawn), the Brennan Center for Justice estimates that twenty-seven new restrictions were passed in eighteen states (Brennan Center for Justice 2012). Figure 6.1 estimates the impact of these changes, as well as changes that occurred after the 2012 presidential election, using data from Quan Li, Michael J. Pomante II, and Scot Schraufnagel. These authors have constructed a cost of voting index for each state and presidential election cycle since 1996 using factor analysis on additive scores that assign value to each state for the following:

- ease of registration,
- restrictions on eligibility,
- restrictions on who can register voters,
- availability of preregistration for sixteen- and seventeen-year-olds before they are eligible,
- opportunities to vote early,
- state assurance of time off work to vote,
- extent of identification requirements,

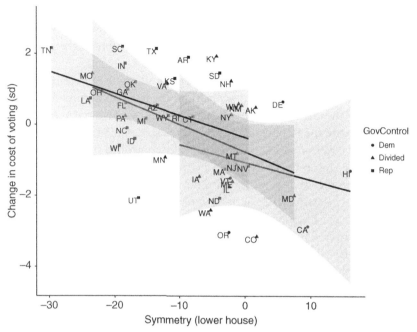

FIGURE 6.1. Partisan symmetry and change in cost of voting 2008–16

- availability of polling stations, and
- the number of hours available for in-person voting (Li, Pomante, and Schraufnagel 2018).

Comparing the change in cost of voting scores from 2008 to 2016, it is clear that Republican-controlled governments imposed substantially higher increases in voting costs compared to divided or Democratic governments over the same time period. Because the scores are standard deviations from the mean state for each election cycle, it is not possible to identify the impact of specific laws in a state. Nevertheless, the magnitude of partisan bias appears to have amplified the impact of government control in shaping voting costs over the last decade.

Within both Republican-controlled and -divided state governments, more gerrymandered legislatures saw significantly higher increases in the cost of voting, compared to unbiased and Democratically controlled legislatures. We should note that while they are not included in the analysis, the Republican states of Alabama and Mississippi saw some of the highest relative increases in voting costs (1.71 and 2.98 standard deviations, respectively). No clear pattern emerges in Democratic-controlled governments, and we don't have enough strong Democratic gerrymanders to draw definitive conclusions, but those states were more likely to expand eligibility and ballot access over the time period.

There are major exceptions, such as Utah's adoption of vote-by-mail in 2013, but the overall pattern demonstrates the partisan nature of changes in election law after 2010. Overall, we find that by 2016, the average cost of voting score for Republican states was 0.407, while the average score for divided governments and Democratically controlled states was −0.206 and −0.581, respectively. Republican-controlled states saw an average voting cost increase of 0.72 standard deviations, compared to an average decline of 1.11 standard deviations in Democratically controlled states.

After the 2013 Supreme Court ruling in *Shelby* v *Holder,* several states formerly covered under preclearance requirements quickly moved to enact new restrictions (some of which were eventually overturned in the courts). Many of the restrictions implemented included voter identification requirements, restrictions on early voting, voter list purging, and proof of citizenship requirements (Brennan Center for Justice 2012). Reducing voting options and complicating voter registration through list purging may have been especially effective at filtering voter participation (Brians and Grofman 2001; Herron and Smith 2014; McDonald 2009; McDonald, Shino, and Smith 2015).

Some of the observed changes are also a function of the implementation of expansive voting laws. Several states have adopted cost-effective reforms like online voter registration and automatic voter registration, an "opt out" program that registers all eligible adults when they interact with state agencies (Brennan Center for Justice 2018). Nevertheless, GOP-controlled legislatures, and extremely gerrymandered legislatures in particular, passed the majority of restrictive election laws leading up to the 2016 presidential election.

Quan and colleagues estimated that a one standard deviation increase in the cost of voting index results in a turnout decline of 2–3 percent (Li, Pomante, and Schraufnagel 2018). A turnout shift of 3 percent may sound low, but that translates into a substantial partisan shift if the decline is concentrated among one party's voters, amplifying the effectiveness of a partisan gerrymander. In turn, with voting strength diluted from both restrictive laws and biased districts, the most vulnerable populations are at greater risk of not being able to protect their interests. Not surprisingly, we find that the types of laws passed (and not passed) in the most gerrymandered legislatures since 2012 look more like what one would expect in heavily Republican states, not states where voters are evenly divided in partisan support.

There is evidence that growing health disparities contribute to geographic shifts in partisan support. For example, comparing the 2008 and 2016 presidential elections, Goldman and colleagues show that counties where Republican vote shares increased had higher age-adjusted death rates compared to counties where Democrats increased their vote shares (Goldman et al. 2019). Similarly, greater healthcare access over the same period may be associated with increased Democratic support (Hollingsworth et al. 2019). In this section, we explore this link between change in government control, political gerrymandering, and health policy responses from governments after the 2010 gerrymanders. We find that the distortion of representation caused by partisan bias has insulated state legislatures from public accountability and made them less responsive, not only to public judgment, but also to the public health and safety of their own constituents.

Dilution of representation in state legislatures should result in a shift in the median assembly member's policy preference away from what would be preferred by representatives of excluded voters. Scholars have measured shifts in policy direction as a result of gerrymandering using ideological points from voting records of newly elected members (Caughey, Tausanovitch, and Warshaw 2017). For example, Devin Caughey and colleagues found that the ideology of the median legislator shifted significantly in the most gerrymandered states during this time period, in the predicted direction of the gerrymander (Caughey, Tausanovitch, and Warshaw 2017). They conclude that in states such as Michigan and Wisconsin, partisan bias enabled legislatures to adopt unpopular policies, including tax increases on pensions, corporate tax cuts, and right-to-work laws, which have weakened organized labor in what were traditionally union strongholds.

Biased legislatures were also less likely to adopt renewable energy or efficient energy standards, which also have widespread health benefits (Dimanchev et al. 2019; Union of Concerned Scientists 2017). For example, in the American Council for an Energy Efficient Economy's energy efficiency scorecard, GOP gerrymandered states are disproportionately located in the lower half of the 2017 rankings (ACEEE 2018). GOP gerrymandered states were also more likely to have passed model legislation from conservative groups such as the American Legislative Exchange Council, including prohibitions against regional climate plans, limitations on corporate liability, and "stand your ground" laws (Jackman 2013).

Similarly, the Center for American Progress has highlighted the connection between gerrymandering and policy implementation in the states (Corriher and Kennedy 2017). Polling conducted in Michigan, North Carolina, Ohio, Rhode Island, Virginia, and Wisconsin has shown that legislatures in these states acted against the preferences of majorities of voters on issues such as the expansion of Medicaid under the Patient Protection and Affordable Care Act (ACA) of 2010, support for marriage equality and same-sex adoption, gun violence prevention, public education, minimum wage increases, and the provision of safe drinking water.

To illustrate how aspects of health policy are linked to partisan gerrymandering, we first describe how states responded to the ACA after its passage, then consider state-level changes in abortion policy after 2010. The ACA, or Obamacare, was signed into law by President Barack Obama on March 23, 2010. The Centers for Medicare and Medicaid Services (CMS) began preparing grants to implement state-based exchanges in twenty-seven states, at the same time that twenty-six states and the National Federation of Independent Businesses filed lawsuits over the constitutionality of the individual mandate and Medicaid expansion requirements (Kaiser Family Foundation 2014; Legal Information Institute 2012). Among the states that sued were Michigan, Ohio, Pennsylvania, and Wisconsin, all of which Barack Obama won in 2008. Michigan was among the states that both sought out and received federal grants while party to the lawsuit, which eventually curtailed Medicaid expansion but upheld the individual mandate. Ohio was among the earliest states to expand Medicaid while continuing to challenge the ACA.

To quantify these policy responses, each state in our database (excluding Alabama and Mississippi) was given a score of "1" if they had not implemented ACA requirements, or a score of 0.5 if they had but were party to the legal challenges before 2016, and a zero otherwise. Figure 6.2 shows that states with extreme Republican gerrymanders were most likely to refuse Medicaid expansion or challenge the ACA. Wisconsin, with its especially egregious gerrymander, was the only Rustbelt state not to expand Medicaid (Ohio, Michigan, and Pennsylvania did), while the three most competitive southern gerrymandered states, Florida, North

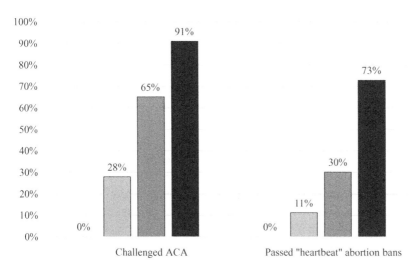

FIGURE 6.2. Republican gerrymandering and public health policy

Carolina, and Virginia, resisted as long as they were under unified Republican control.

The same pattern emerges when we consider extreme limitations to abortion that were passed after 2010. Since 2011, states have enacted over 400 abortion restrictions, with more than 100 of those restrictions passed in the 2011 legislative session (Guttmacher Institute 2018). That year, five states (AL, ID, IN, KS, OK) enacted bans on abortion after twenty weeks of gestation. In addition to these early bans, other restrictions included late term bans, required counseling, waiting periods, ultrasounds, and parental consent, and numerous public funding, insurance coverage, and clinic restrictions. Over the next several years, legislation banning abortion as early as fourteen weeks passed in electorally competitive states like Michigan, North Carolina, Ohio, and Wisconsin.

These early term bans have since been enjoined by state or federal courts. Yet without the partisan advantage gained from gerrymandering, it is unlikely that such extreme policies would have received majority legislative support. They are generally unpopular, in part because they increase health risks to women and children (Keena 2019b). The American Congress of Obstetricians and Gynecologists strongly opposes so-called fetal "heartbeat" (language that is medically inaccurate) legislation.[1] These and similarly extreme laws are not based on scientific or clinical standards, but they provide an accurate metric of the amplification of ideological advantage that results from extreme gerrymandering (Daley 2019; Latner 2019).

The impact of gerrymandering on health policy can also have broader impacts on public safety. Probably the most infamous example comes from Flint, Michigan, already one of the most socioeconomically distressed regions in the country. In 2012, voters rejected a ballot initiative to turn over control of local municipal services to a state-controlled emergency manager, but only a month later, the gerrymandered legislature did it anyway. Two years later, a state-appointed manager switched Flint's water supply to the Flint River without proper treatment, resulting in a contamination outbreak that killed twelve people. Lead poisoning in the area has been linked to a spike in fetal deaths and lower birth weights (Grossman and Slusky 2017).

As we have already noted, the midterm elections of 2018 signaled a reaction to both national politics and the partisan overreach of state governments. Following earlier gubernatorial victories in Pennsylvania, North Carolina, and Virginia, Michigan and Wisconsin elected Democratic governors in a wave that also saw Democrats capture control of government in Connecticut, Maine, and New Hampshire, and legislative control of Colorado's Senate and Maine's House (Stewart 2018). The policy consequences were apparent, and the threatened state legislatures reacted. Following the lead of the North Carolina legislature, after they moved to strip executive power from Democrat Roy Cooper before he took office in 2017 (Thoet 2017), Republican leaders in the Wisconsin and Michigan legislatures acted quickly to remove policymaking authority from newly elected governors Tony Evers and Gretchen Whitmar (Golshan 2018). Notably, both legislatures sought to reduce campaign finance and election administration oversight, and gain control over legal authority involving state laws that the executive might be reluctant to defend. Wisconsin legislators additionally barred the governor from departing from the state's challenge to the Affordable Care Act (White 2020).

Given all the factors that impact health outcomes, assessing the public health costs of these restrictions is difficult, but a study from Sarah Miller, Norman Johnson, and Sara Wherry found that reduction

---

[1] www.acog.org/news/news-releases/2017/01/acog-opposes-fetal-heartbeat-legislation-restricting-womens-legal-right-to-abortion

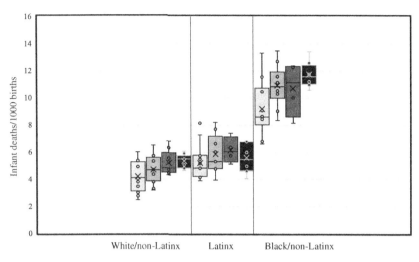

FIGURE 6.3. Republican gerrymandering and infant mortality

in disease-related deaths among near-elderly populations was associated with Medicaid expansion over this period (Miller, Johnson, and Wherry 2019). At the other end of the age spectrum, Chintan Bhatt and Conseulo Beck-Sagué have found that infant mortality has declined at a greater rate in Medicaid expansion states compared to non-Medicaid expansion states, and that there were greater declines among African-American infants (Bhatt and Beck-Sagué 2018).

Racial disparities in infant mortality are an especially troubling indicator of the gap between effective representation and public health. As Figure 6.3 shows, across all types of state government control, 2018 mortality rates for African American infants are twice as high as the rates for white, non-Latinx infants, according to data from the Kaiser Family Foundation (Kaiser Family Foundation 2020). That pattern holds for state governments regardless of partisan control. However, for both white and Black (but not Latinx) infants, average mortality rates are highest in extreme GOP gerrymandered states, though there is not enough evidence to determine whether change in infant mortality rates is causally linked to changes in government control in 2010. Clearly, race is the prevailing effect. The difference between the Black and white/Latinx group is far greater than the difference within, and fixing gerrymandering obviously is not enough to fix such deep racial equities in the United States (see Hajnal 2020).

Rather, the point is to illustrate that extremely gerrymandered states exhibit worse health outcomes across a number of indicators consistent with the anticipated effect of partisan bias. In gerrymandered states like Michigan, Ohio, and Pennsylvania, infant mortality has remained stagnant or declined since 2010, while infant mortality has increased in Wisconsin, North Carolina, Louisiana, and Georgia. Similarly, there is no significant correlation between legislative bias and recent changes in the most common causes of death, including cardiovascular deaths, cancers, and obesity rates. It is quite likely that the primary determinants of such deaths are linked to other long-term economic and social factors. Overall patterns fluctuate considerably, yet the association between partisan bias and infant mortality has become stronger since 2010. The evidence is consistent with a pattern of state legislatures insulating themselves from public accountability through the manipulation of electoral laws.

That said, for opioid deaths, one of the types of death specifically linked to a decline in life expectancy in the later part of the decade, we did find that the increase has been higher in the most gerrymandered high-poverty states. Further, the association is strongest in African American communities, which tend to be in the most distressed regions of these states.

The association between healthcare access, political participation, and representation is also not likely to be linear or unidirectional. Jamila Michener's research has shown that participation in Medicaid is associated with lower voter participation in some states, due to differential success at incorporating clients into the electorate, and that success is lower in states with higher African-American populations (Michener 2016). Our analysis shows how the representation-policy nexus can be distorted when state legislatures, and their health agencies, are insulated from public accountability, potentially amplifying already cumulative inequalities within communities of color and those most likely to be deterred by greater costs of voting (Muennig et al. 2018).

Earlier analyses have shown that states experiencing declining health exhibited shifts in partisan support toward the Republican Party (Bilal, Knapp, and Cooper 2018; Bor 2017; Sund et al. 2017; Wasfy, Stewart III, and Bhambhani 2017). At the county level, frequency of alcohol and suicide deaths has been linked to increasing support for conservative candidates and movements (Goldman et al. 2019). By contrast, gains in healthcare insurance coverage were associated with vote shifts toward the Democratic Party and higher turnout among both those supportive of and opposed to expansion of health services (Haselswerdt 2017;

Hollingsworth et al. 2019). Individual-level analyses also suggest that better health is associated with higher turnout, and that healthier individuals (and those with more resources generally) are more likely to support the Republican Party (Pacheco and Fletcher 2015).

The fact that county-level estimates show a positive correlation between decreasing health and Republican Party support, even though healthier people are more likely to support Republicans is likely an aggregation effect. Similar patterns have been found regarding income. That is, the poorest voters in poorer, Republican-dominated states strongly support Democrats but are less likely to vote (Gelman 2009). Consistent with this pattern is the disproportionate effect that erecting barriers to voting may have less healthy residents. These same states have become more biased in a direction that further dilutes the voting strength of the most vulnerable. States with considerable Republican partisan bias, such as Indiana, Ohio, Pennsylvania, and Wisconsin, experienced some of the sharpest declines in life expectancy since 2010.

Of course, none of the state legislatures, gerrymandered or otherwise, were prepared for what hit them in 2020. The global COVID-19 pandemic shocked political systems across the world, and in the United States, disrupted election season. The political and public health responses from state legislatures revealed once again the broader significance of gerrymandering on the political process.

6.4 STATE RESPONSE TO THE COVID-19 PANDEMIC

By the end of the summer of 2020, nearly one-quarter of a million US residents had perished from the global Coronavirus pandemic that reached US shores at the beginning of the year. It is widely acknowledged that the federal government's response to the novel virus was "astonishing" in having "taken a crisis and turned it into a tragedy" in the words of the *New England Journal of Medicine* (NEJM 2020). The journal notes that not only did most of the world's democracies do better than the United States in managing the threat, "they have outperformed us by orders of magnitude."

The largely decentralized and piecemeal response to the pandemic might seem to provide an opportunity to assess state capacity, but the federal government's uneven support across states, variations in availability of supplies, as well as the virus' failure to respect state borders compound the difficulties of assessment (Gordon, Huberfeld, and Jones 2020; Ollove 2020). Instead, we compare legislative responsiveness to

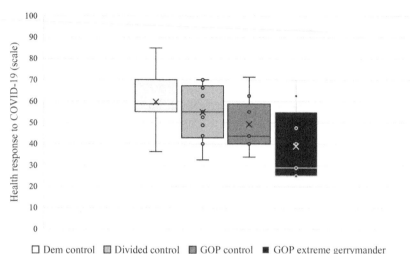

FIGURE 6.4. Republican gerrymandering and health response to COVID-19

COVID-19 as measured by Oxfam America (Oxfam America 2020). Their state healthcare comparison identifies legislatures that had taken the following actions by July 1, 2020: expanded access to Medicaid; expanded access to telehealth services; grace periods for insurance premium payments; waiving costs for COVID-19 treatment; expanded worker compensation; transparency in provision of aggregated COVID-19 data by sex and race.

The legislative response to COVID-19 was lower in extreme GOP gerrymandered legislatures compared to other states, as shown in Figure 6.4. Among the worst performing gerrymandered states like Tennessee, Missouri, and Florida, newly unemployed workers had fewer health and worker protections to fall back on compared to workers in other states.

There are exceptions: Ohio's legislature and governor Tom Dewine responded about as well as any state given their constraints, and the biased Democratic legislature in Hawaii markedly underperformed in providing extended protections. Nevertheless, the overall pattern shows that it was the most biased GOP legislatures that were least responsive in the first several months of the pandemic.

Of course, legislative responsiveness was not limited to health policy. The virus began spreading across the country just as the presidential primaries got under way. Chaotic primary elections in Wisconsin,

Georgia, and elsewhere, with voting places shut down during the morning of the election, demonstrated the need to do more to protect the ability to vote safely.

Sixteen states eventually postponed their primaries, and others postponed special elections or runoffs. The most relevant election changes pertained to options provided to voters in order to cast a ballot safely and securely during the general election. In particular, given the disproportionate COVID-19 death rates recorded among people of color, combined with known racial disparities in long lines and waiting times experienced by voters or color and those living in densely populated urban areas, many experts were advocating a massive expansion in vote-by-mail options for voters (UCLA Voting Rights Project, Voting Rights Lab, and Union of Concern Scientists 2020; Weiser 2020). The degree to which states applied that advice varied considerably by government control and level of partisan bias.

States faced a number of decisions. Every state already had the capacity to allow voters to use absentee or mail ballots under the National Voter Registration Act of 1993, at a minimum for overseas and military voters, who have been using absentee ballots since the Civil War. Prior to 2020, about one-third of states required an excuse for absentee voting or limited use to voters age 65 and over. Several states across the partisan spectrum, from Arkansas and Kentucky to Massachusetts and New York, lifted restrictions on vote-by-mail, as Figure 6.5 shows (NCSL 2020). Most Democratic-controlled states already allowed no-excuse absentee voting, but this was the most common, and often the only expansion among Republican states.

More proactive measures, such as automatically sending all voters a vote-by-mail application, or the optimal and more efficient strategy of simply sending voters ballots, were already in place in some states but newly adopted in others. Michigan, Ohio, and Wisconsin all chose to send their voters vote-by-mail applications for the first time. While sending applications seems like a step in the right direction, it results in more work for election officials and one more opportunity for human error (Lai 2020; Woodward 2020). About a third of Democratic states and states with divided control also sent their voters applications, compared to only about one in ten Republican-controlled states.

The most expansive voting reform for the pandemic was the decision by several states to mail registered voters ballots and allow them to be returned through the post office, at early voting centers, or at official drop boxes (Swasey 2020). California, Nevada, New Jersey, and Vermont, as

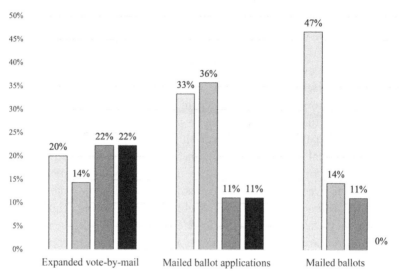

FIGURE 6.5. Republican gerrymandering and ballot access during COVID-19 pandemic

well as select counties in Montana, and in Washington, DC made this move for the 2020 election. Previously, Colorado, Hawaii, Oregon, Washington, and Utah had already relied on universal vote-by-mail. This brought the percentage of Democratic-controlled states automatically sending voters ballots to 47 percent. By contrast, no extremely gerrymandered GOP states sent ballots to their voters in response to the pandemic.

The decision by some states to expand vote-by-mail was part of the basis for President Trump's evidence-free claims questioning the security of vote-by-mail (Barreto et al. 2020). In the final months of the election, it also became clear that the president's rhetoric about "fraudulent" vote-by-mail had damaged his party's mobilization efforts as Democrats gained huge advantages in vote-by-mail requests across crucial swing states (Gardner and Dawsey 2020). By the time of the first presidential debate, in which the president also refused to ensure a peaceful transition of power, he began trying to nuance his language about vote-by-mail, stating that "A solicited ballot is ok ... you're soliciting, you're asking ..." (Blake 2020).

But of the nearly 400 election-related lawsuits being fought across the country *before* Election Day, over one-quarter were filed by the GOP over the eligibility, acceptance, and processing of ballots in Michigan, North Carolina, Ohio, Pennsylvania, and Wisconsin, none of which sent their voters ballots. As we have written elsewhere (Latner et al. 2020), this strategy is consistent with an attempt to pressure those extremely gerry-mandered state legislatures to try to slow or stop counting of the dispro-portionately Democratic mail ballots after Election Day, should the opportunity arise. Had fair districting plans been used to elect these legislatures, there would not likely be such an opportunity.

6.5 CONCLUSION

The United States are increasingly balkanized in terms of the cost of voting, with citizens in high-cost states put at a systematic disadvantage in their ability to express preferences. Across a variety of indicators, we see that people in the least healthy states face additional burdens of discriminatory barriers to voting and equal representation. After 2010, a new wave of restrictive election laws was passed at the same time that governing majorities went to work maximizing their partisan advantage through gerrymandering. Since then, states under unified Republican control have gone further than other states, and in many cases reversed direction, locking down voter eligibility and ballot access while the rest of the country has been expanding political equality through expansive reforms. And, in the wake of President Trump's "Big Lie" that the 2020 presidential election was stolen and the subsequent storming of the US Capitol on January 6, 2021, many state legislatures moved to impose further restrictions on voting access. Collectively, this has been a highly partisan and racialized process. These institutional barriers are likely to exacerbate existing inequalities, compounding the disadvantages that afflict socially distressed communities and communities of color.

Legislatures shape more than just their own electoral ecosystems; government is society's operating system. In principle, the legitimacy of democratic government rests on the consent of the governed, who – through the expression of equally weighted votes, majority rule, and the rule of law – make collective choices to direct the society's future. At its best, democratic government provides an open exchange of information about the nature of social problems and an evidence-based assessment of how to best meet social needs. Democratic processes enable competition over a diverse array of ideas and beliefs to be collectively accepted and implemented for socially beneficial outcomes (Knight and Johnson 2011). In line with this understanding, comparative research has shown that across the globe, there is a positive association between the longevity of democratic institutions, human development, and public health (Gerring, Thacker, and Alfaro, 2012).

The political and social consequences we have documented here have national implications for future elections. Biased legislatures have passed less equitable policies over this time period, even in states where there is approximate parity between partisan voters. The drivers of these social consequences are complex, ranging from the flooding of the prescription drug market with pharmaceutical opioids and a proliferation of firearms over the last several decades, to decades of wage stagnation, rising healthcare costs, and environmental stressors.

However, political institutions also matter. Economic and social conditions are a partial function of the economic and social policies of state governments. Across many states, government has become less responsive to the needs and preferences of their publics because public judgment is being distorted. State legislatures with some of the greatest health declines have insulated themselves from public accountability, while health disparities are exacerbated. We believe that it is no coincidence that many of the same communities bearing a disproportionate burden of the impact of harmful public health policies are the same communities most actively targeted for voter suppression.

7

The Democratic Harms of Gerrymandering

In the previous chapter we assessed the policy and social consequences of extreme partisan gerrymandering, and we found that legislatures with Republican gerrymanders were more likely to enact restrictions on voting rights and public health. In this chapter we consider who gerrymandering harms and how. We start by explaining how *Vieth* v. *Jubelirer* (2004) and the revival of gerrymandering after 2010 can be viewed as an attempt to roll back the voting rights revolution of the 1960s. That is to say, it is a fundamental assault on the principle of one-person, one-vote. We then consider how the harms of state legislative gerrymandering are different than the harms caused by congressional gerrymandering, given the role of state legislatures in redistricting and regulating elections at all levels. We also consider the question of who suffers harm produced by partisan gerrymandering. We show that those suffering harm are not only those in gerrymandered districts or identifying with disadvantaged parties, but rather all citizens. Finally, we consider gerrymandering in the context of the broader crisis of faith in democracy and on American federalism.

7.1 ROLLING BACK THE VOTING RIGHTS REVOLUTION

In *Gerrymandering in America* (2016), we argued that the Supreme Court's decision in *Vieth* – and the gerrymander of 2012 that it greenlighted – was a constitutional revolution, although perhaps "counterrevolution" would have been more appropriate. It struck at the heart of the voting rights revolution of the 1960s and the principle of "one-person, one-vote" on which it was based. The voting rights cases of the 1960s (*Baker* v. *Carr* 1962, *Gray* v. *Sanders* 1963, *Wesberry* v. *Sanders* 1964,

Reynolds v. *Sims* 1964) established that there was not just a constitutional right to vote, but a right to political equality – that all votes need to count equally. This, in turn, logically implies the principle of majority rule. For this reason, it was unconstitutional to advantage some voters by drawing districts with different populations (malapportionment). However, if gerrymandering is allowed, this democratic intent is undermined. State governments may no longer draw districts of different populations, but they can use gerrymandering to achieve exactly the same goals.

In our previous book, we referred to this as "the revenge of the anti-federalists" (McGann et al. 2016, 177). There has been a continual tension in American history between the principle of national, popular government and the principle of state autonomy. At the Federal Convention, there was a division between Federalists who wanted a stronger national government and the "Anti-Federalists," who wanted state governments to continue to be preeminent. This led to the Great Compromise, with the House of Representatives being a national legislature representing the people directly (without dependence on the state government), and the Senate representing the interests of the state governments. However, Article 1§4 of the Constitution gives states authority over the "Times, Places and Manner" of elections. This allowed state governments to exercise control over the branch of government designed to represent the people directly. For example, by simply not updating districts, they could advantage rural over urban populations. By the 1960s, population differences of tenfold were not unknown. The voting rights cases of the 1960s made this practice unconstitutional, and restored popular control of the US House. The revival of gerrymandering after *Vieth* has allowed state governments to reassert themselves and effectively determine who represents the state in Congress.

It is important to recognize that the voting rights cases *Wesberry* v. *Sanders* (1964) and *Reynolds* v. *Sims* (1964) did not simply establish that malapportionment was unconstitutional; they established that the principle of political equality was grounded in the Constitution. The principle of "one-person, one-vote" meant not only that the right to vote could not be taken away, but that every vote had to count equally. This equal right to vote is derived from Article 1§2 in the case of *Wesberry* (the requirement that the US House be elected by "the People of the various States"), and from the Equal Protection Clause of the 14th Amendment in the case of *Reynolds*. This equal right to vote is then shown to imply a strong conception of political equality, which prohibits any distinction and institutional practice that dilutes the effect of that vote in any way. The fact that majority rule is a logical consequence of this kind of political equality is also noted.

It is worth working through this logic. In the case of *Reynolds* (1964, 563), this is based on the principle that the Constitution forbids "sophisticated as well as simple-minded forms of discrimination." It is clearly unconstitutional to deny the right to vote (1964, 554). If this is unconstitutional, then not counting someone's vote is also prohibited, as this would accomplish the same thing. Ballot-box stuffing is also not permissible, because it would be possible to so dilute someone's vote as to make it worthless. Likewise, practices such as racial gerrymanders (*Gomillion* v. *Lightfoot* 1957) and giving some people multiple votes are not allowed. If giving some people multiple votes is not allowed, then assigning people to districts of different sizes must be also, as this would achieve exactly the same thing. Thus, it is concluded (1964, 563) that, "Weighting the votes of citizen differently, *by any method or means*, merely because of where they happen to reside, hardly seems justifiable" (emphasis ours). Or as it is put in *Wesberry* (cited in *Reynolds* v. *Sims* 1964, 559), the principle of equal representation implies that legislatures may not "draw the lines of congressional districts in such a way as to give some voters a greater voice in choosing a Congressman than others."

It is also stated in *Reynolds* that the right to fully and equally participate in government implies the principle of majority rule. "Full and effective participation by all citizens in state government requires, therefore, that each citizen have an equally effective voice in the election of members of his state legislature" (1964, 565). This, in turn, logically implies that "that a majority of the people of a State could elect a majority of that State's legislators."

The arguments in *Reynolds* would certainly seem to prohibit partisan gerrymanders. Malapportionment is not allowed because it dilutes votes in the same way as giving some people multiple votes. However, if it is possible for partisan gerrymandering to achieve the same goal as malapportionment, then surely it is also prohibited. We have shown that partisan gerrymandering can very effectively dilute the effect of certain people's votes, and that it can also give majority control to a minority. Indeed in the years following *Reynolds* the Court did overturn some districting plans on ground of them being partisan gerrymanders (*White* v. *Weiser* 1973, *Karcher* v. *Daggett* 1983), although the decisions were in part justified by there being (very small) population differences between districts (see McGann et al. 2016, 40).

In any case, as we have shown in this volume and in *Gerrymandering in America* (2016), partisan gerrymandering is a powerful enough tool to take control away from the electorate and give it to the state legislatures that draw the districts. An early example we gave was that of Pennsylvania in 2012, where the Republicans were able to win thirteen seats out of eighteen, in spite of the Democrats winning more votes. The elections of 2018 demonstrate how some gerrymanders can withstand even a wave election (see Engstrom 2020). For example, in North Carolina in 2018 the US House vote split was fifty-one to forty-nine in favor of the Republicans, as opposed to sixty-three to thirty-seven in 2016. However, the Republicans took ten seats out of thirteen in both elections.[1] The Democrats gaining twelve points and almost drawing even in votes had literally no effect. And in the state legislative elections, Democrats won majorities in both the state house and the state senate, yet Republicans managed to keep control. Similar Democratic gains in Ohio had likewise no effect with a twelve to four congressional seat split remaining. In Texas there was a fifty-two to forty-eight split to the Republicans in 2018, as opposed to sixty-one to thirty-nine in 2016. As a result, the Democrats gained only two seats in US House, with the Republicans retaining twenty-three seats out of thirty-six. In these examples large vote swings seem to make no difference to the result. It is hard to avoid the conclusion that the outcome depends not on how people vote, but on how the state legislature has drawn the districts.

7.2 THE HARM OF GERRYMANDERING AT THE STATE LEVEL

In *Gerrymandering in America* (2016, 190), we consider the democratic problems that arise from the gerrymandering of the US House of Representatives. These problems become even more pressing when we consider the gerrymandering of state legislatures. This is because they can draw their own districts and also have control over state electoral law. One solution to gerrymandered US House districts would be for the disadvantaged party to compete better at the state level and obtain more advantageous House districts during the next round. However, if state legislative elections are themselves rigged by gerrymandering, this solution becomes far less viable. And indeed, we find that many states have gerrymandered districts at both the US House and state legislature levels.

[1] In 2019 there was a special election in the 9th District due to the 2018 result being voided for voter fraud. The Republican candidate won the special election.

When congressional districts are strongly gerrymandered, the composition of a state's congressional delegation will depend less on how people vote in the congressional elections, and more on which party controls the state legislature at the time when the districts are drawn. We argued that this was problematic for reasons of participation, responsiveness, and transparency. In terms of participation, fewer people may take part in state elections than in national elections, particularly when state elections are held in off-years (nonpresidential even years) or odd-years. In terms of responsiveness, there is less of a direct connection between the people and policymakers (the people choose the state legislatures, then essentially the state legislatures determine the composition of Congress). Furthermore, the composition of the state's congressional delegation is effectively determined every ten years when districts are drawn, instead of every two years. It is notable that Federalist 39 justifies House election being held every two years on the grounds that the House needs to have "an immediate dependence on, and an intimate sympathy with, the people." Finally, and most seriously, there is transparency. It is doubtful that many people who vote in state legislative elections at the end of a decade realize that they are determining the state's Congressional delegation for the next decade. It is far more likely that they are voting on immediate issues of state government.

We confirm that numerous state legislatures do, indeed, draw districts to favor the party that control the legislatures. The states with gerrymandered state legislatures tend to be the same ones we identified in *Gerrymandering in America* as having biased congressional districts. The levels of bias are not quite as extreme as some congressional districts. This makes sense. Once a party has a secure majority in the state legislature, it does not benefit its elected officials to have a larger majority – it just means more competition for resources (see Owen and Grofman 1988). Nevertheless, we do find that the amount of bias has somewhat increased in the last districting round since *Vieth* v. *Jubelirer* (2004). In the US House, however, a larger delegation can make the difference between majority and minority status for the party.

A state legislature drawing biased districts for itself, of course, creates a problem of entrenchment. The only way to change the districts is to get control of the legislative process, and this is unlikely to happen because the districts are biased in favor of the ruling party. This creates obvious problems of democratic accountability. In states that are very finely balanced, it may be possible for the disadvantaged party to get control of the governorship. Since *Gray* v. *Sanders* (1963) the governor and other statewide offices must be elected "at-large" by the entire state, preventing any kind of gerrymandering. The governor can then use their veto to prevent a biased plan in the next districting round (except in Connecticut, Florida, and North Carolina, where the governor does not have a veto on state legislative districting). However, governors are typically elected in off-years, so the turnout in the gubernatorial election may be quite low and not representative of the state. Furthermore, if one party has a persistent advantage, it may be able to hold the governorship for a considerable length of time. It can then use its districting power to increase and entrench its advantage in the state legislature and the US House.

That lawmakers elected in elections that occur once in a decade are able to entrench themselves in power for years to come suggests a radical reformulation of American federalism and a disruption of the balance of power between federal and state government that has existed for the past several decades. The design of federalism built into the US government is reflective of a compromise between framers of the Constitution. The Federalists sought a strong central government to coordinate commerce between the states and to supervise international relations, trade, and economic activity, while the Anti-Federalists were "states' rights" advocates who were skeptical of creating a powerful new government that would undermine the sovereignty of the states and diminish localized rule (see Dow 2017). The federalist system that is embodied in the Constitution represents something of a compromise between these two factions. As Taylor et al. (2014) detail, the framers omitted many details about the nature of federalism and the balance of power between the states. In all likelihood, this was a deliberate necessity to avoid disagreement between participants at the Constitutional Convention. This compromise is reflected in the vague language of the 10th amendment, which defers rights to the states, and in the lack of details in Article I, which addresses the legislative powers of Congress.

Yet, as any introductory US government textbook will attest, many of the questions surrounding ambiguities in the language of the Constitution have been settled, and the Federalists ultimately won the battle in the long-term. Over the course of the first century of the Republic, the power of the national government grew. And the death blow to the Anti-Federalists was the Civil War and the subsequent passage of the 14th amendment, which cemented national supremacy. Several crises, such as the Great Depression and war, resulted in the federal judiciary blessing an expansionist view of the powers of Congress and the Executive Branch over state governments.

Thus, federalism in the United States represents a balance that was negotiated and settled over the course of 150 years. Yet the prevalence of state-level gerrymandering upends this balance that has stabilized federal–state relations for the past several decades. Insofar as elected officials in state government exercise control over congressional districting and they are afforded the same privilege to draw their own lines, this has given the states a powerful tool to dictate national affairs in the interest of political parties and effectively undermines the intent of the House as a "popular branch" of government that would bypass the states.

Another factor that may increase this entrenchment of power is the fact that state governments control the electoral process in matters other than districting. They can use this power to manipulate the electoral competition to their advantage, making it less likely that they will lose at either the state legislature or Congressional level. The Supreme Court's decision in *Shelby County* v. *Holder* (2013) has increased the scope for this. Previously, numerous states were subject to preclearance requirements under the Voting Rights Act when adopting new electoral regulations. Changes in voting regulations required federal approval to ensure the changes did not discriminate against minority groups. However, in *Shelby County* v. *Holder* (2013), the Supreme Court invalidated Section 4(b) of Voting Rights Acts, which defines the jurisdictions covered by preclearance. This makes the preclearance requirements unenforceable. As a result, many states are able to change their electoral regulations, subject only to challenge after the fact. Since 2013 there have been substantial increases in the difficulty of voting in numerous states, including voter ID laws, voter roll purges, closure of polling places, and restrictions on early voting (Li, Pomante, and Schraufnagel 2018). We find that the increase in the cost of voting is greater in those states that engage in partisan gerrymandering. The two practices seem to go together.

In addition to the democratic harm created by gerrymandering, we also find that there is a direct harm in terms of policy outcomes. For example, states with highly biased legislatures have worse health outcomes across a number of measures and were less responsive to the COVID-19 pandemic. Certainly, it is hard to be sure of causality here. In some cases, partisan bias results in one party having complete control, and that produces a different set of policies than would have occurred otherwise. However, it may also be the case that in states with gerrymandered legislatures, the ruling party is insulated from public pressure and able to pursue policies that are unpopular. This is also consistent with the findings of Caughey, Tausanovitch, and Warshaw (2017) who found that the partisan bias increased the extremism of the ruling party.

7.3 WHO IS HARMED? THE ENTIRE PEOPLE

We now turn to the question of who is harmed by partisan gerrymandering. The answer is simple: it is potentially the entire electorate – the entire population of the state for state-level gerrymandering and the entire population of the United States for congressional gerrymandering. This is true when we consider the intrinsic, democratic harm of gerrymandering – the fact that your vote is diluted and your voice is not treated in a fair and equal manner. It is also true if we consider the harm from bad policy due to gerrymandering, perhaps due to lack of accountability or responsiveness to the people. In either case, we are dealing with a harm that is collective in nature. Government decisions and policies apply to the entire population who are subject to that government. Whereas the right to participate in how these policies are made may be individual, the harm from bad policy or undemocratic decision-making applies to everyone. As Justice O'Connor put it in the plurality opinion on *Georgia* v. *Ashcroft*, "Indeed, in a representative democracy, the very purpose of voting is to delegate to chosen representatives the power to make and pass laws" (2003, 482).

In particular, we would emphasize that the harm of gerrymandering does not only affect those living in gerrymandered districts, and does not only affect the partisans of the disadvantaged party. We would note that the Supreme Court in *Gill* v. *Whitford* (2018) asserted that only those whose districts are "packed" or "cracked" have legal standing, while Justice Scalia in the plurality opinion on *Vieth* v. *Jubelirer* (2004, 288) held that gerrymandering complaints necessarily rely on an assertion of the rights of partisans as a group. We will consider both claims in turn.

Let us first consider the argument that gerrymandering only harms those living in the gerrymandered district. For a start, it makes no sense to talk about an individual district being gerrymandered. The standard technique of gerrymandering is to pack your opponents into a few districts, in order to be able to win more districts by a modest, but still safe margin. However, there is nothing intrinsically wrong with an extremely safe seat. If it is balanced by an extremely safe seat for the other party, it produces no bias at all. As we show in Chapter 2, bias results from the overall distribution of districts being skewed, not from an individual district.

However, even if we consider an electoral abuse that does apply to individual districts, the harm would still apply to everyone in the state. Consider something that is unquestionably a violation, such as ballot stuffing. Suppose that in my district there is not ballot stuffing. However, in other districts of the state there is rampant ballot stuffing, and as a result my representative is always outvoted by the opposing ballot stuffing party. Can you seriously claim that I have not been harmed, just because I have been able to elect "my" representative without ballot stuffing? My representative is not an independent magistrate who does tasks for me; rather, they are a member of a legislature and it is the composition of the legislature that determines what policies are enacted. If the legislature is dominated by ballot-stuffing criminals, then I suffer the bad policies they impose and I am denied a fair say in the composition of the legislature. The fact that my representative is honestly elected does not mean I do not suffer harm.

Or consider another abuse that is unquestionably unconstitutional. Suppose there is one corner of a state where there is massive malapportionment, so that this region dominates the state politically. Suppose that most of the people in this region are Democrats, while the majority of people in the state are Republicans. Suppose that, although I live in this region, I am a Republican. In this scenario, I clearly suffer harm from the malapportionment. Although I support the majority party in the state, I have a state government of the minority party imposed on me. The fact that I happened to live in the region that benefits from malapportionment does not mean that I do not suffer harm. The fact that I am mathematically overrepresented is irrelevant. What matters is the overall composition of the state legislature and most of the people who are overrepresented are supporters of the other party.

Neither does partisan gerrymandering only harm partisans of the disadvantaged party. In fact we can show that partisan gerrymandering can cause just as much harm even if there are no partisans at all. Indeed, swing voters may be particularly disadvantaged as Engstrom (2020) argues. If partisan gerrymandering imposes an outcome, then swing voters lose their ability to decide which party governs and what policy concessions it needs to make in order to win them over.

In the plurality opinion of *Vieth* v. *Jubelirer* (2004, 288), Justice Scalia asserts that the plaintiffs case requires a right to the proportional representation of partisan groups, a right Scalia argues does not exist. He claims that partisanship is just another demographic characteristic, and that it is no more relevant than other demographic characteristics like occupation or religion. Thus, the Constitutions does not require "that farmers or urban dwellers, Christian fundamentalists or Jews, Republicans or Democrats, must be accorded political strength proportionate to their numbers."

This line of reasoning results from Justice Scalia's refusal to acknowledge that elections in the United States are in fact partisan, and that this is an objective fact. In a partisan election, the partisan breakdown of the legislature is not simply one way of analyzing the strength of demographics groups; rather it is part of the result. After an election we will say, the Republicans retook the House, or the Democrats retained the Senate. We would not say that Catholics retained the House or farmers took the Senate. Neither do candidates run for office as Catholics or farmers. These factors do not give them automatic access to the ballot without collecting thousands of signatures (as many states require). There is an important difference here. Partisanship is part of the result because the Congress does, in fact, organize itself on partisan lines.

What is it that makes elections objectively partisan? As stated earlier, Congress and nearly all state legislatures organize themselves on partisan lines. Which party is larger determines which party gets to have posts like the Speakership. The majority party will have a number of procedural advantages, in terms of control of the Rules Committee and the Calendar (see Boyce and Bischak 2002; Cox and McCubbins 1993, 2005). The partisan composition of a legislature is an objective institutional fact. As such it is part of the result of the election. If a voter does not have a fair chance to influence this result, then the value of their vote has been diluted.

We would note in passing that the partisan composition of Congress is also likely to have a strong effect on policy outcomes. In recent years, party line voting has become very prevalent. According to CQ Weekly Report party unity voting has been about 90 percent in last decade, as opposed to around 60 percent in the 1970s (Carney 2015; Dancey and Sheagley 2017).[2] The fact that there are partisan elections does not depend on party line voting in Congress, but rather on the fact that the legislature and elections are organized on party lines. Nevertheless, this reinforces the partisan nature of politics.

---

[2] Party unity voting is defined as the percentage of members who vote with their parties on votes where a majority of party members find themselves on opposite sides.

Indeed, it is not necessary for there to be any partisans for there to be partisan elections. Imagine that every voter in a state or in the United States was an independent. No one has a partisan identity, but everyone decides how to vote in each election based on its merits. If the legislature was still organized on party lines, and legislators still worked together as partisans to pursue policy goals, then we would still have partisan elections in an objective sense. The Democrats and the Republicans would still compete for control of the state legislature and the Congress. Whichever party won would still organize the legislature, set the legislative agenda, and attempt to pass its legislative program. Voters would still be able to observe this party in government, and hold it accountable by voting it out if they are dissatisfied with its performance.

Thus, contra Scalia, the claim that elections need to be fair in partisan terms does not depend on a claim from a partisan group to have fair group representation. Rather it comes from the fact the partisan breakdown of the legislature is an essential part of the result of the election. If voters do not have the ability to determine this in a democratic way that makes them politically equal – exactly what partisan gerrymandering deprives them of – then the value of their vote is diluted.

7.4 GERRYMANDERING AND THE CRISIS OF DEMOCRACY

Partisan gerrymandering is a fundamental assault on the principle of democracy. It replaces the rule of the people with the rule of the oligarchy that draws the districts – many of whom have had the privilege of approving their own districts. In this book and its predecessor, we have demonstrated how effectively partisan gerrymandering can determine election outcomes, even against large swings in public opinion. In addition to the harm to democratic government, we show that gerrymandering does concrete material harm to voters. Gerrymandering allows politicians to pursue policies that have real effects on people's lives and health. By protecting politicians from the jeopardy of fair elections, it removes accountability.

The gerrymander of 2012 came during a period when democracy was already facing a crisis of confidence, in the United States and elsewhere. Democracy worldwide continues to face the challenges of economic crisis, rising inequality, the rise of populism, and in 2020 the COVID-19 pandemic. Even before the pandemic, research by the Pew Research Center (Pew Research Center 2020) put trust in government over the last five years at an historical low – about 20 percent. Other survey research finds disturbing increases in support for authoritarian solutions especially among the young and the affluent, even if this is still a minority position (Foa and Mounk 2016).

It might be tempting to argue that democracy is under siege everywhere. There is some evidence that support for democracy is generally in decline, although this is disputed (Dalton 2004; Norris 2011). However, it is certainly the case that support for democracy has held up quite well in some countries. By OECD data, trust in government in the United States was at 30 percent in 2018, considerably below the OECD average of 45 percent. Numerous European countries scored far better (Germany 58 percent, the Netherlands 66 percent, Norway 68 percent, Switzerland 85 percent), although some southern European countries with serious economic problems scored even lower than the United States. It is dangerous to draw causal conclusions, as countries seem to form into geographic clusters. However, the OECD countries where faith in democracy is robust seem to be those characterized by proportional representation, multiparty coalition government, and the emphasis on politics as consensual governing as opposed to a win-at-all-costs contact sport.

Of course, the crisis of American democracy is not simply a matter of public trust. To some degree it reflects institutional reality. The Electoral Integrity Project, an international comparative project, found that in terms of good election practice the United States scores in the second division, far behind most other OECD countries. It is particularly faulted for boundary issues (i.e., gerrymandering), electoral laws (ballot access laws that make it very difficult for new parties to compete), and registration (laws and practices obstructing registration and turnout). There is a tendency for Americans to look to the Supreme Court to protect democracy. However, as we have argued, the Supreme Court has played an active role in bringing about two of these undemocratic practices. As we argued in *Gerrymandering in America* (2016), the Supreme Court's judgment in *Vieth* v. *Jubelirer* gave a green light for state governments to gerrymander after the 2010 Census. Furthermore the Supreme Court has struck down various attempts by federal courts to deal with partisan gerrymandering (as Engstrom 2020 argues, federal courts have been quite willing to consider and strike down partisan gerrymanders), and the Supreme Court's decision in *Shelby County* v. *Holder* (2013) effectively removed Voting Rights Act preclearance requirements and allowed many states to enact laws that made voting more difficult. Perhaps the crisis of faith in democracy is due to the fact that our institutions are not, in fact, that democratic, as Robert Dahl found in his final book *How Democratic Is the American Constitution* (2003).

In the final chapters of this book, we consider various ways to deal with the problem of gerrymandering. In the next chapter, we assess the role of the courts in redressing districting harms. In Chapter 9, we consider the effectiveness of various redistricting reforms.

8

When the Courts Redistrict

We have seen the harms of political districting. Through control of redistricting, political parties are able to achieve extreme partisan advantage and maintain control of state legislatures, even when the other party wins a majority of the vote. As we saw in Chapter 5, Republican legislators are often able to achieve this bias through the drawing of majority-minority districts that dilute the votes of African Americans, thereby denying Democrats strength. And as we showed in Chapter 6, the most biased plans elected Republican legislators who approved restrictions to voting rights, ballot access, and more equitable health policies.

In the next part of this book, we address solutions to problems and harms of political districting. In this chapter, we evaluate the role of the courts in the redistricting process and whether the judiciary is an effective backstop against extreme gerrymandering.

Since the "one-person, one-vote" standard of the 1960s, the judiciary has become a key player in the redistricting process, and litigation has become an increasingly common feature of decennial redistricting. In each redistricting cycle, citizens, reformers, politicians, and interest groups challenge district maps in the courts. In addition, many states grant state courts back-up authority if a primary redistricting authority deadlocks or fails to meet their deadline, and others (Colorado and Florida) subject their redistricting plans to automatic judicial review.

In our investigation of 2011 state legislative redistricting, we found at least fourteen examples of courts imposing changes to district maps. In ten of these cases, courts mandated partial changes to state legislative plans that had been approved during the 2011 redistricting cycle. Of these, four were racial gerrymandering challenges (in Alabama, North

Carolina, Texas, and Virginia), while six involved violations to state constitutional provisions (in Alaska, Colorado, Florida, Hawaii, Idaho, and Kentucky). We also found four examples of state courts taking over the redistricting process entirely from primary redistricting authorities and drawing maps that were subsequently used in elections (in Kansas, Minnesota, Nevada, and New Mexico).

Do state courts provide a significant buffer against gerrymandering when judicial actors intervene? We assess each of these cases in order to understand the promises and limitations of the judiciary in redressing districting harms. First, we consider the federal courts' role in the racial gerrymandering challenges of state legislative maps. In North Carolina and Virginia, federal courts imposed new maps drawn by a special master, which had the effect of reducing bias. By contrast, in Texas, a federal court approved changes to the state legislative plans that resulted in a net increase in bias from the previous districting cycle. The common thread in all three cases is that the reach of the federal judiciary was limited and changes to the maps targeted only a small number of districts. Consequently, judicial intervention had only a limited impact on partisan bias. Nevertheless, these cases underscore our findings from Chapter 5 that suggest that Republican legislatures often achieve partisan bias through minority vote dilution and that the links between racial and political geography are deeply intertwined.

Next we consider the cases of Alaska and Florida, where court action appears to have reduced extreme bias, although this reduction was minimal in the case of Florida. Lastly, we consider the cases in which the courts took over redistricting from primary authorities. In Nevada and New Mexico, the courts drew plans that were free of bias. In the cases of Kansas and Minnesota, however, the courts approved maps with extreme partisan bias.

In sum, our assessment of court intervention suggests that courts are only a partial solution to the problem of gerrymandering, because judicial actors are minimalistic in their treatment of redistricting and have a tendency to avoid extreme changes. While the federal courts have been assertive in combatting racial gerrymandering, state courts have had only a limited effect on partisan bias when they have been delegated the task of redistricting.

8.1 RACIAL GERRYMANDERING AND THE FEDERAL COURTS

In our examination of the processes and outcomes of 2011 state legislative redistricting, we observed four examples of a federal court invalidating district plans for illegal racial gerrymandering. In three of these instances, the federal courts revised the maps to remedy impermissible racial vote dilution. This occurred first in Texas in 2012, after the state house and senate plans, which were approved by the legislature and signed by the governor, were rejected upon mandatory Voting Rights Act preclearance for illegal vote dilution in majority Latinx districts. Federal courts issued remedial plans for the house and senate, which the legislature subsequently adopted.

In North Carolina, a federal district court ruled that the General Assembly "unjustifiably relied on race to draw dozens of state Senate and House of Representatives district lines, in violation of the Equal Protection Clause of the Fourteenth Amendment" (*Covington* v. *North Carolina*, 1:15CV399) and ordered the General Assembly to draw remedial districts. In August of 2017, the General Assembly approved new district plans that altered thirty-five senate districts and seventy-nine house districts from the plans enacted in 2011. However, the court rejected several of these for racial gerrymandering and appointed a special master to revise the impermissible districts in both plans. Although the federal court approved the special master's revisions, a state court in *Common Cause* v. *Lewis* (2019) subsequently invalidated those plans after they were used for the 2018 elections, finding that the General Assembly had violated the Free Elections Clause of the state constitution when it had approved the 2017 remedial maps.

In Virginia, a group of African-American voters challenged the legality of twelve house districts located in Central and Southern Virginia, asserting that the drafters had improperly considered racial demographics when they drew the districts to include at least 55 percent Black voting age population. In 2015, a federal district court ruled that, with the exception of one district (House District 75), the plaintiffs had not shown that race was the "predominant factor in the creation" of the districts (141 F. Supp. 3d 505; E.D. Va. 2015). However, in 2017, the Supreme Court vacated this ruling and remanded the case back to trial court. Writing for the majority opinion in *Bethune-Hill* v. *Virginia State Board of Elections*, Justice Kennedy held that the lower court had not properly applied the legal standard established in *Alabama Legislative Caucus* v. *Alabama* when it determined that the General Assembly's use of race was "narrowly tailored" (*Bethune-Hill* v. *Va. State Bd. of Elections*, 2017; 137 S. Ct. 788) to the goal of complying with the Voting Rights Act.

When the suit was retried in federal district court, a three-judge panel agreed with the plaintiffs and ordered the General Assembly to draw a new House of Delegates map, to "remedy the identified constitutional violations" (368 F. Supp. 3d 872; E.D. Va. 2019). When the Republican-controlled General Assembly failed to pass a plan by the court-imposed deadline of October 30, 2018, the court appointed a special master to redraw the map, to be implemented before the 2019 state legislative elections. An appeal before the Supreme Court was rejected in 2019, on the grounds that the House of Delegates did not have standing to challenge the map, and the new map was given the blessing of the Supreme Court, just days after the primary elections had been held.

Both of the Virginia and North Carolina rulings drew upon an earlier racial gerrymandering case, *Alabama Legislative Black Caucus v. Alabama* (2015), in which the Supreme Court clarified the standards for unlawful racial gerrymandering and remanded the case to a lower court, which ordered the Alabama Legislature to enact remedial plans for twelve districts.

How did the court's correction of racial gerrymandering in these cases affect partisan bias? Because we do not have complete data on districting outcomes in Alabama, we focus on outcomes in Virginia, North Carolina, and Texas. As Table 8.1 reports, judicial intervention in Virginia and North Carolina clearly reduced partisan bias, which suggests that the states were able to achieve a partisan advantage through illegal racial vote dilution. In Virginia, the court-approved plan significantly reduced bias and undoubtedly helped Democrats win a majority in the House of Delegates in 2019. The effect of the remedial map, which was approved by the district court in February of 2019, was that several Democratic and Republican districts that were previously "safe" under the original plan became more competitive, which allowed the Democrats to take 55 percent of the house seats with 53 percent of the two-party vote in 2019. In North Carolina, the federal court's remedial plans substantially reduced bias, but did not eliminate it entirely. Both the house and senate plans preserve extreme bias in favor of the Republicans, and net increases in bias relative to the pre-2011 plans. The effects of this bias were evident in the outcomes of the 2018, when Republicans managed to keep control of both the house and the senate even though Democratic candidates won more than 50 percent of the statewide vote in both chambers. That said, the new map helped Democrats pick up several seats in each chamber and eroded the Republican's seat majority.

In Texas, the original 2011 plans approved by the legislature and signed by the governor were never actually implemented – they were rejected upon mandatory preclearance, so we do not have a baseline to

TABLE 8.1. *When courts redressed racial gerrymandering*

State	Chamber	Bias in pre-2011 plans	Bias in 2011 plans (drawn by state legislature)	Bias in remedial plans (drawn by court)	Outcome
North Carolina	House	−7.16	−18.0	−13.0	Decrease in bias
	Senate	−6.53	−23.8	−17.1	Decrease in bias
Texas	House	−7.71	No data	−13.5	Unclear
	Senate	−12.3	No data	−17.8	Unclear
Virginia	House	−11.4	−12.0	−2.85	Decrease in bias

compare the court-drawn map against. Our estimates show that the interim maps that were drawn by the courts for the 2012 election preserved extreme bias in favor of the Republican Party and actually resulted in a net increase in bias relative to the maps used in the previous districting cycle. However, we have no way of knowing whether the original maps passed by the legislature would have resulted in even more bias than the court-drawn plan. Nevertheless, the legislature was apparently satisfied with the court's remedial plans, because it subsequently adopted them as the permanent maps, even after the federal court's decision not to preclear the original plans was vacated in 2013 after the Supreme Court's ruling in *Shelby County* v. *Holder* (2013), which struck down the formula for preclearance coverage.

8.1.1 Racial Gerrymandering as an Instrument for Partisan Bias

What lessons can we draw from these examples? The outcomes in Virginia, North Carolina, and Texas highlight the complex interrelationship between racial and political geography and show that the courts can have an effect on bias simply by redressing illegal racial vote dilution. In each of these examples, Republicans were able to create a partisan advantage, in part, through the drawing of majority-minority districts, which are required by law under the Voting Rights Act. By "packing" large majorities of African-American or Latinx voters into a small number of majority-minority districts, Republicans were able to "waste" the votes of Democrats in the process, thereby giving themselves a competitive advantage in other parts of the state.

Consider Virginia and North Carolina, which share similar racial geographic features. In Virginia, most of the state's African-American population resides in the Eastern part of the state along the I-95 and I-64 corridors, a region where the state's Democratic support is concentrated. White voters, on the other hand, are evenly distributed across the state, and the Republican Party draws its support from the low population density areas with large white majorities. This, too, is true of North Carolina, where Republicans are able to achieve partisan bias by drawing districts around Black communities in the Piedmont Triad and Tidewater regions of the state.

Because African American voters tend to support Democrats, the Republican gerrymanderers in Virginia and North Carolina were able to use race as a shortcut for party. By drawing lines around African-American communities, they were able to draw majority-Black districts that "wasted" the votes of Black citizens and diluted the Democrats' strength. Ultimately, in all three instances, federal courts stepped in to restore African-American voting rights, but these actions would not come until after several election cycles had already passed, denying Black voters in these states the ability to elect candidates of their choice.

In all three cases, because the courts specifically targeted districts with large African-American or Latinx majorities, the effects of court action on partisan bias was inherently limited. Accordingly, we conclude that the federal courts alone are not an effective remedy for the problem of partisan bias. Although the courts have been aggressive in combating racial vote dilution and have set stringent standards for drawing majority-minority districts, the Supreme Court's decision in *Rucho* forecloses the possibility that citizens can advance partisan gerrymandering claims in federal courts. So, while the dynamics of racial gerrymandering and partisan gerrymandering are deeply intertwined, the federal courts can offer only a partial solution to partisan bias through the lens of racial vote dilution cases.

8.2 STATE COURTS AND INCREMENTALISM IN REDISTRICTING

One of the problems with turning to the courts as a solution to the problem of widespread partisan gerrymandering is that judges are fundamentally incrementalistic when dealing with redistricting. They tend to favor the status quo and rarely draw maps that fundamentally change the political balance of power. In other words, courts tend to move slowly with what has been termed "purposeful incrementalism" (Parsons 2020, 53).

Since courts must be wary that one step leads to another and therefore jurisprudential expansion, incrementalism alone is insufficient to ensure against unintended consequences of actions. Hence, the cautious and deliberate movement – or lack of movement – is a mechanism to ensure judicial modesty to further notions of "legal stability and precision" (Pildes 2004, 66). The underlying rationale is that stability and legitimacy go hand in hand. Accordingly, the courts, generally speaking, avoid deviating far from the status quo and only move as much as is necessary to resolve the disputes before them (Smirnov and Smith 2013). This is particularly true of matters involving the political branches of government, and it explains why state courts are reluctant to make sweeping changes to district plans that violate state law.

In our study of 2011 redistricting, we identified six instances in which a state court ordered a redistricting authority to make changes to its plans. In all of these examples, which occurred in Alaska, Colorado, Florida, Hawaii, Idaho, and Kentucky, the courts found that the redistricting authorities violated state-level legal criteria.

In Colorado and Florida, the state supreme courts are granted automatic judicial review of maps that are approved by redistricting bodies (Florida uses the legislature, Colorado uses a bipartisan politician commission). In Colorado, the supreme court cited redistricting violations that were fairly benign – it found that the commission did not provide adequate justification in splitting county lines (*In re Reapportionment of the Colorado General Assembly*, No. 2011SA282 (Colo. Sup. Ct.)). The commission adopted revisions to the plans that satisfied the court, and the court approved the new plans well in advance of the 2012 state legislative elections.

In Florida, the Republican legislature drew senate plans for 2012 elections that the supreme court subsequently rejected upon review due to improper numbering of districts and unwarranted splitting of municipal boundaries (*In re 2012 Joint Resolution of Apportionment*, No. SC12–460 (Fla. Sup. Ct.)). The legislature revised its plans, and the court approved them in time for 2012. However, those plans were challenged in state courts as an illegal partisan gerrymander, which is prohibited under the state constitution. Faced with the threat of litigation, the legislature voluntarily approved a third set of plans in advance of 2016 elections, and the suit was withdrawn.

In Alaska, Hawaii, Idaho, and Kentucky, the state courts are not granted automatic judicial review of redistricting; however, state courts heard challenges to the state legislative plans and ordered redistricting authorities to implement specific changes. In the cases of Hawaii, Idaho, and Kentucky, these changes were adopted and approved in advance of 2011 and 2012 state legislative elections. In Hawaii, the state supreme court found that the bipartisan politician redistricting commission violated a state constitutional provision when it failed to exclude nonpermanent residents from its population base (*Solomon* v. *Abercrombie*, NO. SCPW-11-0000732 (Sup. Ct. of Hawaii)). The court issued a writ of mandamus that compelled the commission to redraw the plans, which it did, in time for the 2012 elections. In Idaho, the supreme court struck down the original plans approved by the redistricting commission for the unjustifiable splitting of county lines (*Twin Falls County* v. *Idaho Commission on Redistricting*, No. 39373-2011 (Idaho Sup. Ct.)). The commission approved a new set of plans in advance of the 2012 elections. Similarly, in Kentucky, the state supreme court found that the house and senate plans violated state constitutional requirements mandating population equity and the preservation of county lines (*Fischer* v. *Grimes*, No. 2012-SC-000092-T (Ky. Sup. Ct.)). It ordered the 2001 cycle plans to be used for the 2011 elections, and the legislature adopted new plans for subsequent elections.

Like Colorado, the effect of court interventions in Hawaii, Idaho, and Kentucky were minimal and represented minor violations of constitutionally mandated procedural requirements or redistricting criteria. As well, the changes were adopted before the first elections took place, so we have no ability to assess their impact on redistricting outcomes.

However, in Alaska, the state supreme court adopted the state's redistricting plans as interim maps to be used for the 2012 elections, and subsequently ordered new maps to be drawn for elections thereafter, which gives us a baseline to assess the influence of the court. In Alaska, the state's Reapportionment Board, which is a commission of citizens appointed by the three branches of state government, approved redistricting plans early in 2011 that were challenged in the state courts. The state supreme court ruled that the Board had erred in its process for drawing the maps when it followed the instructions of a redistricting consultant who advised the Board to begin the redistricting process first by drawing "Native-influence" districts in order to comply with the Voting Rights Act. Instead, the judge ruled that the Board was required by the Alaska Constitution to follow a procedure known as the *Hickel* process, which requires redistricting authorities to bring the plans into compliance with compactness and "socioeconomic integration" preservation rules and to deviate from these standards only when necessary to comply with the federal Voting Rights Act (*In re 2011 Redistricting Cases*, 274 P.3d 466 (Alaska 2012)). The court instructed the Board to start over, but after the Board submitted the second set of maps to the court for approval in April of 2012, the court found that the Board had again violated the *Hickel* process because the second set of plans preserved twenty-two districts from the first map that were not challenged under the original suit. The court approved the second set of maps to be used as interim plans for the 2012 elections and ordered the Board to draw new maps for subsequent election cycles. The Board approved a third and final set of plans that received the blessings of the court and were used in elections after 2012.

8.2.1 Do State Supreme Courts Affect Redistricting Outcomes?

In all six of these cases, a state supreme court found that redistricting authorities had violated state constitutional provisions and ordered redistricting authorities to make changes to their maps. How did the courts' intervention in these cases affect outcomes in redistricting? In the cases of Colorado, Hawaii, and Idaho the court-mandated changes were approved by redistricting authorities and adopted in advance of the first election of the 2011 redistricting cycle, so we do not have a baseline against which to assess the effects of the courts. In Kentucky, similarly, the supreme court ordered the maps from the previous cycle to be used for the 2011 state elections. However, in the cases of Alaska and Florida, the primary redistricting authorities drew maps that were in place for at least one election cycle after redistricting. In Alaska, the supreme court found procedural flaws with the Redistricting Board's second plans, but implemented those plans as interim maps for the 2012 elections. In Florida, the supreme court approved the legislature's second set of plans upon automatic judicial review, and those plans were in place for the 2012 senate elections. However, those plans were subsequently challenged and the legislature voluntarily drew a third set of plans in the face of court pressure. Accordingly, we can gain insight into the effects of state courts on redistricting outcomes by looking at the maps drawn by redistricting authorities before and after court intervention.

In Alaska, the court mandates evidently had a significant effect on bias in the senate plan, but not the house plan, as reported on Table 8.2. Whereas the Redistricting Board's 2012 senate plan was substantially biased in the Republican Party's favor, the map used in 2016 was largely neutral. Although the court did not invalidate the 2012 plan for partisan gerrymandering, it took issue with the process that the Board used when it

TABLE 8.2. *Court-mandated redistricting in Alaska and Florida*

	Bias in old Map (before 2011)	Bias in 2012 map	Bias in 2016 map
Alaska house map	6.71	0.503	2.72
Alaska senate map	13.0	−15.9	−0.802
Florida senate map	−18.9	−18.1	−11.6

began redistricting by drawing Native-influence districts, in violation of the state constitution. This practice evidently led to an extreme Republican advantage, and although we do not have data on partisan affiliation of Native Alaskan voters, it is possible that the deliberate drawing of Native-influence districts had the effect of "wasting" Democratic votes. Indeed, when drafting the final set of plans, the Board did not set out to draw Native-influence districts and instead focused on compactness and political boundary preservation, which resulted in an unbiased map. In this case, it is clear that the rationale of the Alaska Constitution is to prevent political gerrymandering by requiring mapmakers to focus first on adherence to constitutionally mandated redistricting criteria and only consider deviations to those criteria when necessary to comply with the Voting Rights Act. In the next chapter, we assess the impact of redistricting criteria, like compactness and boundary preservation, on bias in greater detail. However, in the case of Alaska, strict procedural requirements and redistricting criteria served to prevent extreme partisan gerrymandering, in part because the judiciary was assertive in enforcing these requirements.

In Florida, we have no means of assessing the court's initial intervention (which occurred before the 2012 elections) but it is clear that it was limited in scope insofar as the legislature's second set of plans, which were approved for the 2012 elections, did little to curb extreme Republican bias that was present in the pre-2011 plans. However, the second intervention in Florida, which was actually only a threat, reduced bias substantially, but it did not eliminate it entirely.

Florida illustrates another issue with the courts as guardians against gerrymandering. Since the dates of elections are known to all, any litigant that seeks to alter districts must be able to accomplish a judicial outcome with plenty of time left to run an effective campaign to contest the seats in question. Courts can avoid deciding the fate of the redistricting by simply going very slowly or going very incrementally. Either strategy, or even a combination of both, can lead to an abandonment of efforts to alter districting in order to spend political resources and capital in other perhaps winnable contexts. Incrementalism not only keeps policy stable, but it also discourages litigation since the possibility of a positive outcome is tempered by the likelihood of a narrow victory.

8.3 WHEN STATE COURTS REDISTRICT AS CONTINGENCY AUTHORITIES

Unlike the previous cases, where state courts ruled that redistricting plans violated state constitutional provisions and mandated changes to the maps, the courts played a far more assertive role in redistricting in Kansas, Minnesota, Nevada, and New Mexico. In these cases, the courts completely took over the process of redistricting rather than return it to the legislatures. This gives us a window into how the courts approached the task of redistricting and dealt with extreme partisan bias, which was present in maps in all of the states except New Mexico.

In the case of Kansas, the state supreme court serves as a "back-up" authority if the primary redistricting authority (the legislature) fails to enact a plan within a constitutionally imposed deadline. In Minnesota, the Democratic governor vetoed the plans that were approved by the Republican-controlled legislature, and the state supreme court stepped in to end the stalemate and delegated the task of redistricting to a five-judge panel. Similar outcomes occurred in Nevada and New Mexico, where divided government resulted in a stalemate between the legislative branch (held by Democrats) and the executive branch (controlled by Republicans).

Table 8.3 reports the results of those judicial efforts at fair redistricting. While the courts in Nevada and Kansas seem to have made progress in rolling back plans that were previously biased, courts in general made modest gains or, in the case of the Minnesota house plan, made things worse. In New Mexico, the old plans were already unbiased, so it is difficult to determine how the court would have redistricted a plan that was previously biased.

8.3.1 Politicization of the Judiciary

One potential danger of delegating "back-up" authority to the courts is that many state courts use elections to appoint judges. If members of a state supreme court are selected through judicial election then they may be

TABLE 8.3. *When courts controlled redistricting*

State *type of court,* method of appointing judges	Chamber	Bias in pre-2011 map	Bias in court-drawn map	Outcome
Kansas *Supreme Court –* Gubernatorial appointment with popular retention vote every six years	House	−12.0	−10.7	Negligible change in bias
	Senate	−12.8	−6.84	Decreased bias
Minnesota *Supreme Court –* Popularly elected to six-year terms	House	−4.28	−12.2	Increased bias
	Senate	−11.2	−10.1	Negligible change in bias
Nevada *Supreme Court –* Popularly elected to six-year terms	House	14	.415	Decreased bias
	Senate	−5.30	−2.43	Decreased bias
New Mexico *Supreme Court –* Popularly elected to eight-year terms	House	4.42	−.4795	Decreased bias
	Senate	1.71	3.15	Negligible change in bias

prone to protecting political interests. As we noted in the introductory chapter, this was one objection raised by opponents of the redistricting reforms in Virginia, which delegate back-up authority to the Supreme Court of Virginia, in the event of a deadlocked commission. Some vocal opponents predicted that Republicans had set a trap for the Democrats to fall into and that the Republican legislatures would attempt to deadlock the commission, sending it to the Supreme Court of Virginia, which included a majority of judges who were appointed by Republican General Assemblies. Is this a valid critique of the courts?

We can gain insight into the effects of politicization of the judiciary on districting outcomes by comparing the judicial appointment processes for the courts that implemented maps. In Kansas, Supreme Court vacancies are subject to a complex merit selection process that was written into the state constitution in the 1950s. First, a nine-person commission is convened with the purpose of nominating three candidates for the vacancy. Five of the commissioners are attorneys, four of whom are elected by attorneys from each of the state's four congressional districts, with the fifth, the chairperson, elected by attorneys statewide. The other four commissioners are nonattorneys appointed by the governor. Once the commission selects three candidates, the governor makes an appointment. If the governor fails to make an appointment within a sixty-day period, the task falls to the Chief Justice of the Kansas Supreme Court. After the new justice is appointed, their appointment is subject to a retention vote in the next popular vote, and every six years thereafter.

The process used in Kansas is designed to insulate the court from political influence, and similar models are used by twenty-one other state governments to select state supreme court vacancies, including Florida (Reddick and Kourlis 2014). The processes used in Minnesota, Nevada, and New Mexico are inherently political in that they rely on statewide elections to fill Supreme Court vacancies. Although judicial elections in Nevada and Minnesota are nonpartisan, judicial candidates in New Mexico are allowed to affiliate with a political party, and a majority of the five judges who ruled on redistricting challenges in 2011 and 2012 were Democrats.

Did the partisan balance of these state courts mirror the shifts in redistricting bias we observed after court intervention? We do not find compelling evidence that this is the case. In New Mexico, the supreme court ordered the trial court to redraw the state house maps in early 2011, and the end result was a decrease in pro-Democratic bias, despite the Democratic leaning of the Court. The state senate map, which was approved by the New Mexico Supreme Court in 2012, changed only negligibly in its partisan bias, resulting in a neutral plan. Clearly the court was not operating with partisan motives in mind.

In Minnesota, although Supreme Court vacancies are filled through a merit selection system and are then subject to recurring retention elections, mid-term vacancies are filled through gubernatorial appointment. Of the judges who served when the court drew the state house and senate maps, a majority were appointed by Republican Governor Tim Pawlenty. It is possible that, because the court comprised a majority of Republican-appointed judges, this impacted the districting outcomes. However, the court itself did not draw the maps; instead, it convened a five-judge panel to draw the maps. The panel included three state judges appointed by Democratic-Farmer-Labor Party governors, one judge appointed by a Republican governor, and one judge appointed by an independent governor. Indeed, Minnesota is the only court-drawn map that actually increases in bias after court-led redistricting. Yet it does not increase in the Democrats' favor.

There is no evidence that any of the judicial bodies that drew district maps were politically motivated in their decisions, and there are compelling reasons to believe they were not. In the case of Virginia, the balance of the evidence suggests that the redistricting reform opponents' critiques of the courts were overblown. Virginia is just one of two states that delegate the task of appointing judges to the state legislature, which elects judges to twelve-year terms. Although this means that politicians pick judges, in principle this system is no more politicized than appointment methods used in other states, and there is little reason to expect that the Supreme Court of Virginia would advance political interests if it were to draw the lines.

8.4 CONCLUSION

In this chapter, we have assessed the role of the courts in shaping redistricting outcomes and whether they are capable (or willing) to prevent extreme bias. Our analyses yield mixed results. The federal courts have been assertive in redressing racial vote dilution cases, particularly after the Supreme Court's decision in the *Alabama Legislative Black Caucus*. However, in the examples of North Carolina and Virginia, as well as in Texas, the courts' role in redistricting was limited to a small number of districts. Because race and party affiliation are highly correlated in the United States, the court-imposed changes had the effect of reducing bias in the cases of Virginia and North Carolina. However, it did not entirely eliminate bias in North Carolina and Texas, and in North Carolina, the court-imposed maps allowed Republicans to retain the North Carolina General Assembly in 2018 despite losing the two-party vote in both chambers.

Our case study of state courts that revised district maps suggests that the judiciary can be aggressive at enforcing state constitutional provisions, although these provisions are often technical and do not necessarily directly impact partisan bias. As we saw in Florida, in which the supreme court intervened twice, the court's rejection of the first senate map did not result in an unbiased map. Although the court later pressured the legislature to adopt a third map, that too preserved extreme bias in favor of the Republicans who controlled the legislature. By contrast, the state supreme court's procedural objections to Alaska's senate plans appear to have dramatically reduced partisan bias, resulting in an unbiased map, in part because the state supreme court was willing to assert itself aggressively.

Our investigations of court-led redistricting yield similarly mixed findings. On the one hand, we find little evidence that the courts protect political interests through redistricting – even when judges are appointed by politicians and subject to judicial retention elections. On the other hand, there is not compelling evidence that courts act aggressively to neutralize partisan bias. Although many of the courts that controlled redistricting drew unbiased maps, in only two of these cases the courts were working with maps that were previously biased, so it is not possible to draw generalizable conclusions. In the case of Minnesota, the courts approved a plan that dramatically increased bias in favor of the Republicans, although a majority of the judges who served on the panel that drew the maps were appointed by Democratic governors.

Accordingly, we can conclude that, while the courts have a better track record of passing neutral maps than one-party-controlled districting institutions, there are several aspects of the judiciary that limit the effectiveness of the courts as a guardian against overt political bias in gerrymandering. First, courts are inherently incremental. They move slowly out of a concern for the prospects of costs to legitimacy if they move more than necessary (Shapiro 1965; Smirnov and Smith 2013). They avoid future entanglements with other political actors by reducing the value of the judicial payoff even when a litigant wins. Finally, they may lack the expertise to ascertain when they actually are making the situation worse.

When the courts took over the redistricting process, the results were mixed. Courts in Nevada and New Mexico drew plans without partisan bias, while courts in Kansas and Minnesota drew plans with considerable Republican bias. The common thread in all of these cases is that the level of bias in the remedial maps was very similar to the level of bias from the previous plans.

What does this say about the reformers' hopes for the courts to solve the problems of political districting? Courts alone cannot solve the problem, and are at best a partial fix, particularly in the aftermath of *Rucho*. However, as we see in the next chapter, procedural reforms of redistricting can potentially prevent bias from occurring.

9

How to Design Effective Anti-gerrymandering Reforms

In this book, we have investigated the causes and consequences of redistricting outcomes. In the first part of the book, we highlighted the scope of districting bias in the state legislatures and identified the geographic and political determinants of bias. As we saw in Chapter 6, the implications of partisan gerrymandering on policy outcomes are far reaching. Legislatures with extreme Republican gerrymanders were more likely to enact legislation restricting ballot access and voting rights and to limit public health and COVID-19 responsiveness. As we argued in Chapter 7, state legislative gerrymandering additionally harms democratic norms and disrupts the balance of state and federal power.

There are other consequences as well. The story of 2011 redistricting in Virginia shows that gerrymandering can undermine political representation and trust in government. Although Virginia Republicans were able to deny the Democrats seats in the House of Delegates for several election cycles, thanks to their 2011 gerrymander, the court's implementation of a remedial map in 2019 disrupted the relationships between delegates of both parties and their constituents. Many legislators who had not even been in power when the lines were drawn in 2011 saw their districts change dramatically on the eve of the 2019 general election.

Delegate Lashrecse Aird, for example, was elected in 2015 to represent District 63 in Petersburg, which was a majority Black district and a Democratic "safe seat" at the time. However, after the implementation of the remedial map in 2019, the district became competitive and the African American population decreased from 60 percent to under

50 percent.[1] Dozens of other legislators from both parties saw their district lines change just months before Election Day and were forced to familiarize themselves with new constituencies.

These disruptions – and the long-term effects of political districting in Virginia – prompted lawmakers to consider reforms of the redistricting process. In February of 2019, Republicans and Democrats in the General Assembly struck a deal over a redistricting reform proposal to create a semi-independent redistricting commission to draw the state legislative and congressional maps. The proposal would amend the Virginia constitution, transferring redistricting authority from the General Assembly and governor to a sixteen-member commission, comprised equally of politicians and citizens. The eight politician members would be drafted from the General Assembly – two legislators from each party in each chamber. The citizen members would be selected by a group of retired state judges, who would choose from a list of citizens nominated by Republican and Democratic leaders in the General Assembly.

The commission would be tasked with drafting state legislative and congressional maps. In order to advance a districting plan, six of the eight politician members and six of the eight citizen members would have to agree. Then, the package would be sent to the General Assembly for approval by majority vote. If the General Assembly declined to approve the plan, the commission would be given a second opportunity to produce a revised plan. If the second plan was not approved by the General Assembly, or if the commission were to deadlock, redistricting authority would fall to the Supreme Court of Virginia.

In order to enact a constitutional amendment, Virginia requires the General Assembly pass a "reading" of the proposed amendment in two consecutive assemblies, followed by an approval vote in the next general election. In February of 2019, the first reading of the proposed redistricting amendment passed with overwhelming bipartisan support. In the house, the proposal passed by eighty-three to thirteen margin; in the senate, the proposal passed with only a single nay vote. However, after the Democrats won power in November elections, their calculus changed. With control of 2021 redistricting hanging in the balance, Democrats in the House of Delegates opposed the amendment, arguing that the reforms would give the courts too much power and didn't go far enough to ensure independence and racial representation (Moomaw 2020).

---

[1] Source: www.vpap.org/offices/house-of-delegates-63/redistricting/

The Democrats in the house passed a bill that included new districting criteria that prevented the General Assembly from drawing districts "unduly favoring or disfavoring any political party," which they promoted as a more effective alternative to the constitutional amendment (H.B.1255, 2020 General Assembly. 2020 Reg. Sess. (Va. 2020)).

Ultimately, the General Assembly advanced the redistricting reform amendment after eight Democratic delegates broke party ranks and joined Republicans. However, the Democratic Party mounted an aggressive opposition campaign in advance of the general election to cast doubt on the efficacy of the reforms and to undermine public support for the proposal.

The example of the reform debate in Virginia illustrates the difficult challenges that reformers confront. Within the scientific literature, relatively little is known about the effectiveness of commission-based redistricting models, like the one adopted by Virginia, compared to laws that impose rules on existing redistricting authorities, such as the political favoritism ban endorsed by Virginia Democrats. And, without reliable data on "best practices" in redistricting, proponents of reform lack hard evidence to combat the spread of misinformation. In Virginia, reform advocates ultimately prevailed in spite of Democratic opposition, and voters in 2020 approved the redistricting amendment by a nearly two-to-one margin. However, in Missouri, the state GOP succeeded in rolling back many of the reforms approved by voters in 2018, thanks to a deceptively worded ballot initiative that was narrowly approved by voters in 2020 (see Rosenbaum 2020).

In this chapter, we build upon the lessons we have learned in this volume to evaluate redistricting reform options in order to identify "best practices" in redistricting. First, we investigate the effects of common "fair districting" criteria – that is, rules that require (or prohibit) certain outcomes in districting. We find little evidence that adding additional criteria will prevent partisan bias in districting. In many cases, such as district compactness requirements, it appears as though districting authorities frequently ignore the rules. The biggest drawback with rules-based reforms is that they depend upon the judiciary for enforcement. When a politically motivated districting authority wants to create extreme bias through the drawing of irregular district shapes, for example, there is little a court can do to stop them, given the complexities of defining "compactness" and the reluctance of the judicial actors to insert themselves into political debates.

We then evaluate whether "procedural reforms," like citizen redistricting commissions, are effective at preventing bias. We find systemically less bias in districting when the maps are drawn by citizens and other independent bodies. Although the design and mechanics of commissions vary widely, we find the least bias in the maps drawn by redistricting bodies that forbid membership by politicians. This suggests that independent redistricting commissions represent an effective solution against partisan gerrymandering, provided they are staffed by citizens or independent public officials.

9.1 REDISTRICTING REFORMS: RULES VS. PROCESSES

Redistricting reform is not a new concept; indeed, historically, reformers have proposed a variety of methods to promote favorable outcomes and to prevent undesirable outcomes. In the 1960s and 1970s, reformers fought to codify into law districting criteria, such as compactness and community preservation requirements, as a way to prevent lawmakers from exploiting the redistricting process to achieve partisan ends or to disenfranchise minority voters, for example.

The most common redistricting reform proposals tend to fit into one of two classes: rules reforms and procedural reforms. For the sake of simplicity, "rules" are redistricting criteria, or standards, established through law that districting authorities must follow when revising the maps. Rules fall into two categories: requirements and prohibitions. Requirements mandate that districting authorities achieve a certain outcome (or outcomes) with the maps. For example, among the most common criteria are "contiguity" requirements, which require all parts of a district to be physically connected. Prohibitions forbid certain "bad" outcomes, as opposed to requiring "good" outcomes. For example, many states have rules that forbid the deliberate protection of incumbents or the intentional favoring of a political party.

In general, the intent of districting rules is to influence *outcomes* in districting by imposing limits on the decision-making of districting authorities. In this regard, rules are proscriptive, rather than preventative.

Rules reforms don't fundamentally change who is in charge; rather, seek to restrict *what* those in charge can and cannot do. Accordingly, the courts play a key role in the enforcement of redistricting rules when aggrieved citizens challenge the maps in court. Assuming these challenges succeed, a court might instruct the redistricting authority to go back and revise the map in a particular way, in order to comply with the law and redress the harm.

By contrast, procedural reforms concern the institutions and entities that control and coordinate redistricting, as well as the processes that govern how the maps are drawn and who participates in decision-making, rather than the outcomes. Today, independent commissions are a popular form of procedural reform and have been adopted by many states. The first states to adopt commission-based redistricting reforms were in the West (Miller and Grofman 2013). Like Virginia, a number of states in recent years have amended their constitutions to transfer districting control from the state legislature to a commission. In 2018 alone, voters in Michigan, Missouri, and Utah approved commission-based redistricting reforms (although, as we note, this reform was nullified in Missouri in 2020), while the state legislature in Colorado approved a measure to establish a redistricting commission staffed by an equal number of Democratic, Republican, and unaffiliated voters.

One critical distinction between rule-based reforms and procedural reforms is how "good" outcomes are said to be achieved. Rules reforms assume that desirable outcomes can be achieved through legal mandates and prohibitions, and that the threat of a court challenge can be an effective deterrent against noncompliance. By contrast, procedural reforms assume that outcomes are reflective of the design of institutions and processes. Insofar as institutions determine the sets of incentives that actors confront in their decision-making, reforming redistricting institutions to be more inclusive of the electorate yields outcomes that are more representative and thus more desirable to a greater number of people. However, it is important to note that rules reforms and procedural reforms are not mutually exclusive – indeed, it is possible to reform both the rules and institutions, which is often the case when states adopt independent redistricting.

In general, as the example of Virginia suggests, rules reforms tend to be less politically "costly" to implement than procedural reforms. For example, suppose a group of citizens seeks to prevent partisan gerrymandering by pressuring elected officials to advance redistricting reforms. We would expect that it would be an easier sell for the controlling party in the legislature to adopt a new redistricting criterion that forbids partisan advantage, given the symbolic value of such a measure, than it would be to adopt institutional reforms that transfer redistricting authority from the state legislature to an independent citizen commission.

As a general rule, politicians are reluctant to relinquish their power, and election reforms are often opposed by controlling parties that stand to lose power (Kaminski 1999, 2002; Santucci 2018). This is perhaps why most of the states that have switched to independent redistricting commissions have done so through popular referendum, and why in Virginia, where changes to the constitution must first pass through the legislature, the reforms that were approved by the legislature gave the legislature half of the seats on the commission and a veto over the maps drafted by the commission.

9.2 DO REDISTRICTING CRITERIA WORK?

First, we assess the effectiveness of rules-based reforms. We researched the redistricting criteria adopted for each state by referencing state laws and constitutional provisions. We are particularly indebted to National Conference of State Legislatures, which maintains data on the redistricting criteria used in each state. In general, we find considerable variation in terms of the districting criteria in states; however, for our purposes, we focus in detail on the effects of three of the most common types of redistricting criteria adopted by the states: (1) district compactness requirements; (2) political favoritism bans; (3) "competitive elections" clauses. We also considered a number of other criteria, including bans against favoring incumbents, preservation of political boundaries requirements, and preservation of "communities of interest" requirements.

9.2.1 District Compactness Requirements

The requirement that districts be "compact" is one of the oldest and most common districting criteria used in the United States. "Compactness" was legally required by Congress in the Apportionment Act of 1842; however, it was dropped after the Apportionment Act of 1929, when the Supreme Court ruled that, because subsequent apportionment acts had not included the language of "compactness," Congress had not intended to keep it as a standard. Since then, federal law has not mandated compactness as a requirement for congressional districts, although a number of states have added the requirement for their state legislative maps, congressional maps, or both.

Historically, the prevalence of district compactness requirements in state legislative districting increased after the reforms of the 1960s and 1970s. Prior to the 1960s, before the adoption of the "one-person, one-vote" standard and the Voting Rights Act, and before the development of advanced computing, gerrymanderers did not need to draw noncompact districts in order to produce bias. Indeed, because districting authorities were not required to maintain population equality in their districts, malapportionment was the primary tool for achieving partisan advantage (see Grofman, Koetzle, and Brunell 1997). Moreover, as we saw in Chapter 5, state and local governments used a variety of other institutional mechanisms, such as "general ticket" and "at-large" elections, to disenfranchise Black and Latinx voters. However, with the reforms of the 1960s, redistricting authorities were required to achieve population equality and advance minority representation, and the development of advanced GIS software provided them with the means to draw district boundaries with unprecedented precision. Consequently, as Ansolabehere and Palmer (2015) have shown, compactness scores of congressional districts steadily declined in the decades after 1960.

Compactness requirements came into fashion in the 1970s and 1980s, when state governments modernized their state constitutions and adopted single-member districting in their state legislatures. Today, a total of twenty-seven states have a legal requirement, either through statute or constitutional provision, that state legislative districts are to be compact, although the precise definition of "compactness," as well as the language used, varies. For example, when Virginia rewrote its state constitution in 1971, it added the requirement in Article II, Section 6 that districts "be composed of contiguous and compact territory," while a 1983 amendment to the Washington state constitution requires that, "to the extent reasonable, each district ... shall be compact and convenient" (Article II, Section 43). Similarly, the Rhode Island constitution requires districts to be "as compact in territory as possible" (Article VII, Section 1), while Oklahoma requires only that "consideration shall be given to ... compactness, area ... to the extent feasible" (Article V, Section 9A). A number of other states had guidelines in place during 2011 redistricting that recommended districting authorities draw compact districts. We do not include these states in our sample because they were not legal requirements.

To what extent does requiring district "compactness" affect outcomes? In their study of the 2000 redistricting cycle, Forgette and Platt (2005) find that "form-based" redistricting principles, such as compactness laws, had no impact on incumbent vote share. Ladewig (2018) finds a negative association between compactness and voter turnout. As we noted in Chapter 4, there is no direct link between the compactness of a district and partisan bias. In many instances, noncompactness may be necessary to draw unbiased districts, as Nagle has argued in his case study of Pennsylvania (Nagle 2019). However, the shape of a district does have an intuitive appeal as an indicator of stress. That is, when districts are drawn to be highly irregular in shape, this may suggest that districting authorities went to great lengths to accomplish some particular goal or set of goals. For example, when one party is highly segregated from the other party, this can make it easier or more difficult to draw partisan bias. In states where Democratic voting populations are disproportionately concentrated in cities, Republicans have no trouble drawing districting bias, while Democrats must resort to noncompact districts in order to prevent Republican bias. In this regard, compactness requirements may actually cause more harm than good, particularly when we consider the minority districting mandates that stem from the VRA, which require districting authorities to draw districts representing sizable minority communities.

When we look at the correlation between compactness laws and bias, our results do not suggest a relationship between the two. For example, when we compare the average asymmetry in maps (using the absolute value of post-2011 symmetry scores) in states with compactness laws (asymmetry = 9.70 percent) with the maps drawn in states without compactness laws (asymmetry = 12.5 percent), we observe a large and statistically significant difference (p = 0.053), which would suggest that compactness laws lead districting authorities to draw less bias.

However, most of the maps included in the group of states without compactness laws happened to have been those drawn by Republicans. Once we control for partisanship, the difference associated with having a compactness law disappears. When we omit maps drawn by members of one party from the sample, we find no meaningful difference between the compactness law group (8.16 percent) and the no compactness law group (7.12 percent). When we model the effects of partisanship using multi-linear regression analysis, we similarly find no evidence of a statistical relationship between compactness laws and bias.

Although the concept of "compactness" is intuitively appealing, it is inherently difficult to measure (see Kaufman, King, and Komisarchik forthcoming). Neither the federal nor the state courts have embraced a standard for identifying violations of compactness, and to our knowledge, no state court has ever struck down a map for violating a compactness law. Take, for example, a recent lawsuit in Virginia, in which fourteen voters charged that the General Assembly had "subordinated" the constitutional requirement of compact districts in order to achieve partisan advantage in the state legislative plans enacted in 2011 (*Rima Ford Vesilind, et al.* v. *Virginia State Board of Elections, et al.* 2016). The challengers' expert witness, Dr. Michael McDonald, proposed a creative, novel legal standard for identifying violations of district compactness based on a predominance test, comparing the actual district with an "ideally compact district." Despite the intuitive appeal of the proposed standard, the state court agreed with the state's expert witness, Thomas Hofeller, that the proposed standard was too complex and that the compactness of the districts in question "was fairly debatable." It ultimately "upheld the constitutional validity" of the map.

As this example suggests, identifying violations of compactness often relies upon subjective judgment. It is unlikely that a court will ever endorse a uniform, objective standard for unlawful noncompactness given that the language of compactness laws is often vague, and that judges tend to be skeptical of mathematical approaches to election law.

In our investigation, we find little evidence that compactness laws have any effect on the decisions made by districting authorities. Using simple regression analysis, we modeled the effects of having a compactness law (using a binary variable) on the actual average compactness scores of districts, using several different compactness measures, including the convex hull, Polsby–Popper, Schwartzberg, and Reock measures. The presence of a state compactness law was not associated with a statistically significant effect on the actual compactness of a map, using any of the four measures, and the compactness law variable did not contribute to the predictive power of the model. Adding an additional variable representing the average district population (log scale) improved the performance model considerably, accounting for about 10–25 percent of the variance in compactness scores. However, the presence of the district population variable in the model did not fundamentally change the effect associated with the compactness law variable.

In short, we find no evidence that compactness laws are effective. They do not appear to reduce bias, and they apparently do not lead to more compact districts, all else equal. This is not entirely surprising, given the uphill battle that voters confront in challenging violations of compactness in court. For districting authorities who would draw irregularly shaped districts to advance some other goal, the threat of courts invalidating a map for violating a compactness mandate is simply noncredible.

9.2.2 Bans on Party Favoritism, Use of Political Data

A number of states have passed laws or constitutional amendments that forbid districting authorities from using political data or from favoring a political party in their maps, or both. In total, twelve states explicitly ban the practice of drawing maps that favor one party over another, and four of these states, along with Arizona, have specific language that bans the use of political data during redistricting.

For example, California's constitution was amended through ballot proposition in 2008 to include a provision that forbids redistricting authorities from drawing districts "for the purpose of favoring or discriminating against an incumbent, political candidate, or political party" (Article XXI, Sec. 2). The Delaware constitution requires that "Each district shall, insofar as is possible ... Not be created so as to unduly favor any person or political party" (Title 29, Ch. 8, Sec. 804).

Are these prohibitions effective at preventing bias? When we compare the average asymmetry (the absolute value of the post-2011 symmetry score) between the states with and without party favoritism bans, we find that the twenty-four maps drawn in states with favoritism bans are substantially less biased than the maps passed in states without similar rules. When we compare the asymmetry between the states with and without bans on the use of political data, we find comparable results. The nine maps enacted in the states with political data bans were less biased than those enacted in states without such bans ($p = 0.055$).

However, many of the states that have adopted bans against political favoritism also delegate redistricting authority to independent commissions, including California, Idaho, Iowa, Montana, and Washington, while Colorado and Hawaii use bipartisan politician commissions. This makes it difficult to discern whether these effects stem from the controlling institution or the rule itself. Of the remaining states with political favoritism bans, the maps in New York and Oregon were drawn by two parties sharing power in the state legislature, while Nebraska's nonpartisan legislature drew its map.

The maps in Florida (drawn by Republicans in the legislature) and in Delaware (drawn by Democrats in the legislature) were the only examples of a map drawn by politicians from one party in a state with a political favoritism ban. Delaware's house map has only a small amount of bias in favor of the Democrats (6.0), while the Senate map has even less bias (–4.6). However, Florida managed to enact House (–25) and Senate (–18) plans with substantial Republican bias, despite the favoritism ban. As we discussed in Chapter 5, the presence of the ban on political favoritism did give challengers ammunition to force changes to the senate map through the threat of litigation, although the final map adopted in 2016 still had considerable Republican bias (–12).

In order to control for the effects of partisanship, we first looked at the difference in the means between the maps passed by the states with political favoritism bans and the states without similar bans. When we limit our sample to maps not drawn by one party, a simple *t*-test suggests there is no meaningful difference between the states with and without a ban. When we limit our sample to just those maps drawn by one party, we similarly find no statistically significant difference in the bias between the groups.

Like the group of states with bans on political favoritism, each of the five states with bans on the use of political data delegate redistricting authority to bipartisan or citizen commissions, so it is not possible to determine whether a ban on the use of political data would have prevented a political body from drawing bias. However, when we compare these five states to those without political data bans that also approved maps drawn by members of both parties or by independent actors, we find no meaningful difference between the two.

In sum, we do not find definitive evidence that bans on political favoritism or the use of partisanship data *actually* prevent districting authorities from drawing biased maps. Once we take political control of redistricting into account, having such a ban codified into state law does not produce outcomes that are measurably different than not having such a ban. However, in the case of Florida, in which a single party – the Republicans – controlled redistricting, it seems clear that the ban on political favoritism gives aggrieved citizens a means of challenging partisan gerrymanders in the state courts, although the threat of judicial action had only a limited impact on reducing bias.

9.2.3 Competitive Elections Laws

A redistricting rule that has gained popularity in recent years is the mandate that redistricting authorities promote competitive elections in the drawing of districting boundaries. In total, four states have similar rules codified in law: Arizona, Colorado, New York, and Washington. For example, in Arizona the competitive elections requirement was adopted when the constitution was amended in 2002 to establish the independent redistricting commission. As Article IV, Section 1, Part 2 states, "To the extent practicable, competitive districts should be favored where to do so would create no significant detriment to the other goals." In Washington, a statute adopted in 1983 states that the redistricting commission "shall exercise its powers to provide fair and effective representation and to encourage electoral competition" (Revised Code of Washington 44.05.090). In New York, the competition law is in the form of a prohibition, which forbids districting authorities from drawing districts "to discourage competition" (New York State Constitution, Art. II, sec. 5).

While this sample is small, we can gain insights into the effectiveness of this requirement by comparing the level of responsiveness in the maps enacted in these states with the rest of the sample. Based on our responsiveness estimates, which measure the average slope of the vote–seat curve between 45 percent and 55 percent, the average level of responsiveness in the eight maps passed in states with competitive elections is 1.85, while the average responsiveness in the maps drawn in states without a competitive election requirement is 2.40.[2] Thus, it appears that states with competitive election mandates actually draw *less* responsive maps.

For a more precise estimate of the effects of a competition mandate, we regressed the responsiveness scores against a binary variable (representing the existence of a "competitive elections" law), along with a variety of control variables, such as the number of districts included in a map (which reduces responsiveness), the responsiveness in the old plan, political control over redistricting, the type of redistricting institution, and the competitiveness of state politics (using our binary variable from Chapter 4). Although these control variables substantially improved the predictive capabilities of the model ($r^2 \approx 0.50$), the competition mandate variable was statistically insignificant and had a negligible impact on the model. At best, our sample is perhaps too small to make definitive conclusions about the effectiveness of competitive elections laws. At worst, these results seem to suggest that competitive elections requirements are simply ineffective at improving the responsiveness of a map to swings in vote support, particularly when modifying language is included in a provision that can be interpreted by districting authorities as giving them leeway to prioritize other redistricting goals above competition.

9.2.4 Other Criteria

We also studied a number of other common rules and requirements. For example, many states have requirements that districting authorities preserve political boundaries, or prohibitions against splitting political

---

[2] A *t*-test suggests that this difference is statistically significant at the $p = 0.05$ level.

communities (e.g., counties and municipalities) between districts. Similarly, a number of states require districting authorities to preserve "communities of interests." It is possible that such requirements make it more difficult for partisan districting authorities to draw bias, insofar as they add layers of complexity to the redistricting process, as well as rules that in principle might be used to challenge a map in the courts. We also considered laws that require transparency in redistricting (see Green 2018); however, these are very common and widespread and we did not find a clear relationship with bias or responsiveness.

We also studied the effects of bans on the favoring of incumbents. Presumably, such a requirement would result in districting authorities drawing a map that is more responsive and less protective of incumbents and thus more responsive to shifts in the two-party vote support. However, this does not appear to be the case, and we found no clear link between such bans and responsiveness or bias.

9.3 PROCEDURAL REFORMS: THE PROMISE OF CITIZEN COMMISSIONS

Thus far, in this chapter, we have focused on rules-based approaches to redistricting reforms. We have found little evidence that adding additional rules and redistricting criteria is an effective way of neutralizing districting bias. Indeed, as we have discussed earlier, because such measures are intended to shape districting *outcomes*, they are necessarily only as effective as their enforcement. As we saw in the last chapter, courts may provide a remedy for the most egregious violations of districting rules; however, unless the courts pose a credible threat, there is little incentive for redistricting authorities to follow the rules.

In contrast, procedural reforms target the institutions and processes of redistricting. Instead of attempting to define districting outcomes, procedural reforms seek to change who is in charge, as well as the design and operation of redistricting institutions. Today, so-called "independent" redistricting commissions are the most popular procedural reform proposals. Indeed, during the 2018 midterm elections, four states – Colorado, Missouri, Michigan, and Utah – approved procedural redistricting reforms that delegate control of redistricting in 2021 to a commission.

In our investigation of the outcomes of 2011 redistricting, we identify a wide variation in the design of redistricting commissions. Broadly speaking, redistricting commissions are simply bodies that are granted legal control of redistricting that function independently of a state legislature (although in some cases a legislature might be given the opportunity to veto or revise a plan with a supermajority vote). We recognize two classes of commissions: politician commissions and citizen commissions. As we note in Chapter 3, politician commissions are those which are staffed by politicians, aligned with a major political party. In some cases, politician commissions are effectively controlled by members of one party. This was the case in Ohio, Arkansas, and Maryland, which staff their state legislative redistricting commissions with popularly elected, executive branch officials. In other cases, politician commissions are staffed by members of both parties and have rules that require cooperation or balance between the two parties. We refer to these types of commissions as bipartisan politician commissions.

The second class of commissions are those we refer to as "citizen commissions." The critical distinction is that these commissions bar elected officials, politicians, and lobbyists from their membership. While citizen commissions included in our analysis vary in their processes for appointing commissioners, the majority of states with citizen commissions delegate the task of appointing commissioners to the majority and minority party leaders in both branches of the legislature. By contrast, Arizona and California use a complex set of processes to staff their commissions that is designed to ensure independence from the political party leadership, while Alaska assigns the task of appointing commissioners to the heads of all three branches of state government, who are barred from considering prospective commissioners' political affiliation.

There is also the unusual case of Iowa, which delegates redistricting authority to a nonpartisan government agency, which in turn commissions a five-member advisory board to draw the maps. Four of the five members of the commission, the Temporary Redistricting Advisory Commission, are selected by the party leaders in the legislature, who then select a fifth member to serve as chairperson.[3] Because members of the advisory commission are limited to citizens without ties to political parties or elected officials, we classify the Iowa model as a citizen commission.

Given our findings in this book, we expect that citizen commissions are effective insofar as they prevent politicians from dictating districting outcomes. Indeed, our findings thus far underscore the central role of

---

[3] www.ncsl.org/research/redistricting/the-iowa-model-for-redistricting.aspx

politics in districting bias. We can summarize our findings rather simply: we see the most bias when politicians have drawn the maps. Therefore, we expect that keeping politicians out of a commission will lead to plans that are systematically less biased. Is this in fact the case?

In our sample, there are sixteen maps drawn by citizen commissions acting in seven states. In Alaska, as we discuss in the previous chapter, the Redistricting Board approved three sets of plans – the first was rejected by a state court and never used; the second was used in the 2012 election cycle as an interim plan; and a third and final plan used in elections after 2012. Given the unique circumstances of the redistricting process, we use the average of the symmetry scores of the second and third set of plans in our analysis.

When we compare the average asymmetry in these maps with the average asymmetry in the remaining maps, we see less bias. The maps drawn by citizen commissions averaged about 7.5 percent bias, in contrast to the maps drawn by other bodies, which averaged about 11.5 percent, a difference which is statistically significant ($p = 0.05$). Notwithstanding, this is a relatively small n; without more data, we cannot make definitive claims about the effectiveness of citizen commissions. However, when we broaden our subset to include maps drawn by courts, this raises the number of maps in our sample from twelve to twenty. This group, which we shall call "non-political bodies," produced maps that are substantially less biased than the rest of the maps. The maps drawn by nonpolitical bodies average about 6.9 percent bias, compared to 12.1 percent ($p < 0.01$).

As an alternative way of modeling the effects of "nonpolitical" redistricting, we regressed the post-2011 bias estimates (using the absolute value of symmetry) against the pre-2011 bias estimates (using the absolute value of symmetry), along with a binary variable signifying nonpolitical districting. The model estimates that having a nonpolitical body (i.e., a court or citizen commission) draw the maps leads to a reduction in asymmetry of about 4 percent. We find similar results when we use our simple measure of bias, discussed in Chapter 2, which measures the difference in the number of districts that advantage Democrats and the number of districts that advantage Republicans. As an alternative approach to estimating the effect of nonpolitical districting, we also modeled the effects of one-party control in place of the nonpolitical variable. This model's performance improves by about 1 percent. The model estimates that one-party control over redistricting leads to an increase in bias of about 4 percent.

TABLE 9.1. *Citizen commissions, state legislative redistricting, 2011*

State/Name of Commission	Size	Appointment Process	Membership Criteria/ Restrictions
Alaska/ Redistricting Board (Art. 6, sec. 8)	5	To be made "without regard to political affiliation." Governor appoints two presiding officers of House and Senate appoints one each; Chief Justice of Supreme Court appoints one	No public officials or public employees
Arizona/ Independent Redistricting Commission (Art. 4, pt. 2, sec. 1)	5	Must include no more than two members from one political party. Members nominated by the state commission on appellate court appointees; can delegate task of nominations to the redistricting commission	Registered voters only; no elected officials, lobbyists, candidates, party leaders, or campaign officers (previous three years)
California/Citizens Redistricting Commission (Article XXI)	14	Five members from each of two largest parties; four unaffiliated members; members apply; sixty are chosen by State Auditor, after which legislative leaders can veto applicants. First eight members chosen by lottery; eight members subsequently choose remaining six	Registered voters only; members barred from elected office (for ten years), public office and lobbying (for five years); bars those who have in ten years prior been a candidate for office, an officer/employee/ consultant of campaign or party, lobbyist, or have given $2000 to a campaign
Idaho/Citizen Commission for Reapportionment (Idaho Statutes §72-1502)	6	Party leaders in each house pick one member each; chairs of two largest parties pick one each	No appointed or elected officials permitted to serve

State/Name of Commission	Size	Appointment Process	Membership Criteria/ Restrictions
Iowa/Temporary Redistricting Advisory Commission (Iowa Code §42.5)	5	Four members selected by legislative leaders in General Assembly; four members elect a fifth to chair	Must be eligible voters; no political public officeholders or party officeholders; no employees of or relatives of members of General Assembly or US Congress
Montana/ Apportionment Commission (Art. 5, sec. 14)	5	Four members selected by legislative majority and minority leaders; four members elect a fifth to chair	No public officials permitted; barred from running for office for two years
Washington (Art. II, sec. 43)	5	Four members selected by legislative majority and minority leaders; four members elect a fifth to chair	No elected officials, political party officers in two years prior

This evidence suggests that citizen commissions can be an effective way to prevent partisan bias. Transitioning from legislative redistricting to citizen redistricting leads to a measurable reduction in bias. Although citizen commissions vary widely in terms of their design and composition, our findings suggest that many types of procedural reforms are likely to reduce districting bias, provided that reforms prevent politicians from one party from dominating redistricting decisions.

For another window into the links between institutional control and outcomes, we plotted the change in symmetry and responsiveness estimates for maps drawn by citizen commissions, bipartisan politician commissions, and courts. As Figure 9.1a suggests, the citizen commissions tend to reduce bias in revised maps. Although there are one or two outliers (Washington's senate map, for example, increased in bias after redistricting) the bulk of the maps became less biased after redistricting. What is more, the trend line deviates substantially from the dashed line (which signifies no change in outcomes), which suggests that citizen commissions were willing to deviate from the status quo in order to achieve their objectives. Notwithstanding, citizen commissions appear to

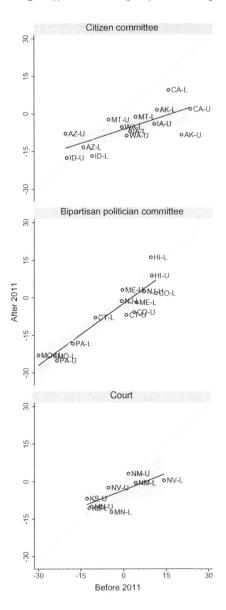

FIGURE 9.1(A). Bias when courts and commissions redistrict

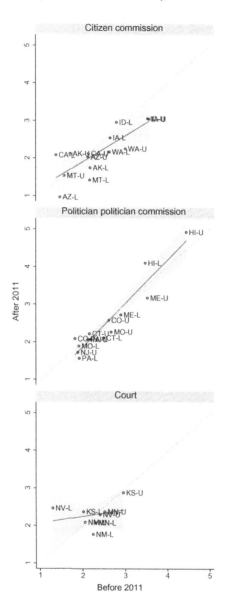

FIGURE 9.1(B). Responsiveness when courts and commissions redistrict

mirror the level of responsiveness in previous plans, which is consistent with findings by Henderson, Hamel, and Goldzimer (2018).

By contrast, the maps drawn by bipartisan politician commissions appear to trend closely to the dashed line in both the bias and responsiveness graphs. As we discuss in Chapter 3, this is not unexpected. In order to reach an agreement, two parties will often agree to preserve the status quo in terms of bias. For example, in Missouri the maps were already biased in favor of the Republicans before redistricting. Because Republicans and Democrats shared power, the politician commission adopted a plan that more or less preserved this preexisting bias. Yet, as Figure 9.1b indicates, the plan ended up reducing the level of seat–vote responsiveness, overall.

9.3.1 Fair Division

In recent years, many have proposed a different type of procedural reform that would give both parties an opportunity to draw districts, by allowing each party to gerrymander part of a state (e.g., Brams 2020; Gaddie 2019; Landau, Reid, and Yershov 2009; Landau and Su 2010; Pegden, Procaccia, and Yu 2017; Scheiber 2013; Sherstyuk 1998; Tucker-Foltz 2018). This process, which is often called "fair division," is based upon the Brams–Taylor procedure for the problem of "envy-free cake-cutting." Brams has applied this solution to the problem of fair districting of electoral districts. The process goes something like this: First, the larger of the two parties would get to draw a line dividing the state into two parts, with population size proportional to the two-party vote divide. The larger party would get to draw districts for the larger piece of the state, while the smaller party would draw districts for the smaller part of the state. In this way, neither of the parties would get to dominate redistricting, and both parties would get an opportunity to draw their own bias. The expected outcome is that for both parties the seat shares would be roughly proportionate to their vote shares.

One of the appeals of this process, according to Brams (2020), is that fair division would be more politically viable to implement than, say, independent redistricting, which is often resisted by parties in charge because it gives each party some power.

The evidence we have presented here would suggest that transferring control of districting from a legislature to a fair division process is unlikely to lead to *more* biased outcomes. Indeed, as we have argued, the most effective reforms are those that prevent one party from monopolizing redistricting. Because fair division would allow both parties to share control of redistricting, we would expect less bias in districting outcomes, although one might argue that it would not ensure a "fair" process if voters and third parties are left on the sidelines.

While fair division might be less *unfair* than one-party districting, it is not clear that it is a viable political alternative to independent redistricting. For example, if a controlling party resists reforms to establish independent redistricting, they are not likely to agree to establish a "fair division" process that guarantees the other party an opportunity to expand its seat share.

As we have seen in this book and in this chapter, parties often resist changes to redistricting. Procedural reforms to redistricting have occurred almost exclusively in states with direct democracy – often Western states, like California and Utah. By comparison, in many other states, it is comparably more difficult to amend the state constitution. In Virginia, this requires a three-step process: approval of a joint resolution by the legislature in two separate general assemblies, then approval by voters through ballot referendum. In Virginia, the first two conditions (approval by the General Assembly in two sessions) were achieved because of unique political circumstances. Republicans, who held a majority, were confronted with the real possibility of losing power in the 2019 elections, which would have given 2021 redistricting to Democrats. They supported the reforms as a hedge against steep losses. Democrats supported the measure when the first reading was up for a vote, but in 2020, after they won control, they opposed it. The measure only passed a second General Assembly because a handful of Democratic delegates joined the Republicans to advance the measure. Thus, these unique conditions created the right incentives to advance reforms. However, such opportunities are rare. And when they do come along, it stands to reason that reformers should pursue the most effective and most popularly appealing reforms, such as independent citizen districting, with broad public support.

9.4 CONCLUSION

In this chapter, we have evaluated redistricting reform options that are used and being considered in several states. We consider two types of redistricting reforms: rules-based reforms and procedural reforms. Rules reforms attempt to proscribe undesirable districting outcomes (such as noncompactness) or mandate certain desirable outcomes (such as community preservation, for example). Rules reforms are appealing, because they are less objectionable to those empowered to redistrict. They do not fundamentally reform the redistricting process or change the balance of power. Yet, as our investigation suggests, they do not appear to be effective buffers against partisan gerrymandering. Because rules must be enforced by the courts, they are only effective at preventing partisan bias when a court is willing to assert itself and aggressively enforce criteria. As we saw in the previous chapter, this happened in Alaska, where court action rolled back severe Republican bias. But this is not common, and judges tend to be incrementalists. Due to the nature of the courts, political redistricting authorities have little to fear from simply disregarding or violating redistricting rules. For these reasons, rules-based reforms are unlikely to succeed without broader procedural reforms.

On the other hand, we see much promise in comprehensive procedural reforms. As we saw in Chapter 3, extreme partisan bias in districting occurs almost exclusively when one party monopolizes the redistricting process. And, as we found in this chapter, maps drawn by nonpolitical actors have on average less bias than maps drawn by political actors. Accordingly, reforms that transfer redistricting authority from a political body (e.g., a legislature or politician commission) to nonpolitical actors, such as citizen commissions or courts, are likely to lead to substantial reductions in partisan bias. In addition, given our analysis in Chapter 5 of the transition to single-member districting, it follows that the adoption of proportional, multimember districting plans would limit partisan bias in the translation of votes into seats.

Conclusion

In this book, we investigated redistricting in the states to understand what happened in the state legislatures after 2011 redistricting and to understand why. We have found that several dozen legislative bodies were drawn with severe bias, and that this bias overwhelmingly favors the Republican Party. The Republicans' advantage in state government is so extreme that the average state legislative plan gives Republicans about 9 percent more seats than Democrats for a similar share of the vote. In many cases, Democrats have to win by a 10 percent vote margin in order to get a majority in the legislature. This is the case in Virginia in 2017 House of Delegates, as well as in North Carolina in the 2018 state house and senate elections, and in Wisconsin in the 2016 State Senate elections and in the 2018 State Assembly elections. In each of these cases, Democrats won vote majorities but were denied a majority of seats, and it could happen in many other maps drawn with extreme levels of bias.

One of our objectives in this book was to understand the causes of these outcomes by identifying their political, demographic, geographic, and institutional determinants. Why do we see gerrymandering where we do? There are two answers: a simple answer and a more complex answer. The simple answer is politics. When one party controls redistricting and can draw the maps by itself, they often draw extreme bias into the maps. This is particularly true in competitive states where both parties stand a reasonable chance at winning control in the future. This gives political parties drawing the maps an incentive to use this power to keep the other party out.

However, there is also a more complex answer. While Democrats and Republicans are both guilty of using political control of redistricting to give themselves an electoral advantage, redistricting bias almost always favors the Republicans. The Republicans controlled most state legislatures during 2011 redistricting, and they approved more than forty maps with extreme bias. The Democrats approved only two maps with extreme bias.

That Republicans have been able to draw extreme gerrymanders, while Democrats have not, is partly because Republicans did very well in the 2010 state-level elections and therefore controlled a greater number of states during redistricting, but it is also because they were willing to exploit political and racial geographies of their states to maximize a trade-off between extreme partisan bias and incumbent safety. Because Democratic voters tend to live in cities, and because African-American and Latinx voters often vote Democratic, Republican mapmakers are able to create efficient gerrymanders by drawing relatively compact districts around urban areas and minority communities. And because these areas are often densely populated, they can often achieve these gerrymanders without having to draw irregularly shaped district lines. In this way, Republicans can get away with gerrymandering while complying with compactness laws and the Voting Rights Act.

By contrast, these geographies hurt Democrats. When Democrats are in charge, they often resort to irregularly shaped district lines in order to pass maps that neutralize these geographic biases. We see far fewer extreme Democratic gerrymanders because it is very difficult for states with large urban areas, like Illinois, to "waste" Republican votes in order to create a seat advantage.

Our study of geography and redistricting bias underscores the interconnectedness of racial and partisan gerrymandering. While the federal courts have treated both issues distinctly, from the perspective of a Republican gerrymanderer, they are two sides of the same coin. In the South, where much of the electorate is geographically segregated by race, race is a simple proxy for partisanship. In addition, the Voting Rights Act and its amendments require state governments to draw district lines in a way that allows minority communities to elect representatives of their choice. This means that Republican gerrymanderers simply draw minority communities into Democratic safe seats that have the effect of wasting Democratic votes. As we saw, this occurred in Virginia, as well as in Alabama, North Carolina, and Texas, and likely in many other states.

The harm of these schemes is not simply that they deny Democrats seats, but that they prevent historically disenfranchised groups from electing candidates of their choosing, leading to distrust and cynicism.

Fortunately, in four of these cases, the federal courts invalidated the Republican maps and installed remedial maps. But these actions did not remedy the harm. In Virginia, it took eight years and four elections before the court installed a new map; in North Carolina, it took seven years and three elections. These delays meant that Black and Latinx voters were denied representation. In many other states, the courts have not provided a remedy.

Our investigation of the political and geographic determinants of bias tell a story about a political party willing to disregard norms and undermine rights in order to gain a partisan advantage. Another part of this story is what the Republicans ultimately did with their power. We studied the laws enacted by gerrymandered state legislatures and found that Republican gerrymandered legislatures approved restrictions to voting rights, divested in public health, and took fewer measures during the COVID-19 pandemic than other Republican-controlled legislatures.

But widespread partisan gerrymandering of state legislatures presents constitutional concerns, as well. As we argued in Chapter 7, the partisan gerrymandering of state legislatures presents unique threats to democracy in the United States and ultimately harms all citizens by denying the right to political equality in elections. In many states, the partisan composition of the US Congress is effectively determined by state legislative elections that occur once a decade, before redistricting. This arrangement means that state governments have expanded their reach into national affairs in ways that undermine the design of the House of Representatives to be responsive to public opinion and unsettle the balance of power between state and federal governments that has been settled for many decades.

Given then the harms of political districting, what solutions do citizens have? The courts have stepped in, although they are not well equipped to stop bias because judicial actors are often reluctant to insert themselves into political matters, or stray too far from incremental change. And when the courts weigh in on districting, it is often to settle a particular issue, and changes to the maps are minimal and narrowly tailored. However, the courts do not appear to show favoritism or protect partisan interests in their decisions, and some cases show that the courts can be aggressive at enforcing constitutional requirements. This happened in Alaska, when the supreme court rejected the first two sets of maps drafted by the Redistricting Board for procedural violations to the state constitution.

At best, the courts are a partial and limited solution to the problems posed by political districting. By contrast, we find that reforms can be very effective, but not all reforms are created equal. Our analysis of redistricting criteria commonly used by the states, such as compactness and community preservation rules, alone do not effectively prevent bias. In the case of compactness laws, redistricting authorities apparently ignore laws that require districts to be drawn in compact shapes and there are no clear standards for identifying violations. Similarly, it is not clear that "competitive elections" laws systematically improve the two-party competition in a state, beyond a few examples. And while bans on political and personal favoritism have an obvious appeal as a means of fighting partisan gerrymandering in the courts (and for their symbolism, rather than substance), it is unclear whether the courts are up for the task.

Because rules-based reforms do not address the processes or institutions tasked with redistricting, they are inherently reliant upon the judiciary for enforcement. Indeed, the threat of a court intervening and forcing a revision to a district plan must be credible. Instead, we find that procedural reforms – those that change who is in charge – are more promising. The lessons from our investigation suggest that partisan bias occurs when districting is political, particularly when one party controls redistricting and is motivated to draw bias. This implies that reforms that insulate redistricting from the influence of politicians are more likely to succeed at reducing bias. For example, we expect that transferring districting control from a political body to an independent body will be most effective, particularly when laws require transparency and bar political favoritism. As well, shifting to multimember districting and proportional representation is likely to prevent political actors from drawing bias into the maps, provided such measures do not undermine minority representation (for example, by giving voters in multimember districts the option of casting more than one vote).

EVALUATING REFORMS IN VIRGINIA

Throughout this book we returned to the example of Virginia, where Republicans gerrymandered the state house plan and denied Democrats a majority until 2019, when the federal courts invalidated several districts for illegal racial vote dilution. After years of litigation, public support for redistricting reform swelled, and lawmakers agreed to advance a constitutional amendment to transfer control to a semi-independent redistricting commission.

However, after the court installed new house maps, the Democrats won back power and opposed the reforms, raising several concerns about the commission design and the role of the courts in the process. Is there any merit to these critiques? Our findings provide some insight. First, during 2011 redistricting, no other state used a model that resembles the commission adopted in Virginia, which is staffed by eight politicians (four from each party) and eight citizens (nominated by the parties and selected by judges). However, several states used bipartisan politician commissions and citizen commissions. Most of these commissions approved maps without extreme bias. Citizen commissions and courts were associated with the lowest levels of bias. Bipartisan commissions tended to produce outcomes that mirrored the bias in the previous maps. In many cases, this resulted in unbiased plans, but in a few cases, bipartisan politician commissions preserved maps with extreme bias. Nevertheless, both models are an improvement above districting by partisans, and our findings suggest that the Virginia model is unlikely to produce the level of bias we observed in the 2011 map.

Another objection raised by opponents of the Virginia reforms was that they gave the courts too much power. In the case of a deadlocked commission, redistricting control shifts to the Supreme Court of Virginia, which currently has more judges appointed by Republicans than Democrats. Would the court approve a Republican gerrymander? It is unlikely. As we show in Chapter 3, it is relatively common for states to give the courts automatic judicial review or "back-up" authority of redistricting – we saw this happen several times during 2011. When the courts did draw the maps, they most often approved maps without extreme bias, but on a few occasions they drew plans with extreme bias. This happened in Minnesota, where a panel of judges drew a map that gave Republicans a considerable advantage. However, most of the judges on the panel were appointed by Democratic governors, and we found no evidence in any of the cases that judges protect the interests of political parties.

Ultimately, the reforms in Virginia are likely to succeed in preventing extreme bias, but they show that reformers should expect to face opposition from politicians who stand to lose power. We hope that this book will help them challenge the spread of disinformation about redistricting reforms and will inform the debate over fairness in districting.

Appendix

A.1. *State House Symmetry 2012*[*]

State	Asymmetry %	sd	5% bound	95% bound	"Simple Symmetry" %[**]
Alaska	0.503	4	−6.41	7.09	−2.5
Arizona	−8.46	3.13	−13.8	−3.21	−6.67
Arkansas	−8.61	2.67	−12.9	−4.08	−6
California	5.64	3.26	0.184	10.9	5
Colorado	−0.195	3.44	−5.86	5.52	−3.08
Connecticut	−4.33	2.13	−7.84	−0.991	−5.3
Delaware	−2.55	4.48	−10	4.58	−4.88
Florida	−17.6	2.69	−22.3	−13.2	−14.2
Georgia	−21.1	1.76	−24	−18.3	−22.2
Hawaii	14.3	4.68	6.44	21.7	3.92
Idaho	−15.8	3.97	−21.9	−9.06	−8.57
Illinois	−2.34	2.26	−6.04	1.41	−5.08
Indiana	−18.3	2.83	−23.3	−13.8	−18
Iowa	−7.29	2.87	−12.1	−2.46	−3
Kansas	−12.9	2.39	−16.7	−9	−16
Kentucky	−7.51	3.02	−12.4	−2.49	−8
Louisiana	−21.8	2.19	−25.3	−18.4	−23.8
Maine	−2.33	2.42	−6.27	1.59	−5.3
Maryland	3.42	1.84	0.507	6.46	4.96
Massachusetts	−4.88	2.39	−8.92	−1.01	−2.5
Michigan	−15.7	2.1	−19.3	−12.4	−15.5
Minnesota	−12.7	2.56	−17	−8.55	−14.2
Missouri	−22.6	2.22	−26.1	−19.1	−25.2
Montana	−1.01	2.57	−5.14	3.23	−1

(*continued*)

Appendix

A.1. *(continued)*

State	Asymmetry %	sd	5% bound	95% bound	"Simple Symmetry" %**
Nevada	−2.08	4.44	−9.21	5.1	−2.38
New Hampshire	−0.0875	1.87	−3.06	3.02	−0.5
New Jersey	−4.89	3.14	−10.2	0.146	−10
New Mexico	−1.53	2.98	−6.08	3.34	2.86
New York	−3.1	2.27	−6.84	0.6	−0.667
North Carolina	−20.6	2.37	−24.5	−16.7	−20
North Dakota	−3.87	3.11	−9.02	1.23	−10.6
Ohio	−18	2.5	−22.1	−13.8	−19.2
Oklahoma	−17.3	2.89	−21.9	−12.5	−17.8
Oregon	−3.52	3.81	−9.65	2.38	−5
Pennsylvania	NA	NA	NA	NA	NA
Rhode Island	−7.6	3.42	−13.1	−1.78	−9.33
South Carolina	−18.2	2.3	−22	−14.3	−19.4
South Dakota	−0.875	3.55	−6.65	5.11	4.29
Tennessee	−28.3	2.42	−32	−24.2	−28.3
Texas	−14.8	1.95	−18.1	−11.6	−13.3
Utah	−16.9	3.25	−22	−11.9	−9.33
Vermont	1.86	2.76	−2.72	6.41	4
Virginia	−13.1	3.16	−18.3	−7.72	−10
Washington	−4.45	2.88	−9.33	−0.0405	−4.08
West Virginia	−1.67	2.73	−6.09	2.86	−7
Wisconsin	−16.6	2.64	−20.8	−12.4	−14.1
Wyoming	−10.7	3.7	−17	−4.68	−16.7

* Data is from 2012 except: Kentucky, Maine, Maryland, Minnesota, Montana (2014); Louisiana (2011); New Jersey (2011–15); North Dakota (2012, 2014).
** The asymmetry measure is calculated from the seats–votes function, while the "simple symmetry" measure is calculated directly from the vote distribution (see Chapter 2). Negative scores represent bias toward the Republican Party.

A.2. *State House Symmetry 2016**

State	Asymmetry %	sd	5% bound	95% bound	"Simple Symmetry" %
Alaska	2.72	3.99	−4.2	9.23	5
Arizona	−18.3	1.43	−20	−15.6	−20
Arkansas	NA	NA	NA	NA	NA
California	13.4	3.15	7.76	18.3	8.75
Colorado	3.7	3.49	−2.4	9.22	0
Connecticut	−11.5	2.32	−15.3	−7.45	−11.3
Delaware	14.1	4.14	7.21	20.8	14.6

State	Asymmetry %	sd	5% bound	95% bound	"Simple Symmetry" %
Florida	NA	NA	NA	NA	NA
Georgia	-14.7	1.74	-17.4	-11.8	-15.6
Hawaii	17.9	4.34	10.7	25.1	13.7
Idaho	-17.9	3.54	-23.6	-12.3	-21.4
Illinois	NA	NA	NA	NA	NA
Indiana	NA	NA	NA	NA	NA
Iowa	-6.67	2.75	-11.2	-2.26	-4
Kansas	-8.47	2.52	-12.7	-4.49	-8
Kentucky	-1.13	2.87	-5.97	3.49	2
Louisiana	-25.6	2.03	-28.8	-22	-26.7
Maine	-1.5	2.5	-5.54	2.61	-3.31
Maryland	11.5	1.78	8.58	14.6	9.93
Massachusetts	-1.25	2.49	-5.46	2.63	1.25
Michigan	-14.6	2.29	-18.5	-10.8	-16.4
Minnesota	-11.7	2.28	-15.3	-7.93	-11.9
Missouri	-24.1	1.93	-27.2	-20.8	-25.8
Montana	-1.34	2.18	-4.88	2.22	-1
Nevada	3.03	4.45	-4.31	10.2	2.38
New Hampshire	-4.07	1.73	-6.97	-1.32	-3.75
New Jersey	2.26	2.92	-2.5	6.87	0
New Mexico	0.465	3.06	-4.44	5.54	2.86
New York	-1.05	2.25	-4.72	2.62	-1.33
North Carolina	-15.5	2.52	-19.7	-11.1	-14.2
North Dakota	NA	NA	NA	NA	-2.13
Ohio	-25.8	2.45	-30	-21.8	-25.3
Oklahoma	-16.1	2.86	-21	-11.7	-17.8
Oregon	-1.37	3.76	-7.62	4.84	-3.33
Pennsylvania	-18.3	1.69	-21.1	-15.6	-18.2
Rhode Island	-12.4	3.5	-18.1	-6.86	-12
South Carolina	-19.2	2.73	-23.7	-14.6	-20.2
South Dakota	-6.76	3.69	-12.6	-0.851	1.43
Tennessee	-31	2.41	-34.8	-26.9	-32.3
Texas	-12.2	2.08	-15.5	-8.7	-11.3
Utah	-15.7	3.25	-21	-10.5	-14.7
Vermont	-6.34	2.5	-10.4	-2.3	-7.33
Virginia	-10.8	2.79	-15.3	-6.27	-10
Washington	-6.05	2.8	-10.7	-1.5	-8.16
West Virginia	-0.256	3.18	-5.6	5	-5
Wisconsin	-21.9	2.67	-26.2	-17.6	-24.2
Wyoming	-12.7	3.54	-18.5	-6.82	-15

* Data is from 2016 except: Louisiana, Virginia (2015); Maryland (2018); North Dakota (2014, 2016); Pennsylvania (2014–16).

A.3. *State Senate Symmetry 2012–14*[*]

State	Asymmetry %	sd	5% bound	95% bound	"Simple Symmetry" %
Alaska	-15.9	5.54	-25	-6.61	-15
Arizona	-8.06	4.74	-15.9	-0.278	-3.33
Arkansas	-5.36	5.42	-14.1	3.34	-8.57
California	0.602	4.38	-6.68	7.68	0
Colorado	-3.09	4.98	-11.1	4.85	-5.71
Connecticut	-4.01	4.67	-11.9	3.6	-5.56
Delaware	-1.23	6.78	-12.5	9.97	-9.52
Florida	-18.1	4.4	-24.9	-10.7	-17.5
Georgia	-27.4	2.76	-31.8	-22.8	-30.4
Hawaii	15.9	6.83	4.69	27.1	16
Idaho	-14.6	5.46	-23.1	-5.55	-5.71
Illinois	-2.5	3.63	-8.63	3.29	0
Indiana	-21.6	4.32	-28.5	-14.5	-22
Iowa	-2.45	4.49	-9.63	4.97	-4
Kansas	-10.9	4.34	-17.8	-3.44	-5
Kentucky	NA	NA	NA	NA	NA
Louisiana	-20.5	4.3	-27.4	-13.4	-25.6
Maine	0.257	5.52	-9.03	8.96	0
Maryland	7.71	3.62	1.73	13.9	6.38
Massachusetts	-3.97	4.96	-12	3.98	-2.5
Michigan	-30.3	3.75	-36.2	-24.1	-28.9
Minnesota	-13.1	3.52	-19.1	-7.32	-8.96
Missouri	-23.2	5.28	-31.9	-14.8	-26.5
Montana	-2.29	3.33	-7.99	3.07	-4
Nebraska	-12.5	4.34	-19.4	-5.55	-16.3
Nevada	-2.29	6.17	-11.9	7.98	4.76
New Hampshire	-5.33	6.36	-15.5	5.29	0
New Jersey	-0.529	4.04	-6.7	6.3	2.5
New Mexico	3.27	4.2	-3.59	10.2	7.14
New York	-12.6	2.69	-16.8	-8.06	-12.7
North Carolina	-22.6	3.58	-28	-16.5	-22
North Dakota	-2.71	4.31	-9.49	4.13	-6.38
Ohio	-27.8	4.77	-35.4	-19.9	-30.3
Oklahoma	-22.4	4.43	-29.3	-15.2	-27.1
Oregon	-1.54	5.59	-11	7.55	3.33
Pennsylvania	NA	NA	NA	NA	NA
Rhode Island	-7.8	5.03	-16	0.559	-10.5
South Carolina	-18.6	3.73	-24.5	-12.1	-19.6
South Dakota	-8.16	4.81	-15.9	-0.328	-2.86

State	Asymmetry %	sd	5% bound	95% bound	"Simple Symmetry" %
Tennessee	−30.6	5.08	−38.7	−22.2	−36.4
Texas	−18.7	3.52	−24	−12.7	−19.4
Utah	−15.7	4.79	−23.5	−8	−20.7
Vermont	6.8	7.97	−6.61	19.6	−6.67
Virginia	2	4.63	−5.34	9.81	−2.5
Washington	−6.12	3.85	−12.6	0.316	−10.2
West Virginia	−8.28	5.16	−16.3	0.643	−17.6
Wisconsin	−18.2	4.99	−26.3	−10	−21.2
Wyoming	−12.3	5.73	−21.9	−3.01	−26.7

* Data from 2012–14 except: Alaska, Arizona, Arkansas, Connecticut, Delaware, Florida, Georgia, Hawaii, Idaho, Illinois, Kansas, Kentucky, Maine, Massachusetts, Minnesota, New Hampshire, New Mexico, New York, North Carolina, Rhode Island, South Carolina, South Dakota, Texas, Vermont, West Virginia (2012); Louisiana, New Jersey, Virginia (2011); Maine, Maryland, Michigan (2014); Montana(2014–16). In states with staggered Senate elections, the results have been adjusted using the statewide swing in state House results (see Chapter 2). Note that Alaska, Delaware, Hawaii, and Illinois have staggered Senate elections, but elect the entire Senate in years following redistricting.

A.4. *State Senate Symmetry 2014–16**

State	Asymmetry %	sd	5% bound	95% bound	"Simple Symmetry" %
Alaska	−0.802	7.09	−12.8	10.8	−5
Arizona	−7.68	4.68	−15.5	0.104	−10
Arkansas	NA	NA	NA	NA	NA
California	3.3	4.6	−4.39	10.8	5
Colorado	−8.48	5.19	−17	0.106	−8.57
Connecticut	−9.78	4.77	−17.7	−2.13	−11.1
Delaware	−7.07	6.76	−17.9	4.35	−4.76
Florida	NA	NA	NA	NA	NA
Georgia	−23.5	2.94	−28	−18.4	−23.2
Hawaii	1.75	6.46	−9.17	12.4	−12
Idaho	−20.6	5.01	−28.6	−12	−25.7
Illinois	NA	NA	NA	NA	NA
Indiana	NA	NA	NA	NA	NA
Iowa	−5.54	4.05	−12.2	1.15	−6
Kansas	−2.79	4.74	−10.6	5.12	−5
Kentucky	−27.9	4.83	−35.7	−20.3	−18.4
Louisiana	−24.3	3.74	−30.2	−17.9	−23.1
Maine	5.87	5.12	−2.53	14.2	5.71

(continued)

A.4. *(continued)*

State	Asymmetry %	sd	5% bound	95% bound	"Simple Symmetry" %
Maryland	9.72	3.41	4.29	15.4	8.51
Massachusetts	-3.06	5.06	-11.7	4.98	-2.5
Michigan	-21.9	4.1	-28.2	-15	-18.4
Minnesota	-7.15	3.49	-12.8	-1.39	-13.4
Missouri	-22.9	4.46	-30.3	-15.6	-20.6
Montana	-2.28	3.3	-7.89	2.75	-4
Nebraska	-7.64	3.91	-13.9	-1.3	-6.12
Nevada	-2.58	5.95	-12	7.35	4.76
New Hampshire	-4.38	6.17	-14.4	5.8	0
New Jersey	5.46	4.11	-1.29	12.3	7.5
New Mexico	3.02	4.38	-3.99	10.6	9.52
New York	-10.7	2.64	-15.3	-6.32	-9.52
North Carolina	-25	3.78	-31	-18.5	-24
North Dakota	-1.39	4.48	-8.73	6.2	0
Ohio	-26.5	4.69	-33.9	-18.7	-30.3
Oklahoma	-6.71	4.49	-14	0.923	-8.33
Oregon	-1.46	5.46	-10.6	7.55	3.33
Pennsylvania	-25.1	4.01	-31.9	-18.3	-32
Rhode Island	-17.1	4.8	-24.8	-9	-18.4
South Carolina	-11.4	4.73	-19.2	-3.57	-8.7
South Dakota	-3.36	5.38	-12.4	5.54	0
Tennessee	-37.1	4.66	-44.8	-29.8	-39.4
Texas	-16.8	3.97	-22.8	-9.99	-19.4
Utah	-16	5.44	-24.6	-7.11	-10.3
Vermont	13.7	7.64	0.771	25.9	0
Virginia	3.01	3.73	-3.19	8.97	2.5
Washington	-11.2	3.92	-17.5	-4.8	-14.3
West Virginia	0.917	5.65	-8.67	9.63	0
Wisconsin	-21.9	5.4	-30.8	-12.9	-24.2
Wyoming	-11.1	5.94	-21.1	-1.12	-10

* Data from 2014–16 except: Arizona, Connecticut, Georgia, Idaho, Kansas, Massachusetts, Minnesota, New Hampshire, New Mexico, New York, North Carolina, Rhode Island, South Carolina, South Dakota, Vermont, West Virginia (2016); Louisiana, Virginia (2015); Maine(2014); Maryland, Michigan (2018); New Jersey (2013). In states with staggered Senate elections, the results have been adjusted using the statewide swing in state House results (see Chapter 2).

A.5. *State House Responsiveness 2012 (see A.1 for details)*

State	Responsiveness	sd	5% bound	95% bound
Arizona	1.58	0.331	1.04	2.13
Arkansas	1.98	0.301	1.47	2.47
California	2.2	0.334	1.65	2.75
Colorado	2.14	0.383	1.54	2.77
Connecticut	2.05	0.232	1.67	2.41
Delaware	2.17	0.466	1.42	2.93
Florida	2.7	0.288	2.24	3.19
Georgia	1.31	0.173	1.01	1.59
Hawaii	4.08	0.55	3.18	4.95
Idaho	3.08	0.392	2.4	3.71
Illinois	1.6	0.24	1.23	1.99
Indiana	2.47	0.305	1.97	2.96
Iowa	2.85	0.352	2.28	3.44
Kansas	2.37	0.28	1.92	2.84
Kentucky	3.15	0.355	2.54	3.71
Louisiana	1.18	0.222	0.826	1.56
Maine	2.83	0.269	2.41	3.29
Maryland	1.13	0.182	0.829	1.42
Massachusetts	2.76	0.261	2.34	3.19
Michigan	1.23	0.243	0.825	1.62
Minnesota	2.33	0.263	1.88	2.72
Missouri	2.1	0.237	1.72	2.49
Montana	1.54	0.265	1.11	1.97
Nevada	2.4	0.479	1.64	3.2
New Hampshire	3.31	0.176	3.03	3.61
New Jersey	2.19	0.306	1.69	2.69
New Mexico	1.77	0.329	1.24	2.33
New York	1.8	0.204	1.44	2.13
North Carolina	1.97	0.26	1.55	2.39
North Dakota	3.15	0.369	2.55	3.73
Ohio	1.67	0.272	1.21	2.13
Oklahoma	3.04	0.356	2.46	3.63
Oregon	2.01	0.355	1.42	2.6
Pennsylvania	NA	NA	NA	NA
Rhode Island	3.19	0.414	2.52	3.87
South Carolina	1.7	0.253	1.28	2.11
South Dakota	2.93	0.383	2.33	3.6
Tennessee	1.65	0.271	1.22	2.1
Texas	1.36	0.184	1.07	1.67
Utah	2.06	0.329	1.52	2.6
Vermont	3.29	0.297	2.82	3.78

(*continued*)

A.5. *(continued)*

State	Responsiveness	sd	5% bound	95% bound
Virginia	2.86	0.32	2.34	3.37
Washington	2.38	0.334	1.87	2.91
West Virginia	2.26	0.297	1.78	2.77
Wisconsin	2.03	0.311	1.53	2.56
Wyoming	2.46	0.42	1.76	3.15

A.6. *State House Responsiveness 2016 (see A.2 for details)*

State	Responsiveness	sd	5% bound	95% bound
Alaska	1.71	0.424	1.0	2.40
Arizona	0.35	0.182	0.054	0.667
Arkansas	NA	NA	NA	NA
California	1.96	0.317	1.45	2.46
Colorado	2.04	0.384	1.4	2.65
Connecticut	2.17	0.245	1.79	2.57
Delaware	1.9	0.409	1.22	2.58
Florida	NA	NA	NA	NA
Georgia	1.39	0.177	1.1	1.67
Hawaii	4.12	0.539	3.19	4.99
Idaho	2.84	0.395	2.16	3.51
Illinois	NA	NA	NA	NA
Indiana	NA	NA	NA	NA
Iowa	2.24	0.305	1.74	2.75
Kansas	2.37	0.278	1.91	2.81
Kentucky	2.34	0.322	1.84	2.88
Louisiana	1.09	0.226	0.736	1.48
Maine	2.61	0.274	2.16	3.03
Maryland	0.993	0.165	0.719	1.26
Massachusetts	2.66	0.26	2.24	3.08
Michigan	1.34	0.235	0.945	1.74
Minnesota	1.82	0.252	1.42	2.23
Missouri	1.68	0.207	1.32	2.01
Montana	1.3	0.261	0.864	1.73
Nevada	2.52	0.507	1.67	3.34
New Hampshire	2.75	0.174	2.45	3.04
New Jersey	1.95	0.317	1.44	2.5
New Mexico	1.77	0.328	1.24	2.3
New York	1.66	0.194	1.35	1.98
North Carolina	2.09	0.261	1.67	2.53
North Dakota	NA	NA	NA	NA
Ohio	1.65	0.268	1.21	2.09

State	Responsiveness	sd	5% bound	95% bound
Oklahoma	2.31	0.317	1.8	2.83
Oregon	1.91	0.357	1.31	2.52
Pennsylvania	1.56	0.186	1.26	1.88
Rhode Island	2.8	0.385	2.18	3.41
South Carolina	1.91	0.25	1.5	2.32
South Dakota	3.82	0.439	3.1	4.57
Tennessee	1.47	0.255	1.05	1.89
Texas	1.59	0.207	1.26	1.94
Utah	1.81	0.323	1.27	2.36
Vermont	2.42	0.254	1.99	2.85
Virginia	2.13	0.294	1.63	2.62
Washington	1.95	0.299	1.45	2.45
West Virginia	3.16	0.339	2.57	3.69
Wisconsin	1.96	0.285	1.49	2.43
Wyoming	1.94	0.362	1.35	2.5

A.7. *State Senate Responsiveness 2012–14 (see A.3 for details)*

State	Responsiveness	sd	5% bound	95% bound
Alaska	1.69	0.628	0.667	2.77
Arizona	2.11	0.578	1.17	3.08
Arkansas	2.96	0.557	2.05	3.89
California	2.12	0.473	1.34	2.88
Colorado	2.59	0.559	1.69	3.52
Connecticut	2.17	0.52	1.32	3.05
Delaware	2.71	0.669	1.62	3.81
Florida	2.06	0.438	1.39	2.78
Georgia	1.11	0.287	0.67	1.62
Hawaii	4.43	0.783	3.15	5.76
Idaho	3.53	0.554	2.67	4.46
Illinois	2.19	0.37	1.57	2.8
Indiana	3.03	0.457	2.23	3.77
Iowa	3.51	0.531	2.64	4.4
Kansas	2.93	0.557	2.04	3.89
Kentucky	NA	NA	NA	NA
Louisiana	2.15	0.476	1.34	2.93
Maine	3.53	0.613	2.49	4.53
Maryland	1.62	0.366	1.06	2.24
Massachusetts	3.41	0.609	2.4	4.39
Michigan	1.67	0.396	1.03	2.32
Minnesota	2.5	0.38	1.89	3.14

(*continued*)

A.7. (*continued*)

State	Responsiveness	sd	5% bound	95% bound
Missouri	2.69	0.527	1.84	3.54
Montana	1.58	0.387	0.954	2.24
Nebraska	3.01	0.469	2.27	3.77
Nevada	2.42	0.713	1.28	3.67
New Hampshire	2.92	0.721	1.73	4.09
New Jersey	1.88	0.433	1.2	2.57
New Mexico	2.06	0.437	1.4	2.83
New York	1.09	0.285	0.635	1.55
North Carolina	1.65	0.364	1.05	2.24
North Dakota	2.74	0.514	1.89	3.56
Ohio	2.2	0.506	1.36	3.03
Oklahoma	3.48	0.522	2.64	4.34
Oregon	2.66	0.59	1.67	3.63
Pennsylvania	NA	NA	NA	NA
Rhode Island	3.34	0.602	2.37	4.36
South Carolina	1.83	0.433	1.09	2.52
South Dakota	4.21	0.645	3.16	5.3
Tennessee	2.81	0.592	1.83	3.75
Texas	0.967	0.391	0.326	1.61
Utah	2.04	0.579	1.1	3.05
Vermont	3.07	0.601	2.1	4.09
Virginia	2.62	0.532	1.77	3.52
Washington	2.33	0.463	1.58	3.07
West Virginia	3.41	0.668	2.35	4.49
Wisconsin	2.48	0.562	1.56	3.36
Wyoming	4.02	0.687	2.89	5.14

A.8. *State Senate Responsiveness 2014–16 (see A.4 for details)*

State	Responsiveness	sd	5% bound	95% bound
Alaska	2.55	0.634	1.5	3.57
Arizona	1.95	0.517	1.12	2.81
Arkansas	NA	NA	NA	NA
California	2.12	0.471	1.33	2.9
Colorado	2.56	0.512	1.71	3.43
Connecticut	2.27	0.522	1.4	3.12
Delaware	2.62	0.671	1.51	3.75
Florida	NA	NA	NA	NA
Georgia	1.2	0.295	0.729	1.71
Hawaii	5.41	0.85	4.02	6.75

State	Responsiveness	sd	5% bound	95% bound
Idaho	2.58	0.534	1.71	3.47
Illinois	NA	NA	NA	NA
Indiana	NA	NA	NA	NA
Iowa	2.58	0.465	1.82	3.32
Kansas	2.82	0.497	1.98	3.61
Kentucky	3.68	0.551	2.75	4.6
Louisiana	1.35	0.382	0.756	2.01
Maine	2.81	0.574	1.83	3.68
Maryland	1.08	0.285	0.618	1.57
Massachusetts	3.28	0.559	2.37	4.19
Michigan	1.79	0.448	1.06	2.54
Minnesota	2.24	0.346	1.66	2.84
Missouri	1.84	0.473	1.08	2.65
Montana	1.49	0.392	0.862	2.14
Nebraska	2.18	0.427	1.46	2.88
Nevada	2.17	0.668	1.08	3.32
New Hampshire	3.36	0.724	2.21	4.56
New Jersey	1.56	0.398	0.929	2.22
New Mexico	2.12	0.444	1.39	2.88
New York	0.981	0.261	0.544	1.4
North Carolina	1.78	0.379	1.18	2.41
North Dakota	2.94	0.517	2.13	3.82
Ohio	2.26	0.517	1.44	3.12
Oklahoma	3.89	0.552	3.01	4.77
Oregon	2.42	0.571	1.45	3.33
Pennsylvania	2.07	0.425	1.41	2.79
Rhode Island	2.92	0.547	2.03	3.82
South Carolina	2.15	0.471	1.38	2.96
South Dakota	4.35	0.661	3.24	5.45
Tennessee	2.49	0.537	1.66	3.4
Texas	1.26	0.43	0.598	2.02
Utah	2.53	0.611	1.47	3.5
Vermont	3.49	0.59	2.54	4.47
Virginia	1.69	0.447	1	2.44
Washington	2.17	0.435	1.45	2.89
West Virginia	4.3	0.638	3.26	5.33
Wisconsin	2.62	0.526	1.72	3.51
Wyoming	3.78	0.655	2.69	4.83

A.9. *State House Symmetry, Remedial Maps*

State	Asymmetry %	sd	5% bound	95% bound	"Simple Symmetry" %
North Carolina 2018	−13	2.42	−17	−9.21	NA
Virginia 2019	−2.85	2.79	−7.31	1.82	NA

A.10. *State Senate Symmetry, Remedial Maps*

State	Asymmetry %	sd	5% bound	95% bound	"Simple Symmetry" %
Florida 2016	−11.6	4.55	−19	−4.39	−5
North Carolina 2018	−17.1	3.89	−23.6	−10.4	−16

A.11. *State House Responsiveness, Remedial Maps*

State	Responsiveness	sd	5% bound	95% bound
North Carolina 2018	1.86	0.244	1.46	2.27
Virginia 2019	2.19	0.298	1.71	2.67

A.12. *State Senate Responsiveness, Remedial Maps*

State	Responsiveness	sd	5% bound	95% bound
Florida 2016	2.5	0.491	1.67	3.3099999
North Carolina 2018	1.98	0.384	1.33	2.63

A.13. *State House Symmetry 2008**

State	Asymmetry %	sd	5% bound	95% bound	"Simple Symmetry" %
Alaska	6.71	5.06	−1.94	15.2	7.5
Arizona	−12.2	3.11	−17.4	−6.97	−10
Arkansas	−16.5	3.09	−21.4	−11.2	−12
California	9.66	2.47	5.33	13.5	11.2
Colorado	6.42	3.36	1.01	11.9	6.15
Connecticut	−9.11	2.35	−13	−5.31	−13.2
Delaware	−13.6	4.36	−20.8	−6.23	−9.76
Florida	−15.4	2.58	−19.6	−11.2	−15

State	Asymmetry %	sd	5% bound	95% bound	"Simple Symmetry" %
Georgia	−14.8	1.8	−17.8	−12	−14.4
Hawaii	5.1	4.45	−2.2	12.3	1.96
Idaho	−9.95	3.64	−16	−3.81	−5.71
Illinois	−9.94	1.93	−13.2	−6.71	−11
Indiana	−4.75	2.76	−9.3	−0.325	−5
Iowa	−0.165	3.05	−5.18	4.75	−2
Kansas	−12	2.36	−15.9	−8.09	−12.8
Kentucky	−8.55	3.36	−14.2	−3.31	−9
Louisiana	−4.7	3.01	−9.55	0.259	−10.5
Maine	1.42	2.56	−2.91	5.5	−1.99
Maryland	−1.04	2.05	−4.35	2.25	−1.42
Massachusetts	2.73	2.72	−1.65	7.47	−1.25
Michigan	−2.48	2.46	−6.76	1.77	−0.909
Minnesota	−4.28	2.44	−8.33	−0.144	−0.746
Missouri	−19.7	2.01	−23.1	−16.3	−22.7
Montana	1.23	2.83	−3.34	6.01	0
Nevada	14.2	3.51	8.3	19.9	19
New Hampshire	−9.44	1.74	−12.2	−6.52	−6
New Jersey	−2.37	3.33	−7.97	3	−5
New Mexico	4.27	3.53	−1.61	10.5	4.29
New York	3.84	2.27	0.157	7.49	2
North Carolina	−7.16	2.5	−11.2	−2.96	−5
North Dakota	−12.3	3.61	−18	−6.25	−8.51
Ohio	−10.4	2.57	−14.6	−5.9	−11.1
Oklahoma	−18	3.23	−23.4	−12.5	−9.9
Oregon	−8.42	3.82	−14.8	−2.2	−15
Pennsylvania	−15	1.92	−18.1	−11.9	−14.3
Rhode Island	−8.76	3.54	−14.8	−3.04	−8
South Carolina	−19.2	2.31	−22.9	−15.4	−20.2
South Dakota	−12.6	3.27	−17.9	−7.07	−12.9
Tennessee	−18.1	2.7	−22.4	−13.7	−20.2
Texas	−7.71	2.16	−11.3	−4.13	−9.33
Utah	−7.88	4.2	−15	−0.995	−14.7
Vermont	11.1	2.28	7.33	14.9	14
Virginia	−11.4	2.77	−16	−6.94	−11
Washington	−2.26	2.96	−7.14	2.73	−4.08
West Virginia	12.3	3.37	6.51	17.6	14
Wisconsin	−5.45	2.7	−9.96	−1.09	−7.07
Wyoming	−17.6	2.97	−22.4	−12.7	−20

* Data from 2008 except: Louisiana, New Jersey, Virginia (2007); Maryland (2010).

A.14. *State Senate Symmetry 2008–10* *

State	Asymmetry %	sd	5% bound	95% bound	"Simple Symmetry" %
Alaska	13	6.45	2.43	23	10
Arizona	−16.8	4.7	−24.3	−8.8	−16.7
Arkansas	−18.6	5.32	−27.4	−10.1	−8.57
California	15.3	3.75	8.45	21.4	15
Colorado	0.798	4.73	−6.83	8.26	0
Connecticut	−1.19	5.2	−9.98	6.94	2.78
Delaware	−1.74	6.07	−11.4	7.99	−4.76
Florida	−18.9	4.78	−26.6	−11	−20
Georgia	−21.8	2.63	−26.1	−17.3	−19.6
Hawaii	5.36	6.33	−5.37	15.2	12
Idaho	−16.5	5.31	−24.9	−7.48	−17.1
Illinois	−9.93	3.74	−15.8	−3.71	−11.9
Indiana	−20.3	3.86	−26.6	−14.1	−18
Iowa	6.04	4.43	−1.22	13.3	−2
Kansas	−12.8	4.43	−19.8	−5.48	−20
Kentucky	−10.6	5.36	−19.2	−2.09	−13.2
Louisiana	−6.93	2.9	−11.8	−2.05	−7.69
Maine	−2.18	4.47	−9.27	5.21	−5.71
Maryland	1.84	4.12	−4.87	8.57	8.51
Massachusetts	−3.92	5.06	−12.6	4.53	2.5
Michigan	−26.6	3.95	−32.9	−19.8	−26.3
Minnesota	−11.2	3.67	−17.3	−5.21	−13.4
Missouri	−23.9	5.19	−32.3	−15.4	−26.5
Montana	−5.67	4.08	−12.2	0.817	−4
Nebraska	−11.2	4.36	−18.2	−4.19	−8.16
Nevada	−5.3	4.62	−12.7	2.81	−4.76
New Hampshire	0.764	6.34	−9.4	11	0
New Jersey	3.4	3.97	−3.19	9.87	2.5
New Mexico	1.71	4.34	−4.97	8.99	4.76
New York	−14	3.06	−19	−8.97	−16.1
North Carolina	−6.53	4.23	−13.6	0.468	−4
North Dakota	−6.89	5	−15.4	1.16	−6.38
Ohio	−17.6	4.55	−25.2	−10.2	−21.2
Oklahoma	−16.9	4.58	−24.3	−9.27	−22.9
Oregon	8.44	6.03	−1.25	18.6	6.67
Pennsylvania	−19.1	3.51	−24.8	−13.1	−14
Rhode Island	−18.5	4.84	−26.5	−10.4	−15.8
South Carolina	−11	4.12	−18	−4.29	−10.9
South Dakota	−0.509	5.08	−8.97	7.95	2.86
Tennessee	−11.7	4.55	−19.1	−4.09	−9.09
Texas	−12.3	4.54	−19.6	−4.87	−6.45
Utah	−13.8	5.33	−22.3	−4.83	−13.8
Vermont	9.39	5.69	0.451	18.4	3.33

State	Asymmetry %	sd	5% bound	95% bound	"Simple Symmetry" %
Virginia	3.16	4.33	−4.28	10.5	0
Washington	−1.03	4.17	−7.75	6.06	−4.08
West Virginia	16.9	5.62	8.13	25.8	14.7
Wisconsin	−2.56	4.99	−11.1	5.81	−6.06
Wyoming	−27	4.77	−34.5	−18.7	−26.7

* Data from 2008–10 except: Arizona, Connecticut, Kansas, Maine, Massachusetts, New Hampshire, New Mexico, North Carolina, Rhode Island, South Carolina, South Dakota, Vermont (2008); Louisiana, New Jersey, Virginia (2007); Maryland, Michigan, Minnesota (2010). In states with staggered Senate elections, the results have been adjusted using the statewide swing in state House results (see Chapter 2).

A.15. *State House Responsiveness 2008 (see A.13 for details)*

State	Responsiveness	sd	5% bound	95% bound
Alaska	2.17	0.456	1.42	2.9
Arizona	1.46	0.293	0.994	1.94
Arkansas	3.97	0.358	3.38	4.51
California	1.37	0.292	0.901	1.85
Colorado	1.81	0.36	1.22	2.4
Connecticut	2.48	0.252	2.08	2.92
Delaware	2.01	0.438	1.31	2.72
Florida	2.45	0.285	1.99	2.94
Georgia	1.27	0.167	0.996	1.55
Hawaii	3.47	0.498	2.64	4.28
Idaho	2.79	0.396	2.16	3.46
Illinois	1.05	0.206	0.737	1.38
Indiana	1.83	0.276	1.38	2.29
Iowa	2.64	0.336	2.09	3.2
Kansas	2.01	0.276	1.56	2.48
Kentucky	3.94	0.391	3.29	4.61
Louisiana	2.64	0.313	2.13	3.16
Maine	2.89	0.275	2.45	3.33
Maryland	1.29	0.183	1	1.6
Massachusetts	6.01	0.315	5.48	6.52
Michigan	1.58	0.255	1.19	2.02
Minnesota	2.3	0.269	1.87	2.74
Missouri	1.9	0.223	1.52	2.26
Montana	2.16	0.311	1.66	2.65
Nevada	1.3	0.423	0.628	2.01
New Hampshire	2.93	0.159	2.67	3.2

(continued)

A.15. (*continued*)

State	Responsiveness	sd	5% bound	95% bound
New Jersey	2.17	0.314	1.67	2.69
New Mexico	2.24	0.38	1.63	2.86
New York	1.86	0.219	1.48	2.2
North Carolina	2.2	0.281	1.74	2.68
North Dakota	4.56	0.393	3.9	5.18
Ohio	1.61	0.254	1.22	2.03
Oklahoma	3.57	0.338	3	4.11
Oregon	2.17	0.393	1.53	2.81
Pennsylvania	1.91	0.198	1.6	2.24
Rhode Island	2.97	0.406	2.29	3.6
South Carolina	1.82	0.248	1.4	2.23
South Dakota	2.67	0.396	2.03	3.34
Tennessee	1.84	0.284	1.38	2.32
Texas	1.57	0.216	1.23	1.92
Utah	2.11	0.335	1.56	2.66
Vermont	2.62	0.27	2.19	3.06
Virginia	2.73	0.33	2.18	3.25
Washington	2.62	0.353	2.04	3.2
West Virginia	3.21	0.352	2.63	3.77
Wisconsin	2.26	0.315	1.72	2.79
Wyoming	1.52	0.357	0.977	2.1

A.16. *State Senate Responsiveness 2008 (see A.14 for details)*

State	Responsiveness	sd	5% bound	95% bound
Alaska	1.7	0.622	0.725	2.77
Arizona	2.12	0.594	1.15	3.12
Arkansas	2.94	0.581	2.03	3.9
California	2.13	0.461	1.36	2.9
Colorado	2.6	0.544	1.73	3.49
Connecticut	2.15	0.532	1.29	3.09
Delaware	2.66	0.682	1.56	3.8
Florida	2.07	0.468	1.3	2.83
Georgia	1.09	0.286	0.619	1.57
Hawaii	4.44	0.775	3.17	5.68
Idaho	3.53	0.589	2.57	4.49
Illinois	2.18	0.391	1.53	2.81
Indiana	3	0.467	2.21	3.76
Iowa	3.56	0.514	2.75	4.42
Kansas	2.95	0.57	2.01	3.91
Kentucky	4.32	0.604	3.31	5.29
Louisiana	2.15	0.448	1.4	2.88

State	Responsiveness	sd	5% bound	95% bound
Maine	3.52	0.616	2.55	4.54
Maryland	1.61	0.358	1.04	2.19
Massachusetts	3.46	0.578	2.51	4.43
Michigan	1.65	0.398	1.01	2.31
Minnesota	2.51	0.389	1.87	3.19
Missouri	2.66	0.547	1.77	3.56
Montana	1.56	0.391	0.933	2.23
Nebraska	2.99	0.474	2.2	3.77
Nevada	2.4	0.735	1.24	3.64
New Hampshire	2.94	0.737	1.77	4.17
New Jersey	1.88	0.439	1.18	2.61
New Mexico	2.05	0.429	1.34	2.73
New York	1.07	0.276	0.632	1.53
North Carolina	1.57	0.372	0.981	2.2
North Dakota	2.78	0.515	1.9	3.59
Ohio	2.02	0.469	1.26	2.79
Oklahoma	3.55	0.498	2.73	4.4
Oregon	2.67	0.589	1.69	3.65
Pennsylvania	2.11	0.433	1.4	2.8
Rhode Island	3.31	0.599	2.37	4.33
South Carolina	1.77	0.414	1.12	2.45
South Dakota	2.81	0.539	1.9	3.68
Tennessee	0.979	0.382	0.374	1.63
Texas	1.9	0.554	1	2.82
Utah	3.41	0.607	2.37	4.42
Vermont	2.47	0.624	1.48	3.53
Virginia	2.71	0.506	1.89	3.54
Washington	3	0.512	2.15	3.84
West Virginia	2.36	0.536	1.49	3.24
Wisconsin	NA	NA	NA	NA
Wyoming	NA	NA	NA	NA

References

Alabama Legislative Black Caucus *v.* Alabama, No. 13-895, 575 U.S. ___, 135 S. Ct. 1257 (2015).

Baker *v.* Carr, 369 U.S. 186 (1962).

Bandemer *v.* Davis, 478 US 109 (1986).

Bethune-Hill *v.* Va. State Bd. of Elections, 137 S. Ct. 788 (2017).

Beverly R. Gill, et al. *v.* William Whitford, et al., No. 16-1161, 585 138 (US Supreme Court 2018).

Common Cause *v.* Lewis (2019), 18 CVS 014001 (NC Superior Court Division).

Covington *v.* North Carolina (2018), 15CV399 (M.D.N.C. Jan. 26, 2018).

Davis *v.* Bandemer, 478 US 109 (1986).

Fischer *v.* Grimes, No. 2012-SC-000092-T (Ky. Sup. Ct.).

Georgia *v.* Ashcroft, 539 US 461 (2003).

Gomillion *v.* Lightfoot, 364 US 339 (1960).

In re 2011 Redistricting Cases, 274 P.3d 466 (Alaska 2012).

In re 2012 Joint Resolution of Apportionment, No. SC12-460 (Fla. Sup. Ct.).

In re Reapportionment of the Colorado General Assembly, No. 2011SA282 (Colo. Sup. Ct.).

Karcher *v.* Daggett, 462 US 725 (1983).

Mobile *v.* Bolden (1980).

Rene Romo, et al. *v.* Ken Detzner, et al. (2014).

Reynolds *v.* Sims 377 US 533,563(1964).

Richard Vieth, et al. *v.* Robert C. Jubelirer, President of the Pennsylvania Senate, et al., 541 US 267 (2004).

Rima Ford Vesilind, et al. *v.* Virginia State Board of Elections, et al., 91 Va. Cir. 490 (2016).

Rucho *v.* Common Cause, No. 18-422, 588 U.S. ___ (2019).

Shelby County *v.* Holder, No. 12-96, 570 U.S. 529 (2013).

Solomon *v.* Abercrombie, No. SCPW-11-0000732 (Sup. Ct. of Hawaii).

Thornburg *v.* Gingles, 478 U.S. 30 (1986).

Twin Falls County v. Idaho Commission on Redistricting, No. 39373-2011 (Idaho Sup. Ct.).

Wood v. Broom, 287 US 1 (1932).

Abramowitz, Alan I., Brad Alexander, and Matthew Gunning. 2006. Incumbenc., Redistricting, and the Decline of Competition in US House Election. *The Journal of Politics* 68 (1): 75–88.

ACEEE. 2018, June 23. The State Energy Efficiency Scorecard [Text]. Retrieved September 27, 2019, from American Council for an Energy-Efficient Economy website: https://aceee.org/state-policy/scorecard

Aldrich, John H. 1995. *Why Parties?: The Origin and Transformation of Political Parties in America*. 1st Edition. Chicago: University of Chicago Press.

Alexeev, Boris, and Dustin G. Mixon. 2018. Partisan Gerrymandering with Geographically Compact Districts. *Journal of Applied Probability* 17 (4): 1046–59. https://doi.org/10.1017/jpr.2018.70

Altman, Micah. 1998. Modeling the Effects of Mandatory District Compactness on Partisan Gerrymanders. *Political Geography* 17 (8): 989–1012.

Altman, Micah, Brian Amos, Michael P. McDonald, and Daniel A. Smith. 2015. Revealing Preferences: Why Gerrymanders Are Hard to Prove, and What to Do about It. Social Science Research Network.

Altman, Micah, Karin MacDonald, and Michael McDonald. 2005. From Crayons to Computers: The Evolution of Computer Use in Redistricting. *Social Science Computer Review* 23 (3): 334–46.

Altman, Micah, and Michael P. McDonald. 2011a. BARD: Better Automated Redistricting. *Journal of Statistical Software* 42 (4): 1–28.

2011b. Redistricting Principles for the Twenty-First Century. *Case Western Reserve Law Review* 62: 1179.

2013. A Half-Century of Virginia Redistricting Battles: Shifting from Rural Malapportionment to Voting Rights to Public Participation. *University of Richmond Law Review* 47: 771–831.

2014. Redistricting by Formula: An Ohio Reform Experiment. http://ssrn.com/abstract=2450645

2015. Paradoxes of Political Reform: Congressional Redistricting in Florida. In *Jigsaw Puzzle Politics in the Sunshine State*, edited by S. C. McKee. Gainesville: University of Florida Press.

Ansolabehere, Stephen, and Jonathan Rodden. 2011. *Washington Data Files*. Harvard Dataverse.

Ansolabehere, Stephen, and Maxwell Palmer. 2016. A two-hundred year statistical history of the gerrymander. *Ohio State Law Journal* 77: 741.

Ansolabehere, Stephen, Maxwell Palmer, and Amanda Lee. 2014. Precinct-Level Election Data. Harvard Dataverse V1. https://doi.org/10.7910/DVN/YN4TLR

Ansolabehere, Stephen, Nathaniel Persily, and Charles Stewart III. 2013. Regional Differences in Racial Polarization in the 2012 Presidential Election: Implications for the Constitutionality of Section 5 of the Voting Rights Act, *Harvard Law Review Forum* 126: 205-220.

Arrington, Theodore S. 2016. A Practical Procedure for Detecting a Partisan Gerrymander. *Election Law Journal* 15 (4): 385–402.

Barreto, Matt A., Chad Dunn, Sonni Waknin, Michael Cohen, Michael S. Latner, and Gabriel Sanchez. 2020. Analysis of H.R.1 and the Immediate Need for Expanded Access to Vote-by-Mail. *UCLA Latino Policy and Politics Initiative, A Joint Project with the Union of Concerned Scientists and The University of New Mexico Center for Social Policy.* https://latino.ucla.edu/wp-content/uploads/2020/04/UCLA-VRP-Memo-on-HR1.pdf

Bawn, Kathleen, Martin Cohen, David Karol, Seth Masket, Hans Noel, and John Zaller. 2012. A Theory of Political Parties: Groups, Policy Demands and Nominations in American Politics. *Perspectives on Politics* 10 (3): 571–97.

Bentele, Keith G., and Erin E. O'Brien. 2013. Jim Crow 2.0? Why States Consider and Adopt Restrictive Voter Access Policies. *Perspectives on Politics* 11 (4): 1088–116. https://doi.org/10.1017/S1537592713002843

Bernstein, Mira, and Moon Duchin. 2017. A Formula Goes to Court: Partisan Gerrymandering and the Efficiency Gap. *Notices of the AMS* 64 (9): 1020–24.

Best, Robin E., Shawn J. Donahue, Jonathan Krasno, Daniel B. Magleby, and Michael D. McDonald. 2018. Considering the Prospects for Establishing a Packing Gerrymandering Standard. *Election Law Journal* 17 (1): 1-20.

Bhatt, Chintan B., and Consuelo M. Beck-Sagué. 2018. Medicaid Expansion and Infant Mortality in the United States. *American Journal of Public Health* 108 (4): 565–67. https://doi.org/10.2105/AJPH.2017.304218

Bilal, Usama, Emily A. Knapp, and Richard S. Cooper. 2018. Swing Voting in the 2016 Presidential Election in Counties Where Midlife Mortality Has Been Rising in White Non-Hispanic Americans. *Social Science & Medicine (1982)* 197: 33–38. https://doi.org/10.1016/j.socscimed.2017.11.050

Blake, Aaron. 2020. Analysis: Trump Unleashed a Torrent of Voter Fraud Disinformation at the Debate. *Washington Post,* October 1, 2020. www.washingtonpost.com/politics/2020/09/30/trump-unleashed-torrent-disinformation-about-voter-fraud-debate/

Bor, Jacob. 2017. Diverging Life Expectancies and Voting Patterns in the 2016 US Presidential Election. *American Journal of Public Health* 107 (10): 1560–62. https://doi.org/10.2105/AJPH.2017.303945

Bowen, Daniel C. 2010. *District Characteristics and the Representational Relationship.* Doctoral Dissertation, The University of Iowa.

Boyce, John R., and Diane P. Bischak. 2002. The Role of Political Parties in the Organization of Congress. *Journal of Law Economics & Organization* 18 (1): 1–38.

Bradlee, Dave. 2014. *Dave's Redistricting App.* www.davesredistricting.org

Brams, Steven J. 2020. Making Partisan Gerrymandering Fair: One Old and Two New Methods. *Social Science Quarterly* 101: 68–72.

Brennan Center for Justice. 2012. Election 2012: Voting Laws Roundup. Retrieved February 5, 2019, from www.brennancenter.org/analysis/election-2012-voting-laws-roundup

Brennan Center for Justice. 2018. Automatic Voter Registration and Modernization in the States | Brennan Center for Justice. Retrieved July 10, 2018, from www.brennancenter.org/analysis/voter-registration-modernization-states

Brians, Craig Leonard, and Bernard Grofman. 2001. Election Day Registration's Effect on U.S. Voter Turnout. *Social Science Quarterly* 82 (1): 170–83. https://doi.org/10.1111/0038-4941.00015

Browning, Robert X., and Gary King. 1987. Seats, Votes, and Gerrymandering: Estimating Representation and Bias in State Legislative Redistricting. *Law & Policy* 9: 305–22. doi:10.1111/j.1467-9930.1987.tb00413.x

Bullock, Charles S., and Ronald K. Gaddie. 1993. Changing from Multimember to Single-Member Districts: Partisan, Racial, and Gender Consequences. *State and Local Government Review* 25: 155–63.

Burden, Barry C., and Rochelle Snyder. 2020. Explaining Uncontested Seats in Congress and State Legislatures. *American Politics Research* (forthcoming). doi:10.1177/1532673X20960565

Butler, David, and Bruce E. Cain. 1992. *Congressional Redistricting: Comparative and Theoretical Perspectives, New Topics in Politics*. New York, Toronto: Macmillan Pub. Co.; Maxwell Macmillan Canada.

Cain, Bruce E., Wendy K. Tam Cho, Yan Y. Liu, and Emily R. Zhang. 2018. Reasonable Bias Approach to Gerrymandering: Using Automated Plan Generation to Evaluate Redistricting Proposals. *William & Mary Law Review* 59 (5): 1521–58.

Canon, David T. 1999. *Race, Redistricting, and Representation: The Unintended Consequences of Black Majority Districts*. Chicago: University of Chicago Press.

Carney, Eliza Newlin. 2015, March 16. Standing Together against Any Action. *CQ Weekly Report* 2015: 37–40.

Carson, James L., and Michael H. Crespin. 2004. The Effect of State Redistricting Methods on Electoral Competition in United States House Races. *State Politics & Policy Quarterly* 4 (4): 455–69.

Carson, Jamie L., Michael H. Crespin, and Ryan D. Williamson. 2014. Reevaluating the Effects of Redistricting on Electoral Competition, 1972–2012. *State Politics & Policy Quarterly* 14 (2): 165–77.

Caughey, Devin, Chris Tausanovitch, and Christopher Warshaw. 2017. Partisan Gerrymandering and the Political Process: Effects on Roll-Call Voting and State Policies. *Election Law Journal: Rules, Politics, and Policy* 16 (4): 453–69. https://doi.org/10.1089/elj.2017.0452

Chen, Jowei. 2017. The Impact of Political Geography on Wisconsin Redistricting: An Analysis of Wisconsin's Act 43 Assembly Districting Plan. *Election Law Journal* 16 (4): 417–42.

Chen, Jowei, and David Cottrell. 2016. Evaluating Partisan Gains from Congressional Gerrymandering: Using Computer Simulations to Estimate the Effect of Gerrymandering in the US House. *Electoral Studies* 44: 329–40. [Computer simulations to show that much of the bias is geographic.]

Chen, Jowei, and Jonathan Rodden. 2013a. Unintentional Gerrymandering: Political Geography and Electoral Bias in Legislatures. *Quarterly Journal of Political Science* 8: 239–69.

2013b. Report on Computer Simulations of Florida Congressional Districting Plans. https://sites.tufts.edu/vrdi/files/2018/06/Chen-FL.pdf. Unpublished working paper.

2015. Cutting Through the Thicket: Redistricting Simulations and the Detection of Partisan Gerrymanders. *Election Law Journal* 14 (4): 331–45.

Cirincione, Carmen, Thomas A. Darling, and Timothy G. O'Rourke. 2000. Assessing South Carolina's 1990 Congressional Districting. *Political Geography* 19: 189–211.

Clayton, Dewey M. 2004. *African Americans and the Politics of Congressional Redistricting.* New York: Garland Publishing.

Corriher, Billy, and Liz Kennedy. 2017. Distorted Districts, Distorted Laws. Retrieved July 26, 2018, from Center for American Progress website: www.americanprogress.org/issues/democracy/reports/2017/09/19/439164/distorted-districts-distorted-laws/

Cottrell, David. 2019. Using Computer Simulations to Measure the Effect of Gerrymandering on Electoral Competition in the US Congress. *Legislative Studies Quarterly* 44 (3): 487–514.

Cox, Gary W., and Mathew D. McCubbins. 1993. *Legislative Leviathan: Party Government in the House, California Series on Social Choice and Political Economy.* Berkeley: University of California Press.

2005. *Setting the Agenda: Responsible Party Government in the U.S. House of Representatives.* Cambridge; New York: Cambridge University Press.

Curiel, John A. and Tyler Steelman. 2018. Redistricting Out Representation: Democratic Harms in Splitting Zip Codes. *Election Law Journal* 17 (4): 328–53.

Dahl, Robert A. 2003. *How Democratic Is the American Constitution.* New Haven, CT: Yale University Press.

Daley, David. 2017. *Ratf**ked: Why Your Vote Doesn't Count.* New York: Liveright.

2019. How Gerrymandering Leads to Radical Abortion Laws. *The New Republic*, May 14, 2019. https://newrepublic.com/article/153901/gerrymandering-leads-radical-abortion-laws

Dalton, Russell J. 2004. *Democratic Challenges, Democratic Choices: The Erosion of Political Support in Advanced Industrial Democracies, Comparative Politics.* Oxford; New York: Oxford University Press.

Dancey, Logan, and Geoffrey Sheagley. 2017. Partisanship and Perceptions of Party-Line Voting in Congress. *Political Research Quarterly* 71 (1): 32–45.

Derfner, Armand. 1972. Multi-Member Districts and Black Voters. *National Black Law Journal* 2 (2): 120–28.

Dimanchev, Emil G., Sergey Paltsev, Mei Yuan, Daniel Rothenberg, Christopher W. Tessum, Julian D. Marshall, and Noelle E. Selin. 2019. Health Co-Benefits of Sub-National Renewable Energy Policy in the US. *Environmental Research Letters* 14 (8): 085012. https://doi.org/10.1088/1748-9326/ab31d9

Donnovan, Todd (ed.). 2017. *Changing How America Votes.* Lanham, MD: Rowman and Littlefield.

Dow, Jay K. 2017. *Electing the House: The Adoption and Performance of the US Single-Member District Electoral System.* Lawrence, KS: University Press of Kansas.

Engstrom, Erik J. 2006. Stacking the States, Stacking the House: The Partisan Consequences of Congressional Redistricting in the 19th Century. *The American Political Science Review* 100 (3): 419–27.

2013. *Partisan Gerrymandering and the Construction of American Democracy*. Illustrated Edition. Ann Arbor: University of Michigan Press.

Engstrom, Richard L. 2020. Partisan Gerrymandering: Weeds in the Political Thicket. *Social Science Quarterly* 101: 23–36.

Epperly, Brad, Christopher Witko, Ryan Strickler, and Paul White. 2019. Rule by Violence, Rule by Law: Lynching, Jim Crow, and the Continuing Evolution of Voter Suppression in the U.S. *Perspectives on Politics* 1–14. https://doi.org/10.1017/S1537592718003584

Erikson, Robert S. 1972. Malapportionment, Gerrymandering, and Party Fortunes in Congressional Elections. *American Political Science Review* 66 (4): 1234–45.

Fairvote, 2019. Where Ranked Choice Voting Is Used. Accessed November 17, 2019, www.fairvote.org/where_is_ranked_choice_voting_used

Fields, Reginald. 2010, November 3. Republican John Kasich Victorious in Ohio; Jobs Message Overcomes Wall Street Baggage. *The Plain Dealer*. Accessed September 9, 2019, www.cleveland.com/politics/2010/11/republican_john_kasich_headed.html

Foa, Roberto Stefan, and Yascha Mounk. 2016. The Danger of Deconsolidation: The Democratic Disconnect. *Journal of Democracy* 27 (3): 5–7.

Forgette, Richard, and Glenn Platt. 2005. Redistricting Principles and Incumbency Protection in the U.S. Congress. *Political Geography* 24 (8): 934–51.

Fraga, Bernard. 2016. Redistricting and the Causal Impact of Race on Voter Turnout. *Journal of Politics* 78 (1): 19–34.

Frederick, Brian. 2008. Constituency Population and Representation in the US House. *American Politics Research* 36 (358): 27.

Friedman, John N., and Richard T. Holden. 2009. The Rising Incumbent Reelection Rate: What's Gerrymandering Got to Do with It? *Journal of Politics* 71 (2): 593–611.

Gaddie, Keith. 2019, April. *Applied Fair Division Systems for Redistricting*. Presented at the annual meeting of the American Association of Geographers, Washington, DC.

Gardner, Amy, and Josh Dawsey. 2020, August 3. As Trump Leans into Attacks on Mail Voting, GOP Officials Confront Signs of Republican Turnout Crisis. *Washington Post*. www.washingtonpost.com/politics/republicans-race-to-promote-mail-voting-as-trumps-attacks-discourage-his-own-supporters-from-embracing-the-practice/2020/08/03/9dd1d988-d1d9-11ea-9038-af089b63ac21_story.html

Gelman, Andrew. 2009. *Red State, Blue State, Rich State, Poor State: Why Americans Vote the Way They Do – Expanded Edition*. Expanded edition. Princeton, NJ: Princeton University Press.

Gelman, Andrew, and Gary King. 1990. Estimating the Electoral Consequences of Legislative Redistricting. *Journal of the American Statistical Association* 85 (410): 274–82.

1994a. Enhancing Democracy through Legislative Redistricting. *American Political Science Review* 88 (3): 541–59.

1994b. A Unified Method of Evaluating Electoral Systems and Redistricting Plans. *American Journal of Political Science* 38 (2): 514–54.

Gerber, Elisabeth, R. Rebecca Morton, and Thomas A. Rietz. 1998. Minority Representation in Multimember Districts. *American Political Science Review* 92 (1): 127–44.

Gerring, John, Strom C. Thacker and Rodrigo Alfaro. 2012. Democracy and Human Development. *Journal of Politics* 74(1): 1-17.

Goedert, Nicholas. 2014a. Redistricting, Risk, and Representation: How Five State Gerrymanders Weathered the Tides of the 2000s. *Election Law Journal: Rules, Politics, and Policy* 13 (3): 406–18. http://doi.org/10.1089/elj.2014.0261

2014b. Gerrymandering or Geography? How Democrats Won the Popular Vote but Lost the Congress in 2012. *Research & Politics* 1 (1): 1–8. doi:10.1177/2053168014528683

Goedert, Nicholas. 2017. The Pseudoparadox of Partisan Mapmaking and Congressional Competition. *State Politics & Policy Quarterly* 17 (1): 47–75. https://doi.org/10.1177/1532440016659234

2020. *Ground War: Court, Commissions, and the Fight Over Partisan Gerrymanders* [Manuscript submitted for publication]. Department of Political Science, Virginia Tech.

Goldman, Lee, Maribel P. Lim, Qixuan Chen, Peng Jin, Peter Muennig, and Andrew Vagelos. 2019. Independent Relationship of Changes in Death Rates with Changes in US Presidential Voting. *Journal of General Internal Medicine* 34 (3): 363–71. https://doi.org/10.1007/s11606-018-4568-6

Golshan, Tara. 2018. Wisconsin Gov. Scott Walker Signs into Law Sweeping Bills Stripping Powers from the Democrats. *Vox*. December 4, 2018. www.vox.com/policy-and-politics/2018/12/4/18123784/gop-legislature-wisconsin-michigan-power-grab-lame-duck

Gordon, Sarah H., Nicole Huberfeld, and David K. Jones. 2020. What Federalism Means for the US Response to Coronavirus Disease 2019. *JAMA Health Forum* 1 (5): e200510. https://doi.org/10.1001/jamahealthforum.2020.0510

Green, Rebecca. 2018. Redistricting Transparency. *William & Mary Law Review* 59 (5): 1787–836.

Grofman, Bernard. 2018. Crafting a Judicially Manageable Standard for Partisan Gerrymandering: Five Necessary Elements. *Election Law Journal: Rules, Politics, and Policy* 17 (2): 117–36.

1981. Alternatives to Single-Member Plurality Districts: Legal and Empirical Issues. *Policy Studies Journal* 9: 6, doi: 10.1111/j.1541-0072.1981.tb00992.x

Grofman, Bernard, and Thomas Brunell. 2005. The Art of the Dummymander: The Impact of Recent Redistrictings on the Partisan Makeup of Southern House Seats. In *Redistricting in the New Millennium*, edited by Peter F. Galderisi. Lanham, MD: Lexington Books, 183–200.

Grofman, Bernard, and Jonathan R. Cervas. 2018. Gerrymandering: Lessons from *League of Women Voters v. Commonwealth of Pennsylvania* (2018). *Election Law Journal: Rules, Politics, and Policy* 17 (4):264–85. http://doi.org/10.1089/elj.2018.0496

Grofman, Bernard, and Chandler Davidson. 1992. *Controversies in Minority Voting: The Voting Rights Act in Perspective*. The Bookings Institution: Washington, DC.

Grofman, Bernard, and Lisa Handley. 1991. The impact of the Voting Rights Act on black representation in southern state legislatures. *Legislative Studies Quarterly* 16(1): 111-128

Grofman, Bernard, and Gary King. 2007. The Future of Partisan Symmetry as a Judicial Test for Partisan Gerrymandering after *LULAC v. Perry. Election Law Journal* 6 (1): 2–35.

Grofman, Bernard, William Koetzle, and Thomas Brunell. 1997. An Integrated Perspective on the Three Potential Sources of Partisan Bias: Malapportionment, Turnout Differences, and the Geographic Distribution of Party Vote Shares. *Electoral Studies* 16 (4): 457–70.

Grossman, Daniel S., and David J.G. Slusky. 2017. The Effect of an Increase in Lead in the Water System on Fertility and Birth Outcomes: The Case of Flint, Michigan. www2.ku.edu/~kuwpaper/2017Papers/201703.pdf

Grossman, Matt, and David A. Hopkins. 2016. *Asymmetric Politics: Ideological Republicans and Group Interest Democrats. Asymmetric Politics*. New York: Oxford University Press. https://oxford.universitypressscholarship.com/view/ 10.1093/acprof:oso/9780190626594.001.0001/acprof-9780190626594

Guest, Olivia, Frank J. Kanayet, and Bradley C. Love. 2019. Gerrymandering and Computational Redistricting. *Journal of Computational Social Science* 2 (2): 119–31.

Guttmacher Institute. 2018. Policy Trends in the States, 2017. Guttmacher Institute. January 2, 2018. www.guttmacher.org/article/2018/01/policy-trends-states-2017

Hajnal, Zoltan L. 2020. *Dangerously Divided: How Race and Class Shape Winning and Losing in American Politics*. New York: Cambridge University Press.

Haselswerdt, Jake. 2017. Expanding Medicaid, Expanding the Electorate: The Affordable Care Act's Short-Term Impact on Political Participation. *Journal of Health Politics, Policy and Law* 42 (4); 667–95. https://doi.org/10.1215/ 03616878-3856107

Hasen, Richard. 2018. Race or Party, Race as Party, or Party All the Time: Three Uneasy Approaches to Conjoined Polarization in Redistricting and Voting Cases. *William and Mary Law Review* 59: 1837, https://scholarship.law.wm .edu/wmlr/vol59/iss5/8

Hayes, Danny, and Seth C. McKee. 2012. The Intersection of Redistricting, Race, and Participation. *American Journal of Political Science* 56 (1): 115–30.

Henderson, John A., Brian T. Hamel, and Aaron M. Goldzimer. 2018. Gerrymandering Incumbency: Does Nonpartisan Redistricting Increase Electoral Competition? *Journal of Politics* 80 (3): 1011–16.

Herron, Michael C., and Daniel A. Smith. 2014. Race, Party, and the Consequences of Restricting Early Voting in Florida in the 2012 General Election. *Political Research Quarterly* 67 (3): 646–65. https://doi.org/10 .1177/1065912914524831

Hill, Kevin A. 1995. Does the creation of majority black districts aid Republicans? An analysis of the 1992 congressional elections in eight southern states. *The Journal of Politics* 57(2): 384-401.

Hill, Steven. 2013. How the Voting Rights Act Hurts Democrats and Minorities. *The Atlantic*. Accessed February 8, 2019. www.theatlantic.com/politics/archive/2013/06/how-the-voting-rights-act-hurts-democrats-and-minorities/276893/

Hirsch, Sam. 2003. The United States House of Unrepresentatives: What Went Wrong in the Latest Round of Congressional Redistricting. *Election Law Journal* 2 (2):179–216.

Hollingsworth, Alex, Aparna Soni, Aaron E. Carroll, John Cawley, and Kosali Simon. 2019. Gains in Health Insurance Coverage Explain Variation in Democratic Vote Share in the 2008-2016 Presidential Elections. *PLOS ONE* 14 (4): e0214206. https://doi.org/10.1371/journal.pone.0214206

Hood, M. V., III, and Seth C. McKee. 2008. Gerrymandering on Georgia's Mind: The Effects of Redistricting on Vote Choice in the 2006 Midterm Election. *Social Science Quarterly* 89: 60–77. doi:10.1111/j.1540-6237.2008.00521.x

  2010. Stranger Danger: Redistricting, Incumbent Recognition, and Vote Choice. *Social Science Quarterly* 91: 344–58.

  2013. Unwelcome Constituents: Redistricting and Countervailing Partisan Tides. *State Politics & Policy Quarterly* 13 (2): 203–24.

Hopkins, Dan. 2018, August 21. What We Know About Voter ID Laws. Retrieved September 27, 2019, from FiveThirtyEight website: https://fivethirtyeight.com/features/what-we-know-about-voter-id-laws/

Ingraham, Christopher. 2014. America's Most Gerrymandered Congressional Districts. *The Washington Post*, May 15, 2014.

Jackman, Molly. 2013. ALEC's Influence over Lawmaking in State Legislatures. *Brookings* (blog). www.brookings.edu/articles/alecs-influence-over-lawmaking-in-state-legislatures/

Johnston, Ron, David Manley, Kelvyn Jones, and Ryne Rohla. 2020. The Geographical Polarization of the American Electorate: A Country of Increasing Electoral Landslides?. *GeoJournal* 85: 187–204. https://doi.org/10.1007/s10708-018-9955-3

Jones, Jeffrey. 2010, September 1. Americans Give GOP Edge on Most Election Issues. *Gallup*. Accessed September 9, 2010, https://news.gallup.com/poll/142730/americans-give-gop-edge-election-issues.aspx.

Kaiser Family Foundation. 2014. States' Positions in the Affordable Care Act Case at the Supreme Court. *KFF* (blog). August 27, 2014. www.kff.org/health-reform/state-indicator/state-positions-on-aca-case/

Kaminski, Marek M. (1999). How Communism Could Have Been Saved: Formal Analysis of Electoral Bargaining in Poland in 1989. *Public Choice* 98 (1): 83–109.

  (2002). Do Parties Benefit from Electoral Manipulation? Electoral Laws and Heresthetics in Poland, 1989–93. *Journal of Theoretical Politics* 14 (3): 325–58.

Kaminski, Marek M., and Monika A. Nalepa. 2004. Poland: Learning to Manipulate Electoral Rules. In *The Handbook of Electoral System Choice*, edited by Josep M. Colomer. London: Palgrave Macmillan UK, 369–81. https://doi.org/10.1057/9780230522749_21

Katz, Jonathan N., Gary King, and Elizabeth Rosenblatt. 2020. Theoretical Foundations and Empirical Evaluations of Partisan Fairness in District-Based Democracies. *American Political Science Review* 114 (1): 164–78.

Kaufman, Aaron, Gary King, and Mayya Komisarchik. Forthcoming. How to Measure Legislative District Compactness If You Only Know It When You See It. *American Journal of Political Science.*

Keena, Alex. 2019a. Who Needs the Wealthy? The Effects of Size Scaling on Money in Senate Elections. *Congress & the Presidency* 46 (2): 235–52.

2019b. The GOP's "Supply-Side" Abortion Bans Won't Work and Will Have Dire Consequences for Women's Health. *USAPP* (blog). May 23, 2019. https://blogs.lse.ac.uk/usappblog/2019/05/23/the-gops-supply-side-abortion-bans-wont-work-and-will-have-dire-consequences-for-womens-health/

King, Gary. 1990. Electoral Responsiveness and Partisan Bias in Multiparty Democracies. *Legislative Studies Quarterly* XV: 159–81.

Klain, Maurice. 1955. A New Look at the Constituencies: The Need for a Recount and a Reappraisal. *American Political Science Review* 49 (12): 1105–19.

Klarner, Carl. 2018. State Legislative Election Returns, 1967–2016, https://doi.org/10.7910/DVN/3WZFK9, Harvard Dataverse, V3, UNF:6:pV4h1CP/B8pHthjjQThTTw== [fileUNF]

Knight, Jack and James Johnson. 2011. *The Priority of Democracy: Political Consequences of Pragmatism.* Princeton: Princeton University Press.

Kovalov, Maksym. 2014. Electoral Manipulations and Fraud in Parliamentary Elections: The Case of Ukraine. *East European Politics and Societies* 28 (4): 781–807. https://doi.org/10.1177/0888325414545671

Krasno, Jonathan, Daniel B. Magleby, Michael D. McDonald, Shawn Donahue, and Robin E. Best. 2019. Can Gerrymanders Be Detected? An Examination of Wisconsin's State Assembly. *American Political Research* 47 (5):1162–201.

Ladewig, Jeffrey W. 2018. "Appearances Do Matter": Congressional District Compactness and Electoral Turnout. *Election Law Journal: Rules, Politics, and Policy* 17 (2): 137–50. http://doi.org/10.1089/elj.2017.0466

Landau, Zeph, O. Reid, and I. Yershov. 2009. A Fair Division Solution to the Problem of Redistricting. *Social Choice and Welfare* 32 (3): 479–92.

Landau, Zeph, and Frances Edward Su. 2010. Fair Division and Redistricting. In *The Mathematics of Decisions, Elections, and Games,* edited by Karl-Dieter Crisman and Michael A. Jones. Providence, RI: Contemporary Mathematics, 17–36, 624.

Latner, Michael. 2019. Let's Stop Letting Minority Rule Give Us Science Fiction Abortion Laws. Union of Concerned Scientists. June 3, 2019. https://blog.ucsusa.org/michael-latner/lets-stop-letting-minority-rule-give-us-science-fiction-abortion-laws

Latner, Michael, Alex Keena, Charles Anthony Smith, and Anthony McGann. 2020. How Gerrymandering in the States Could Lead to President Trump's Re-Election. *USAPP* (blog). August 12, 2020. https://blogs.lse.ac.uk/usappblog/2020/08/12/how-gerrymandering-in-the-states-could-lead-to-president-trumps-re-election/

Lee, Frances E., and Oppenheimer, Bruce I. 1999. *Sizing Up the Senate: The Unequal Consequences of Equal Representation.* Chicago: University of Chicago Press.

Legal Information Institute. 2012. NFIB v Sebelius. LII / Legal Information Institute. www.law.cornell.edu/supremecourt/text/11-393

Leighley, Jan E., and Jonathan Nagler. 2013. *Who Votes Now?: Demographics, Issues, Inequality, and Turnout in the United States.* 1st Edition. Princeton: Princeton University Press.

Li, Quan, Michael J. Pomante, and Scot Schraufnagel. 2018. Cost of Voting in the American States. *Election Law Journal: Rules, Politics, and Policy* 17 (3): 234–47. https://doi.org/10.1089/elj.2017.0478

Lublin, David. 1997. *The Paradox of Representation: Racial Gerrymandering and Minority Interests in Congress.* Princeton, NJ: Princeton University Press.

  1999. Racial Redistricting and African-American Representation: A Critique of "Do Majority-Minority Districts Maximize Substantive Black Representation in Congress?". *American Political Science Review* 93(1): 183–86.

Lyons, Michael, and Peter F. Galderisi. 1995. Incumbency, Reapportionment, and U.S. House Redistricting. *Political Research Quarterly* 48 (4): 857–71.

Magleby, Daniel B., and Daniel B. Mosesson. 2018. A New Approach for Developing Neutral Redistricting Plans. *Political Analysis* 26 (2): 147–67.

Makse, Todd. 2012. Strategic Constituency Manipulation in State Legislative Redistricting. *Legislative Studies Quarterly* 37: 225–50. doi:10.1111/j.1939-9162.2012.00044.x

Makse, Todd. 2014. The Redistricting Cycle, Partisan Tides, and Party Strength in State Legislative Elections. *State Politics and Policy Quarterly* 14 (3): 342–63.

Masket, Seth E., Jonathan Winburn, and Gerald C. Wright. 2012. The Gerrymanderers Are Coming! Legislative Redistricting Won't Affect Competition or Polarization Much, No Matter Who Does It. *Political Science & Politics* 45 (1): 39–43.

Massey, Douglas S., and Nancy A. Denton. 1988. The Dimensions of Residential Segregation. *Social Forces* 67 (2): 281–315.

Mayhew, David R. 2014. *Placing Parties in American Politics: Organization, Electoral Settings, and Government Activity in the Twentieth Century. Placing Parties in American Politics.* Princeton, NJ: Princeton University Press. www.degruyter.com/princetonup/view/title/508848

McCarthy, Ryan, Derek Willis, and Jonathan Lai. 2020. Pennsylvania's Rejection of 372,000 Ballot Applications Bewilders Voters and Strains Election Staff. *ProPublica.* October 15, 2020. www.propublica.org/article/pennsylvanias-rejection-of-372-000-ballot-applications-bewilders-voters-and-strains-election-staff?token=XSO7CCiM7DoudJrFYQeZnvAitR3ZTosj

McDonald, Michael P. 2004. A Comparative Analysis of Redistricting Institutions in the United States, 2001–02. *State Politics & Policy Quarterly* 4 (4): 371–95.

  2009. *Voter Preregistration Programs.* George Mason University. https://cses.org/wp-content/uploads/2019/04/CSES_2009Toronto_McDonald.pdf

  2013. Geography Does Not Necessarily Lead to Pro-Republican Gerrymandering. *Huffington Post.* www.huffpost.com/entry/geography-does-not-necess_b_3530099.

McDonald, Michael D., and Robin E. Best. 2015. Unfair Partisan Gerrymanders in Politics and Law: A Diagnostic Applied to Six Cases. *Election Law Journal* 14 (4): 312–30.

McDonald, Michael P., Enrijeta Shino, and Daniel A. Smith. 2015. *Convenience Voting and Turnout: Reassessing the Effects of Election Reforms* . Prepared for the New Research on Election Administration and Reform Conference at MIT, June 8, 2015.

McElwain, Kenneth Mori. 2018. Manipulating Electoral Rules to Manufacture Single-Party Dominance. *Critical Readings on the Liberal Democratic Party in Japan* September: 430–59. https://doi.org/10.1163/9789004380523_018.

McGann, Anthony J., Charles A. Smith, Michael Latner, and J. Alex Keena. 2015. A Discernable and Manageable Standard for Partisan Gerrymandering. *Election Law Journal* 14 (4): 295–311.

McGann, Anthony J., Charles Anthony Smith, Michael Latner, and Alex Keena. 2016. *Gerrymandering in America: The House of Representatives, the Supreme Court and the Future of Popular Sovereignty*. New York: Cambridge University Press.

McGhee, Eric. 2014. Measuring Partisan Bias in Single-Member District Electoral Systems. *Legislative Studies Quarterly* 39 (1): 55–85.

McKee, Seth C., Jeremy M. Teigen, and Mathieu Turgeon. 2006. The Partisan Impact of Congressional Redistricting: The Case of Texas, 2001–2003. *Social Science Quarterly* 87: 308–17. doi:10.1111/j.1540-6237.2006.2006.00382.x

Michener, Jamila. 2016. Race, Poverty, and the Redistribution of Voting Rights. *Poverty & Public Policy* 8 (2):106–28 doi: 10.1002/pop4.137

Miller, Peter, and Bernard Grofman. 2013. Redistricting Commissions in the Western United States. *U.C. Irvine Law Review* 3: 637.

Miller, Sarah, Norman Johnson, and Laura R. Wherry. 2019. Medicaid and Mortality: New Evidence from Linked Survey and Administrative Data. Working Paper 26081. Working Paper Series. National Bureau of Economic Research. https://doi.org/10.3386/w26081

Moomaw, Graham. 2020. Virginia Democratic Party Urges Voters to Defeat Redistricting Reform Amendment. *Virginia Mercury*. June 24, 2020. www .virginiamercury.com/2020/06/24/virginia-democratic-party-urges-voters-to-defeat-redistricting-reform-amendment/ Accessed October 16, 2020.

Muennig, Peter A., Megan Reynolds, David S. Fink, Zafar Zafari, and Arline T. Geronimus. 2018, November. America's Declining Well- Being, Health, and Life Expectancy: Not Just a White Problem. *American Journal of Public Health* 108 (12): 1626–631. https://doi.org/10.2105/AJPH.2018.304585

Murphy, Chad, and Antoine Yoshinaka. 2009. Are Mapmakers Able to Target and Protect Congressional Incumbents? The Institutional Dynamics of Electoral Competition." *American Politics Research* 37 (6): 955–82.

Nagle, John F. 2019. What Criteria Should Be Used for Redistricting Reform? *Election Law Journal: Rules, Politics, and Policy* 18 (1): 63–77. http://doi .org/10.1089/elj.2018.0514

Nakao, Keisuke. 2011. Racial Redistricting for Minority Representation Without Partisan Bias: A Theoretical Approach. *Economics & Politics* 23 (1): 132–51.

NCSL. 2020. Absentee and Mail Voting Policies in Effect for the 2020 Election. National Conference of State Legislatures. www.ncsl.org/research/ elections-and-campaigns/absentee-and-mail-voting-policies-in-effect-for-the-2020-election.aspx

NEJM. 2020. Dying in a Leadership Vacuum. *New England Journal of Medicine* 383 (15): 1479–80. https://doi.org/10.1056/NEJMe2029812

Niemi, R. G., and Abramowitz, A. I. 1994. Partisan redistricting and the 1992 congressional elections. *The Journal of Politics* 56(3): 811-817.

Niemi, Richard G., and Jackman, Simon. 1991. Bias and Responsiveness in State Legislative Districting. *Legislative Studies Quarterly* 16 (2): 183–202.

Norris, Pippa. 2011. *Democratic Deficit: Critical Citizens Revisited*. Cambridge: Cambridge University Press.

Oliver, J. Eric. 2000. City Size and Civic Involvement in Metropolitan America. *American Political Science Review* 94 (June): 361–73.

Ollove, Michael. 2020. How Misinformation, Federalism and Selfishness Hampered America's Virus Response. Pew Stateline. July 18, 2020. https:// pew.org/3g94a3A

Oppenheimer, Bruce I. 1996. The Representational Experience: The Effect of State Population on Senator-Constituency Linkages. *American Journal of Political Science* 40 (4): 1280–99.

Overby, L. Marvin, and Kenneth M. Cosgrove. 1996. Unintended Consequences? Racial Redistricting and the Representation of Minority Interests. *The Journal of Politics* 58 (2): 540–50.

Owen, Guillermo, and Bernard Grofman. 1988. Optimal Partisan Gerrymandering. *Political Geography* 7 (1): 5–22.

Oxfam America. 2020. The Best and Worst States to Work in America – during COVID-19. /explore/issues/economic-well-being/covid-map/

Pacheco, Julianna, and Jason Fletcher 2015. Incorporating Health into Studies of Political Behavior: Evidence for Turnout and Partisanship. *Political Research Quarterly* 68 (1): 104–16. https://doi.org/10.1177/1065912914563548

Parsons, G. Michael. 2020. Gerrymandering & Justiciability: The Political Question Doctrine After Rucho v. Common Cause. *Indiana Law Journal* 95(4): 1295-1364.

Pegden, Wesley, Ariel D. Procaccia, and Dingli Yu. 2017. A Partisan Districting Protocol with Provably Nonpartisan Outcomes. ArXiv. Accessed at https:// arxiv.org/abs/1710.08781.

Perkins, Alec. 2014. *FairDistrict.US* 2014 [cited November 6, 2014]. Available from fairdistrict.us.

Petrocik, John R., and Scott W. Desposato. 1998. The partisan consequences of majority-minority redistricting in the South, 1992 and 1994. *The Journal of Politics* 60 (3): 613-633.

Pew Research Center. 2020. Americans' Views of Government: Low Trust, but Some Positive Performance Ratings. www.pewresearch.org/politics/ 2020/09/14/americans-views-of-government-low-trust-but-some-positive-performance-ratings/

Pildes, Richard H. 2004. Forward: The Constitutionalization of Democratic Politics. *Harvard Law Review* 118 (1): 28-154.

Powell, R. J., Clark, J. T., and Dube, M. P. 2020. Partisan Gerrymandering, Clustering, or Both? A New Approach to a Persistent Question. *Election Law Journal: Rules, Politics, and Policy* 19(1), 79-100.

Pritchard, Anita. 1992. Changes in Electoral Structures and the Success of Women Candidates: The Case of Florida. *Social Science Quarterly* 73: 62–70.

The Public Mapping Project, Michael Altman, Michael P. McDonald, and Azavea. 2014. *District Builder*. www.publicmapping.org

Reddick, Malia, and Rebecca Love Kourlis. 2014. Choosing Judges: Judicial Nominating Commissions and the Selection of Supreme Court Justices. *Institute for the Advancement of the American Legal System*. https://iaals.du .edu/sites/default/files/documents/publications/choosing_judges_jnc_report.pdf

Rhola, Ryne, Ron Johnson, Kelvyn Jones, and David Manley. 2018. Spatial Scale and the Geographical Polarization of the American Electorate. *Political Geography* 65: 117–22. https://doi.org/10.1016/j.polgeo.2018.05.010

Rodden, Johnathan A. 2019. *Why Cities Lose: The Deep Roots of the Urban-Rural Political Divide*. New York: Basic Books.

Rosenbaum, Jason. Missourians Scrap Clean Missouri Redistricting Plan, Pass Amendment 3. November 4, 2020. *St. Louis Public Radio*. Accessed March 1, 2021. https://news.stlpublicradio.org/government-politics-issues/2020-11-04/missourians-scrap-clean-missouri-redistricting-plan-pass-amendment-3

Rosentiel, Tom. 2010. A Clear Rejection of the Status Quo, No Consensus about Future Policies. *Pew Research Center* (blog). November 3, 2010. www .pewresearch.org/2010/11/03/a-clear-rejection-of-the-status-quo-no-consen sus-about-future-policies/

Rove, Karl. The GOP Targets State Legislatures. March 4, 2010. *Wall Street Journal*. Accessed September 9, 2019, www.wsj.com/articles/ SB10001424052748703862704575099670689398044

Santucci, Jack. 2017. Party Splits, Not Progressives: The Origins of Proportional Representation in American Local Government. *American Politics Research* 45: 3, https://doi.org/10.1177/1532673X16674774

2018. Maine Ranked-choice Voting as a Case of Electoral System Change. *Representation* 54 (3): 297–311.

Schattschneider, Elmer E., and David Adamany. 1975. *The Semisovereign People: A Realist's View of Democracy in America*. 1st Edition. Hinsdale, IL: Cengage Learning.

Scheiber, Stuart. 2013. Can Gerrymandering Be Solved with Cut-and-Choose? October 28. Accessed at https://blogs.harvard.edu/pamphlet/2013/10/28/can-gerrymandering-be-solved-with-cut-and-choose/

Schlozman, Kay Lehman, Henry E. Brady, and Sidney Verba. 2018. *Unequal and Unrepresented: Political Inequality and the People's Voice in the New Gilded Age*. Princeton, NJ: Princeton University Press.

Schlozman, Kay Lehman, S. Verba, and Henry E. Brady. 2012. *The Unheavenly Chorus: Unequal Political Voice and the Broken Promise of American Democracy*. Princeton, NJ: Princeton University Press.

Seabrook, Nicholas R. 2017. *Drawing the Lines: Constraints on Partisan Gerrymandering in US Politics*. Ithaca, NY: Cornell University Press.

Shapiro, Martin. 1965. Stability and Change in Judicial Decision-Making: Incrementalism or Stare Decisis. *Law in Transition Quarterly* 2 (3): 134–57

Sherstyuk, Katerina. 1998. How to Gerrymander: A Formal Analysis. *Public Choice* 95: 27–49.

Smirnov, Oleg, and Charles Anthony Smith. 2013. Drift, Draft, or Drag: How U.S. Supreme Court Justices React to New Members. *The Justice System Journal* 34 (2): 228–45.

Spicuzza, Mary, and Dee J. Hall. 2010, November 3. Walker Defeats Barrett to win Governor's Race. *Wisconsin State Journal.* Accessed September 9, 2010, https://madison.com/wsj/news/local/govt-and-politics/elections/walker-defeats-barrett-to-win-governor-s-race/article_d112cfd0-e6f9-11df-83c9-001cc4c002e0.html

Stephanopoulos, Nicholas O., and Eric M. McGhee. 2015. Partisan Gerrymandering and the Efficiency Gap. *University of Chicago Law Review* 82: 831–900.

  2018. The Measure of a Metric: The Debate over Quantifying Partisan Gerrymandering. *Stanford Law Review* 70: 1503–68.

Stephanopoulos, Nicholas O. and Christopher Warshaw. 2020. The Impact of Partisan Gerrymandering on Political Parties. *Legislative Studies Quarterly* 45(4): 609–43. doi:10.1111/lsq.12276

Stewart, Emily. 2018. State Legislatures Democrats Have Flipped so Far in the 2018 Elections. *Vox.* November 7, 2018. www.vox.com/policy-and-politics/2018/11/7/18071410/democrat-state-legislature-colorado-minnesota-election-results

Sund, Reijo, Hannu Lahtinen, Hanna Wass, Mikko Mattila, and Pekka Martikainen. 2017. How Voter Turnout Varies between Different Chronic Conditions? A Population-Based Register Study. *Journal of Epidemiology and Community Health* 71 (5): 475–79. https://doi.org/10.1136/jech-2016-208314

Swasey, Benjamin. 2020. Map: Mail-In Voting Rules By State – And The Deadlines You Need. NPR.Org. October 14, 2020. www.npr.org/2020/09/14/909338758/map-mail-in-voting-rules-by-state

Tam Cho, Wendy K., and Yan Y. Liu. 2016. Toward a Talismanic Redistricting Tool: A Computational Method for Identifying Extreme Redistricting Plans. *Election Law Journal* 15 (4):351–66.

Tam Cho, Wendy K and Yan Y. Liu. 2018. Sampling from Complicated and Unknown Distributions: Monte Carlo and Markov Chain Monte Carlo Methods for Redistricting. *Physica* 506:170-178.

Tan, Netina, and Bernard Grofman. 2018. Electoral Rules and Manufacturing Legislative Supermajority: Evidence from Singapore. *Commonwealth & Comparative Politics* 56 (3): 273–97. https://doi.org/10.1080/14662043.2018.1468238

Taylor, Steven L., Matthew S. Shugart, Arend Lijphart, and Bernard Groftman. 2014. *A Different Democracy: American Government in a Thirty-One Country Perspective.* New Haven: Yale University Press.

Thoet, Alison. 2017. What North Carolina's Power-Stripping Laws Mean for New Gov. Roy Cooper. PBS NewsHour. January 3, 2017. www.pbs.org/newshour/politics/north-carolinas-power-stripping-laws-mean-new-gov-roy-cooper

Trounstine, Jessica, and Melody E. Valdini. 2008. The Context Matters: The Effects of Single-Member versus At-Large Districts on City Council Diversity. *American Journal of Political Science* 52 (3): 554–69.

Tucker-Foltz, Jamie. 2018. A Cut-And-Choose Mechanism to Prevent Gerrymandering. ArXiv. Accessed at https://arxiv.org/abs/1802.08351/

Tufte, Edward R. 1973. The Relationship between Seats and Votes in Two-Party Systems. *American Political Science Review* 67 (2): 540–54.

UCLA Voting Rights Project, Voting Rights Lab, and Union of Concern Scientists. 2020. Protecting Public Health in the 2020 Election. https://d3267f1c-3110-4540-a458-82b406b9ec8a.usrfiles.com/ugd/d3267f_bof4283b924d4d289bf8862eb58c2dce.pdf

Union of Concerned Scientists. 2017. Benefits of Renewable Energy Use. www.ucsusa.org/clean-energy/renewable-energy/public-benefits-of-renewable-power

United Health Foundation. 2018. America's Health Rankings | AHR. Retrieved February 6, 2019, from America's Health Rankings website: www.americashealthrankings.org/

Veomett, Ellen. 2018. Efficiency Gap, Voter Turnout, and the Efficiency Principle. *Election Law Journal: Rules, Politics, and Policy* 17 (4): 249–63. http://doi.org/10.1089/elj.2018.0488

Vickrey, William. 1961. On the Prevention of Gerrymandering. *Political Science Quarterly* 76(1): 105–10.

Wang, Samuel S.-H. 2016. Three Tests for Practical Evaluation of Partisan Gerrymandering. *Stanford Law Review* 68: 1263–320.

Warrington, Gregory S. 2018. Quantifying Gerrymandering Using the Vote Distribution. *Election Law Journal* 17(1): 39-57.

2019. A comparison of partisan-gerrymandering measures. *Election Law Journal: Rules, Politics, and Policy* 18(3): 262–81.

Wasfy, Jason H., Charles Stewart III, and Vijeta Bhambhani. 2017. County Community Health Associations of Net Voting Shift in the 2016 U.S. Presidential Election. *PLOS ONE* 12 (10): e0185051. https://doi.org/10.1371/journal.pone.0185051

Washington, E. (2012). Do Majority-Black Districts Limit Blacks' Representation? The Case of the 1990 Redistricting. *The Journal of Law and Economics* 55 (2): 251–74.

Waymer, Damion, and Robert L. Heath. 2016. Black Voter Dilution, American Exceptionalism, and Racial Gerrymandering: The Paradox of the Positive in Political Public Relations. *Journal of Black Studies* 47 (7): 635–58.

Weeks, Linton. 2010. 10 Takeaways from The 2010 Midterms. NPR.Org. November 3, 2010. www.npr.org/templates/story/story.php?storyId=131039717

Weiser, Wendy. 2020. To Protect Democracy, Expand Vote by Mail | Brennan Center for Justice. June 30, 2020. www.brennancenter.org/our-work/analysis-opinion/protect-democracy-expand-vote-mail

Welch, Susan, and Donley T. Studlar. 1990. Multimember Districts and the Representation of Women: Evidence from Britain and the United States. *The Journal of Politics* 52 (2): 391–412.

Whitby, Kenny J. 2000. *The Color of Representation: Congressional Behavior and Black Interests*. Ann Arbor: University of Michigan Press.

White, Laurel. 2020. Wisconsin Supreme Court Upholds GOP-Backed Lame-Duck Laws Limiting Power Of Governor, AG. Wisconsin Public Radio. July 9, 2020. www.wpr.org/wisconsin-supreme-court-upholds-gop-backed-lame-duck-laws-limiting-power-governor-ag

Wolf, Stephen. 2015. *What If We Had Non-Gerrymandered Redistricting Nationwide? The Daily Kos*, August 6, 2012 [cited July 21, 2015]. Available from www.dailykos.com/story/2012/08/06/1115538/-What-if-We-Had-Non-Partisan-Redistricting-Nationwide

Wolfinger, Raymond E., and Steven J. Rosenstone. 1980. *Who Votes?* New Haven: Yale University Press.

Woodward, Kelly. 2020. Ohioans Should Fill Their Absentee Ballot Request Carefully, Or Risk Having It Rejected. October 6, 2020. https://radio.wosu.org/post/ohioans-should-fill-their-absentee-ballot-request-carefully-or-risk-having-it-rejected

Index

Made in United States
North Haven, CT
09 September 2024

57195951R00146